MOSES OF THE NEW WORLD:
THE WORK OF BARON DE HIRSCH

MOSES
OF THE NEW WORLD
THE WORK OF BARON DE HIRSCH

Samuel J. Lee

THOMAS YOSELOFF
NEW YORK • SOUTH BRUNSWICK • LONDON

© 1970 by A. S. Barnes and Co., Inc.
Library of Congress Catalogue Card Number: 79-88281

Thomas Yoseloff, *Publisher*
Cranbury, New Jersey 08512

Thomas Yoseloff Ltd
108 New Bond Street
London W1Y OQX, England

ISBN 0-498-07378-5
Printed in the United States of America

FOR LEONIE

CONTENTS

PREFACE

It has been said that to learn European history one should study the history of the Jews of Europe, for where history was made, there the Jews were to be found. But, to understand Jewish history, one must know the conditions under which Jews lived in Europe as an integral part of the European scene, yet completely insulated from everyday life in the community in which they lived. Who put them behind ghetto walls; what forces kept them there; and why did they remain a people apart for so many centuries? Only by understanding Jewish life during those dark years can one realize the tremendous impact on European Jewry of the liberalism that the French Revolution spread throughout Europe as Napoleon's conquering armies broke down ghetto walls wherever they penetrated. This new freedom coincided with the emergence of the many small European principalities from feudalism into a capitalistic society, for which Jews were uniquely suited. It was an interesting era, an exciting period in which conflict built upon conflict, with the struggle for control of the economic and industrial system leading to war after war, finally culminating in the great World Wars of the twentieth century.

Out of this era of emancipation, the names of five great Jews emerge: Adolphe Isaac Crémieux, France's most illustrious Jew—statesman, politician, and president of the Alliance Israélite Universelle for many years; Sir Moses Montefiore, dean of the large group of English Jews who were noted statesmen, titled millionaires, and philanthropists; Theodor Herzl, Viennese journalist and writer, father of the Zionist movement; the Rothschilds, a family that spread its influence over England, France, Germany, Italy, and Austria, probably the best known of these names; and Baron Maurice de Hirsch auf Gereuth, the greatest and most famous of them all—entrepreneur, banker, railroad builder, philanthropist, hailed as the wealthiest man in the world, the nineteenth-century Moses who started the exodus of Russia's Jews to the Western world—and probably the least known today of the great Jewish figures of the last century.

While this book revolves around Baron de Hirsch as the central figure, it can in no sense be considered a biography. As happens so frequently when attempts are made to write the story of a great man, there is little known of the intimate, everyday happenings of a lifetime occupied with great undertakings, and only too often there is little documentation of the events in which he played a part. In the case of Baron de Hirsch much of what might have been documented about him in Germany, or stored in Belgian and French archives, has been destroyed by the Nazis.

Actually, the biography of a man who spent the better part of his life, and a fortune of somewhere around three hundred million dollars, in an attempt to relieve the sufferings of the oppressed Jews of Russia and the Near East, cannot be told except in the context of the entire period during which he lived. It is the purpose of this book to try to recreate that period and to use the great events in which Baron de Hirsch participated to depict the way in which Jewish life in the nineteenth century was affected by the rise of the capitalist system and the spread of the industrial revolution.

Baron Maurice de Hirsch auf Gereuth played a leading role in that period of transition. Unwittingly, he contributed in no small measure to the buildup of tensions that led to the outbreak of the First World War, which historians have labeled "a culmination of the struggle for control of the avenues of commerce into the Near East that started with the opening of the Suez Canal and the building of Baron de Hirsch's railroad from Vienna to Constantinople." It was in this connection, too, that he became a leading victim of political anti-Semitism, which first manifested itself when an anti-Semitic party appeared in Germany and, with no platform other than the elimination of Jews from European life, captured five seats in the German Reichstag. From there it spread rapidly through the Balkans into Poland and Russia, bringing on violent persecution and pogroms, which finally led to Baron de Hirsch's attempt to move the millions of Russian Jews out of the land of the Czars to colonies in the Argentine, clashing head-on with Theodor Herzl's grandiose scheme of resettling the Jews in a national homeland in Palestine. Both Baron de Hirsch and Theodor Herzl, while they could not possibly foresee the coming of the Nazis, each in his own way tried to stop the march toward the complete annihilation of Europe's Jews, whether by force or by assimilation.

Baron de Hirsch cannot be measured by ordinary standards. His business activities were colossal and spectacular; his antics in the frivolous society of the Victorian era were notorious, and yet he was the friend and confidant of princes and potentates, diplomats and statesmen. Thoroughly cosmopolitan, speaking three or four languages with easy fluency, living in princely splendor, maintaining palatial homes in Paris and London and a large estate in Hungary, he was recognized by bankers and industrialists alike as one of the leading financial figures in the world, reputed to be one of the wealthiest men of his time. But he dropped all this activity at the very zenith of his career so that he might devote his time and his fortune to relieving the distress of his less fortunate fellow Jews. Why? What brought him to the decision that he alone, against the advice of the recognized leaders of world Jewry, could remove millions of Jews from Russia and settle them in the western hemisphere?

In discussing his plan in the July, 1891, issue of *North American Review*, he said:

The only means to raise their (the Russian Jews) condition is to remove them from the soil to which they are rooted and to transport them to other countries where they will enjoy the same rights as the people among whom they live and where they will cease to be pariahs, and become citizens. . . . What I desire to accomplish, what, after many failures has come to be the object of my life, and that for which I am ready to stake my wealth and my intellectual powers, is to give to a portion of my companions in faith the possibility of finding a new existence, primarily as farmers and also as handicraftsmen in those lands where the laws and religious tolerance permit them to carry on the struggle for existence as noble and responsible subjects of a humane government. The Government of the Czar means to get rid of five million Jews who inhabit Russian territory. Let him allow the many who, like myself, are interested in the fate of these victims of persecution and who will certainly be prepared to make the greatest sacrifices on their behalf, to save them. Without such help it would be impossible for the government to get rid of five million Jews except by slaughtering them in a mass.

Little did he realize that his words would come true fifty years later—not in Russia, but in the land of his birth, brought about by a movement that started in Munich, the city of his birth. Nor did he think that the Baron de Hirsch Fund, which he incorporated under the laws of the State of New York in 1891 to help refugees from Czarist Russia, would one day be called upon to do exactly the same kind of rehabilitation work for that new group of Jewish refugees who were able to flee from the very land in which his father and his grandfather had received such high honors.

It is strange that Americans should have so little knowledge of the man who was responsible for breaking down the barriers that held their parents and grandparents captive in the Russian Pale of Settlement and starting them on the road to freedom in the New World. For he alone set the stage for the emigration from the Czar's ghettos that caused Oscar Straus, the U.S. Minister to Turkey in the 1880s, to label Baron de Hirsch "the Napoleon of the Great Exodus." A large segment of American Jewry owes its very presence in America, directly or indirectly, to the activities of this one man whose genius for organizing large projects led him to undertake the staggering task of transplanting millions of persecuted Russian Jews to new lands, where they might find peace and happiness and the opportunity of becoming respected, self-supporting citizens.

On the occasion of the death in 1899 of his widow,

Baroness Clara de Hirsch, the *American Hebrew* said, editorially:

> Baron and Baroness de Hirsch will ever occupy a foremost place among the great ones in history, not on account of the millions they lavishly bestowed upon their unfortunate brethren, but because they by their matchless philanthropy became the redeemers and saviors of thousands and hundreds of thousands of their race.
>
> The Baron, and still more so the Baroness de Hirsch, never looked upon their millions as something they could boast of and glory in before the world. On every occasion they voiced the right spirit of Jewish charity in stating that wealth is a trust, a stewardship, and in managing it they have responsibilities for the life and happiness of those who are less fortunate than they. Children of the 19th Century, which was essentially an age of intellectual and social emancipation, Baron and Baroness de Hirsch will shine forth throughout all the centuries to come as emancipators of their brethren from social and mental thraldom by the educational institutions they founded in almost every part of the globe.

Why did these prophecies of immortality fail to come true? Why is the name of Baron de Hirsch practically unknown to the descendants of those Jews who were released from the ghettos and brought to the New World by this nineteenth-century Moses? Why are there no monuments to Baron or Baroness de Hirsch anywhere in the world? Why are their pictures, which once adorned the walls of ghetto homes all over eastern Europe, unavailable anywhere today?

Perhaps one answer is that they and their works were totally eclipsed by Theodor Herzl and the Zionist movement, which came on the scene shortly before their deaths. Baron de Hirsch was one of the first of the millionaires Herzl went to see with his dream of a Jewish homeland, and the interview between the two makes interesting reading. Baron de Hirsch, while not enthusiastic about Herzl's ideal of a Jewish state, nevertheless asked Herzl to submit a written proposal that would explain his plan in more detail and be more specific about just how his Zionist organization would function. Three months later, Baron de Hirsch was dead. The report Herzl was writing to present him actually became Herzl's *The Jewish State,* the plea for Jewish nationhood that was to lead to the Basle Convention and the organization of the Zionist movement.

Many writers have speculated as to what would have happened had Baron de Hirsch lived a few years longer. Some have written of what a great team these two giants would have made, with Herzl's idealism and Baron de Hirsch's millions. It is doubtful, however, that Baron de Hirsch would have joined hands with Herzl at any time, because he was an assimilationist whose ideals were completely at variance with any notions of Jewish nationalism. For him there existed only two types of Jew, the ghetto Jew—coarse, ignorant, fanatical in his religious practices—and the emancipated Jew. All that was necessary was to remove Jews in large numbers from the first group into the second group and anti-Semitism would vanish. He recognized only one avenue through which Jews might achieve equality among their neighbors: Education! He was sure that Jews could be taught to work and live like their neighbors; that they could be educated away from the Talmud and the Cheder; that they could be educated out of the ghetto. He had seen this happen many times in the struggle for Jewish emancipation. Where ghetto walls had been broken down and Jews were allowed to mingle with the rest of the population they had readily assimilated, becoming tradesmen and artisans and business and professional men. The schools the Alliance Israélite Universelle had established with his money were turning out skilled craftsmen by the thousands—shoemakers, tailors, saddlers, bookbinders, bakers, weavers, locksmiths, printers, watchmakers, furriers, and workers of all kinds. He once told Clara, "The conception that the only difference between Jew and Christian is one of religious beliefs must be given wider circulation, and what better way can this be accomplished than to have them work side by side at the same workbench or till the same ground together."

Commenting editorially on the almost unexplainable indifference on the part of the American public to Baron de Hirsch, even at a time when he was donating $2,-400,000 to establish the American Baron de Hirsch Fund for the purpose of helping immigrant Jews who had come to the United States, the *New York Sun,* in its issue of October 9, 1892, said:

> Although the Baron de Hirsch has, for several years been known to all the peoples of the civilized world, his name does not appear in any of the books devoted to the biographies of great men. Strange as it may seem, this wonderful man, who has undertaken the most gigantic enterprises in the most magnificent manner, whose fortune is so vast that no one seems to know its limit, whose courage is so splendid, whose achievements bid fair to have a lasting effect upon the world's history, is not even mentioned among the notables of the day in any of the better known publications.

There are two possible reasons for this omission. One is that within a few years he has arisen before the world like another Monte Cristo. Another is that the information concerning him is so contradictory in most of its features that are essential, that a biographer would find an effort to search for the truth most laborious and the results most unsatisfactory. As described by the men who claim personal knowledge of him, he is selfish, generous, vainglorious, modest, ill-mannered, boorish, gentlemanly. All these opposite characteristics are attributed to him by men who stoutly disclaim any prejudice for or against the object of their criticism. Evidence would seem to favor, however, those who speak well of him. The mean man would never expend millions for charitable purposes, and even if he were vainglorious, the boor would scarcely be selected for a host by the Prince of Wales, though he possessed all the millions of Europe.

Baron Maurice de Hirsch died on April 21, 1896, but the many organizations he created still carry on his activities in the spirit of the founder. Whatever was left of his fortune he willed to the Jewish Colonization Association, which was thus enriched by the huge sum of $45,000,000, making it the largest trust fund the world has ever known. It was characteristic of him that he should reply to a well-wisher who was consoling him on the loss of his only son and heir in 1887, "My son I have lost, but not my heir; humanity is my heir." Such was the philosophy of the man who had spent so many years in the service of his fellow Jews.

Jacob Schiff suggested to the Baroness when Baron de Hirsch died that their great contribution to Jewry should be perpetuated through a monument in stone and iron, to which Clara replied, "If the ideas and endeavors which my husband and I have embodied permanently into the foundations which we have instituted the world over cannot secure honor and permanency to his memory, no words or monuments could or should do this." Perhaps they should have built the monument.

ACKNOWLEDGMENTS

I would like to thank the following publishers for permission to quote from copyrighted material:

Alliance Israélite Universelle, Paris, France, for the use of its library and for permission to quote from its publications.

Baron de Hirsch Fund, New York, for permission to quote from its book, *History of the Baron de Hirsch Fund,*

B'nai B'rith, for its permission to quote from its booklet on The Exhibit in Klutznick Exhibit Hall, Washington, D.C., on the 75th Anniversary of the Baron de Hirsch Fund, and for loan of the picture of Baron de Hirsch.

The Day, for permission to quote from featured articles in several publications that have been merged into *The Day* and *The Jewish Morning Journal,* New York.

Jewish Publication Society of America, Philadelphia, for permission to quote from the following three books:

Alex Bein, *Theodore Herzl, A Biography of the Founder of Modern Zionism,* 1945

S. M. Dubnow, *History of the Jews in Russia and Poland: From the earliest times until the present day,* 1916

Marvin Lowenthal, *The Jews of Germany: A Story of Sixteen Centuries,* 1936

Keter Publishing House Ltd. for permission to quote from Kurt Grunwald, *Turkenhirsch,* 1966 (Israel Program for Scientific Translation), reprinted by permission of Keter Publishing House Ltd., Jerusalem.
The Zionist Organization of America for permission to quote from its book *Edmond de Rothschild* by Isaac Naiditch, 1945.

I would also like to extend my sincere thanks and appreciation to Dr. Isidore S. Meyer, who was for many years the librarian of the American Jewish Historical Society, and without whose help I probably would not have been able to complete this book. Dr. Meyer not only helped me find references to Baron de Hirsch but was instrumental in having about 300 documents microfilmed for me so that I could take them home and work on this book at my own convenience.

I am especially grateful to Dr. Bernard Wax, Director of the American Jewish Historical Society, for allowing me to use the material contained in the Society's Max J. Kohler collection of material on Baron de Hirsch.

I would like to thank Dr. Victor Girmounsky, Director of the Jewish Colonization Association in London, for allowing me to use information from that organization's records and publications.

I would be remiss if I did not acknowledge the help Mrs. Janet Silverman gave me in doing the early typing, which was most helpful in organizing the book.

INTRODUCTION

Jewish history divides into two separate and distinct phases. The Biblical period is well known. It is the glorious tale of the ancient Hebrews as recorded in the books of the Bible, telling the story of the People of the Book from the beginning of time to the coming of the Christian era and the dispersion of the Jews throughout the civilized world. The post-biblical era is not nearly so well known, perhaps because there is so little about it to stir the imagination. There are no great battles won or lost, no history of great accomplishment, no periods to which Jews can point with pride, no romanticism, and no heroics. Rather, the history of the post-biblical two thousand years is a dreary repetition of persecution heaped upon persecution, each period of discrimination worse than that which preceded it. It is a story of the degradation of a people. The English historian, W. E. H. Lecky, graphically sums up this sordid history in one brief paragraph when he says

Certainly the heroism of the defenders of every other creed fades into insignificance before this martyr people who, for thirteen centuries, confronted all the evils that the fiercest fanaticism could devise, enduring obloquy and spoliation and the violation of the dearest ties, and the infliction of the most hideous sufferings, rather than abandon their faith. . . . Persecution came to the Jewish nation in its most horrible forms, yet surrounded by every circumstance of petty annoyance that could destroy its grandeur, and it continued for centuries their abiding portion.

Physical violence toward the Jews of Europe first manifested itself during the Crusades, for what was more logical than to liquidate those defamers of Christ who were close at hand before starting off to fight the infidels who had taken possession of the Holy Land. The first Crusade in 1096 resulted in the murder of 20,000 Jews in Germany alone. It set the pattern for the many Crusades that were to follow at periodic intervals, each of which was to bring in its wake widespread pillage and death to Jewish communities lying in the path of the crusading hordes. The precedent was established, too, that all Jews were henceforth to be known as enemies of Christendom. While, up to the time of the Crusades, Jews had been regarded more or less as members of a quaint sect, disdaining to preach their religion abroad or to compete with Christianity in its proselytizing efforts, they now were considered veritable demons, capable of the most horrible crimes, the special enemy of the Church that was to make Jews their primary target for a thousand years to come.

Nothing was too infamous to attribute to these "killers of Christ." As Marvin Lowenthal says in his *History of the Jews of Germany:* "Once aroused and fed by a rich booty, religious hatred proved ingenious in providing new charges. To the crucifixion of Jesus was added the ritual murder of children, desecration of the Host, conspiracy with the enemy, plots to destroy Christendom, and congenital greed and treachery—each leading to further humiliation and plunder."

The Age of Degradation had set in. From the day of the First Crusade the Jews were doomed to a life of humiliation and scorn. For over a thousand years they were destined to spend their lives in fear behind ghetto walls, living precariously off their Christian neighbors, buying and selling old clothes, or following trades and professions that the Gentile spurned. Their history is one long tale of misery and woe, written in sorrow and grief in the memory books of the ghetto synagogues and telling the stark, cruel story of Jewish persecution with a realism that few historians have ever been able to achieve and which writers of fiction have seldom surpassed in vividness of detail. Told in words simple and clear and yet most pungent, the pages of the memory books tell the story of not one tragedy alone but of a thousand tragedies spread over a thousand years.

The keeping of memory books is a distinctly Jewish custom of ancient origin, based on the practice in Judaism of honoring the dead by offering up special prayers for their souls during services for the High Holidays. The typical memory book consists of a simple list of the dead of the congregation, with mention of their activities on behalf of their coreligionists and the community as a whole. In addition to this general part of the book and the introductory prayers, there follows a special listing of the names of those who have, by their many charitable and pious acts during their lifetime, earned the right to special mention. A list of the localities in which persecutions had taken place either preceded the necrologies or was added to them. In recent years historians have found these synagogue memory books to be of inestimable value in providing a source material from which they have been able to reconstruct many phases of European life during the

Dark Ages. The memory books of the Jews throw much light on conditions prevailing in the Christian communities as well as in the ghettos.

Although Jews are known to have been in the Germanic countries as early as the fourth century, the oldest memory book of which we have any record is that of the Jewish congregation of Nuremberg, which was started in the year 1296. The martyrology of this book is of special interest because it contains a summary of the persecutions during the Crusades from 1096 to 1298, listing not only the names of the victims but a list of the cities and villages throughout Germany in which massacres occurred. The horrors the Jews endured during the dark ages are depicted in graphic language in the earliest portion of the Nuremberg memory book, where it says:

> May God remember, as He has remembered the souls of Abraham, Isaac, and Jacob, the souls of all members of the communities who have been killed, stoned, burned, strangled, slaughtered, drowned, broken on the wheel, hanged, or buried alive because they remained true to their belief in the One God. Since they have suffered this grievous pain, may God remember them, together with all pious men and women who rest in Paradise. To this we respond: Amen!

There has been no kingdom in Germany in which hatred has raged so furiously against the Jews as it has in Bavaria, and nowhere else have exceptional discriminatory laws and special disabilities been so persistently maintained. Though its Jewish community was not at any time large enough to warrant special notice by historians, it was subject to all the waves of fanaticism that rolled over Europe, in addition to the many outbreaks of violence nurtured locally by the Bavarian princes and clerics. Perhaps it is only a logical finale to its history of Jew hatred that Bavaria was the birthplace of the Nazi movement that attempted to annihilate the Jews completely.

The earliest documentary reference we have to the Jews of Bavaria relates that during the reign of Duke Otto I (1120-1183), certain Jews of Munich advanced a loan to the monarch to finance the building of "Land-shuth." In return they were granted special privileges, which were enlarged upon by Ludwig I, who reigned from 1184 to 1231. In the year 1210 he granted the Jews of Munich permission to build a synagogue, to which a cemetery was added in the year 1225. The earliest reference to any Jew's participation in a legal matter is recorded in a document dated in the year 1299, in which one "Abraham de Munichem" acted as a witness to the sale of a house in Ratisbon. The Jewish community of Munich consisted of around two hundred souls at that time, all of whom resided in the "Judengasse," or Jew's street, on which were located the synagogue, a communal house, a ritual bath, a slaughter house, and a hospital.

In 1248 a ritual murder charge was raised against the Jewish community, but there is no record that violence reached serious proportions and the commotion this charge caused quickly subsided. A similar charge in the year 1285, however, was not treated so lightly and brought much suffering in its wake. The temper of the populace had been raised to such a pitch by the clergy that a mob was formed with the avowed intention of avenging the death of the "Christian child the Jews had purchased and murdered for ritual purposes." The Jews, seeking to avoid the fury of the mob, sought sanctuary in their synagogue, which was promptly set afire by the enraged burghers; one hundred and sixty-eight terrified Jews perished in the flames. The names of sixty-eight of these martyrs were inscribed in the Nuremberg memory book when it was inaugurated in 1296, the names of the additional one hundred souls being omitted because they were children. History records that at the instigation of the King an investigation was held which proved the charges against the Jews to be completely false. The ringleaders of the mob were duly punished and those Jews who had been imprisoned were set free.

Another massacre in Nuremberg, brought on by an accusation of desecration of the Host, claimed 628 victims on August 1, 1298. In 1338 a similar charge was made against the Jews of Deggendorff, and the entire Jewish population of that town was murdered. Following a superficial investigation of that massacre the ring-leaders were not only fully pardoned but were actually honored by a royal edict of commendation. A memorial church was erected on the spot where the massacre took place, which, until comparatively recent times, was a pilgrimage center for the faithful of Bavaria. This incident too was dramatized in a play which was shown throughout Germany for 500 years, with a performance actually being given as late as the year 1800 in Regen.

And then came Black Death—twelve years of plague running riot over Europe, during which the population of the continent was depleted by at least twenty-five percent! The plague first made its appearance in Provence early in the year 1348 and swept like wild-fire through a continent impoverished by continual warfare. With a populace ill fed and ill housed, completely ignorant of even the most elementary rules of sanitation, there was no stopping the death-dealing scourge. And with the spreading of the plague came terror.

A few Jews in Switzerland, under the strain of the most horrible tortures the medieval mind could devise, "confessed" that they had poisoned the wells. Without testing the wells to see if they had been tampered with, the officials allowed the confessions to become public knowledge, encouraging wide circulation throughout Europe of the idea that a simple way to prevent the plague from reaching the gates of the city was to kill off all Jews before they had a chance to poison the wells. Henricus, the poet of Erfurt, describes in a few well-chosen words the tragic fate of those Jews unfortunate enough to fall victim to the blood-bath that followed:

> The pestilence like fury broke
> And took its thousands of our folk;
> The Earth against us fiercely turned
> And many Jews were therefore burned.

Ten thousand Jews of Bavaria fell victim to the massacres. The *Martyrologium des Nurnberger Memor-Buchs* lists nearly eighty congregations that suffered almost complete extinction. Through the medium of widespread burnings and hangings, Germany almost rid herself completely of Jews for within two years close to three hundred and fifty German Jewish communities were completely exterminated.

In 1475 the accidental drowning of a boy, Simon of Trent, in the Austrian Tyrol set off another ritual murder charge. Pilgrims who came to view the body claimed they saw a halo hovering over it, giving rise to the rumor that the area where the boy was buried was hallowed ground.

A church was erected at the boy's grave, which became a famous place of pilgrimage for several centuries. Despite the official denial of the ritual murder charge by Pope Sixtus IV, and his refusal to permit canonization of the boy, this ritual murder charge was recorded in the "The Acts of the Saints," triggering a wave of massacres all over Bavaria that soon spread into other Germanic principalities. Anti-Jewish outbreaks then became common throughout Germany for the next several decades.

Those who were able to flee this new series of massacres started a huge exodus to Austria and Bohemia and as far east as Poland where the Jews found, to their surprise, a welcoming hand extended to them by Casimir the Great, whose friendship for the Jews earned him the nickname "King of the Serfs and the Jews." He set the pattern for the tolerant attitude of the Polish people toward the Jews for the next few centuries. Jewish communities prospered and grew in Poland until it was generally recognized that Poland had become the cultural and religious center of the Jewish world.

On December 23, 1551, another expulsion decree was issued in Bavaria, followed by a law written into the legal statutes of the land classifying Jews as being among the "dangerous, frivolous, and suspicious persons" who were to be prevented from residing within the borders of the country and who were to be denied the right to carry on trade and industry anywhere in Bavaria.

During the next century-and-a-half, few, if any, Jews were able to settle within the borders of the Bavarian Kingdom, and little is known of those who did manage to filter back under the watchful eye of the authorities. It is apparent, though, that the restrictions must have been relaxed considerably toward the end of the seventeenth century for we find a new expulsion order issued on March 12, 1715, by the Elector Max Emanuel, once again clearing the country of Jews. In 1773 a new regulation was issued, barring Jews from settling permanently anywhere in Bavaria, this restriction remaining in effect until the year 1785, when Jews were once again given the right to settle in the country. Primarily because of the new financial rules of exchange, the authorities were frank to admit that the unfavorable condition of Bavarian finances made it advisable to import Jews into the country so as to make use of their acknowledged ability in the manipulation of financial matters. From that time on Jews lived uninterruptedly in Bavaria, with no further expulsion orders upsetting the normal routine of their lives, until the coming of the Nazis one hundred and fifty years later.

A mere recital of persecutions and expulsions, however violent these periodic outbursts were, does not begin to picture the wretchedness and misery of Jewish life in the Germanic communities during the years when comparative quiet reigned. Nor does it portray the complete degradation to which the Jews of Europe were subjected under the drastic regulations placed against their activities for over a thousand years. Persecution, physical violence, expulsion, and economic discrimination could not have been so soul-destroying as the complete isolation from social and civil life established by the Lateran Council of 1215. Summoned by Pope Innocent III to take measures that would "prevent infection of Christian souls by contamination with the infidel," the Lateran Council prescribed the formula that was to ostracize Jews completely from Christian society for centuries, making communication between Jew and Christian virtually impossible except in business affairs, and even then only under the strictest of controls.

A Christian might not enter into partnership with Jews;
he might not eat with them; he might not use the same
bath; he might not employ Jews as physicians; he might
not even purchase their drugs. Intermarriage with them
was deemed a horrible pollution. Excommunication was
held out as the penalty for any Christian layman who discussed matters of faith with a Jew. No Jew was allowed
to enter a church, or cathedral, or any Christian house of
God, under any pretext. During the Holy Week, Jews
were to remain completely out of sight, and woe betide
any Jew found outside his home. At no time were Christians allowed to attend Jewish social functions, whether
weddings, dances, patriotic assemblies, or other festivi-
ties. Not satisfied with these measures, the Lateran Council undertook to prescribe the dress the Jew must wear in
order to distinguish him from the true believer. In the
words of Marvin Lowenthal in his *History of the Jews of
Germany:*

The sign which the Lateran Council prescribed to
distinguish the Jews as moral lepers suffering from
noxious and contagious beliefs, received general en-
forcement by the fourteenth century in Germany, where
it usually took the form of a yellow-fabric ring stitched
on the sleeve or breast. In addition, a high peaked hat,
the "Judenhut," probably first adopted by the Jews out
of choice, was made obligatory, in case, no doubt, the
ring escaped notice. Still not satisfied, the authorities
often ordered the use of a long cloak, sometimes speci-
fying the color and the inches. Yet despite these precau-
tions, the Jews apparently looked too much like Germans to suit the popular taste. So, in a number of cities,
the cloaks were not only ordered lengthened, but the
beards shortened. For the women there were blue
strips on the veil or headgear, bells on the skirts, and,

on occasion, their finger-rings numbered and weighted. Mediaeval life, to be sure, ran riot with distinctive and obligatory costumes; but for the Christians they meant badges of honor—uniforms of rank, calling or craft. For the Jew, these bizarre regulations shut every man and woman in, as it were, a personal walking ghetto. Clothes made the man, and of the Jew, a marked man, ringed or striped like a convict.

And then came the two crowning indignities, the walled ghetto in which Jews were forced to spend their days in ignominy and shame, and the "More Judaico," or Jew's oath, which, of all the special disabilities placed against the Jews in their long history of life in the diaspora, was the most difficult to dispose of, and which persisted long after most of the other legislation against Jews had been removed. In describing this "Jew's Oath," Lowenthal says: "Before the bar of justice he (the Jew) was made to feel his inferiority as a witness and a man of honor by being compelled to take a blood-curdling oath while standing barefoot on the hide of a swine—a procedure which lingered in the statutes of Germany until 1877."

The first compulsory ghetto was ordained in Silesia by the Synod of Breslau "to prevent the Christians from falling under the influence of Judaism." It was not long before the idea spread throughout the rest of Europe, and by the beginning of the fourteenth century there was not a Jewish community in all of Germany that was without its ghetto walls. Each night the gates were locked from the outside, as in a prison, and no Jew dared leave its confines without special permission. The Jews now were, in every sense of the word, a people apart.

Cut off from the outside world, Jews turned to the synagogue as the center of Jewish life and activity. It was the house of worship, the school, the theater, the communal center, and the court of law of every ghetto community. In vermin-infested ghetto quarters, however, the synagogue was rarely a place of beauty. Entering a synagogue was like descending into a musty dungeon filled with the smell of closely packed bodies mingled with all the odors of the ghetto—the musty old clothes bought originally from the Christians and handed down from father to son—the smell of old leather, of rotting wood, and of smoke from the oil lamps—the old men wailing, the children noisily singing hymns, the women in the balconies silently watching their loved ones below. The almost complete lack of decorum made the whole scene seem like some underground chamber for clandestine meetings rather than a House of God.

Secular knowledge was not needed in the ghetto and for centuries all Jewish thought was channeled into interpreting and splitting hairs over phrases and passages in the Talmud. With rare exceptions, each Jewish boy received a thorough Talmudic education, which did not cease with maturity. Every minute that could be spared from the struggle for a bare existence was devoted to poring over the writings of the Talmudic scholars. The Jew lost himself in a world of letters, where he remained in complete isolation. With a thorough knowledge of philosophy and of all the laws by which he was to regulate his personal way of life, he was completely and abysmally ignorant of the ways of the outside world. The ghetto was his home. He was born there and he would die there. He was not German, nor Bavarian, nor a citizen of Munich. He was a Jew.

The ghetto was virtually a state within a state. The community governed itself, maintaining a system of courts with power to enforce decisions in civil and criminal cases.

It supported the synagogues, schools, bath-houses, and the slaughtering houses. It levied taxes on a pro rata basis based on ability to pay, and in this manner it raised the money with which to pay the taxes the government assessed upon the Jewish community as a whole. Jews lived by the Torah as interpreted by the rabbis. Their life was a hard one, but there were compensating factors. The ghetto developed a sense of closeness and a sense of unity, for everyone knew everyone else. Their interests were identical and they lived in close communion with each other, with the synagogue the center of all their activities.

But the ghetto was not a pretty place. Bayard Taylor, in his widely read travel book of over a century ago, *Views Afoot,* has given us this picturesque description of the Prague ghetto, which might have been any ghetto in any city in Eastern Europe:

There is another part of Prague which is not less interesting, though much less poetical—the Jew's City. In our rambles we got into it before we were aware, but hurried immediately out of it again, perfectly satisfied with one visit. We entered first a dark, narrow street, whose sides were lined with booths of old clothes and second-hand articles. A sharp-featured old woman thrust a coat before my face, exclaiming, "Herr, buy a fine coat!" Instantly a man assailed me on the other side, "Here are vests! pantalons! shirts!" I broke loose from them and ran on, but it only became worse. One seized me by the arm, crying "Lieber Herr, buy some stockings!" and another grasped my coat; "Hats, Herr! Hats! Buy something, or sell me something!" I rushed desperately on, shouting, "No! No!" with all my might, and finally got safely through. My friend having escaped their clutches also, we found our way to the old Jewish Cemetery.

The unlocking of the ghettos began with the coming of the French Revolution, which was to upset the equilibrium of all of Europe, awakening its peoples from the lethargy that had held them in its grip for so long, bringing an entirely new concept of the social order, denying for the first time the divine right of kings and establishing the principle of the dignity of man—of all men, not only in France, but everywhere. From out of the masses, for centuries mere pawns in the hands of the aristocracy, sprang a new force, which denied that men were serfs whose very existence was subject to the whim or caprice of a duke or a princeling and whose loyalties could be swayed back and forth in the perennial tug of war between state and church. The newly formulated constitution of the United States of America, too, established beyond doubt that sovereignty rested with the people, and that government of the people, by the people, and for the people was not only a plausible theory—it was already an established fact.

Napoleon's victorious legions carried "Liberty, Fraternity, and Equality" to ever corner of Europe, to the Jews as well as to the peasants and serfs. The proclamation by the French Assembly on September 28, 1791, announcing the civil emancipation of the Jews lent hope to Jewish communities everywhere that the Age of Reason was meant for them too. It took more than a century, however, completely to eradicate ghettos from the European scene. With each wave of liberalism, Jews were carried along with the tide, but with the return of reaction, the rights they had gained were again wiped out. Gradually the Jews of Germany, Italy, the Balkan States, and the countries of Northern Europe were granted political rights and civic equality. Only in Russia and Poland did the ghetto linger on into the twentieth century.

MOSES OF THE NEW WORLD:
THE WORK OF BARON DE HIRSCH

1
MUNICH

Moritz von Hirsch first saw the light of day on
December 9, 1831, in Munich, the wind-swept
capital of the ancient Kingdom of Bavaria, a city in the
midst of a great transformation, a city in which the old
was rapidly giving way to the new and in which the contrast between the two emphasized forcibly the passing of
medieval feudalism and the emergence of the new capitalism that was slowly spreading over Europe.

An insignificant provincial town but thirty years before,
Munich had, since the beginning of the nineteenth century,
more than doubled its population and its size. Magnificent
buildings lined the newly laid-out spacious streets and tree-
lined boulevards. Cathedrals, theaters, colleges, art insti-
tutes, and music centers had been built, with a lavish
disregard of the cost, with no expense spared in filling
these halls of culture with the most prized paintings and
statuary that money could buy. Munich, in this short time,
had become an art and music center scarcely second to
any in all of Europe. It had become a city of splendor.

This rapid transformation of the typically German
small town into a glittering, cosmopolitan city was owing
entirely to one man, King Ludwig I. In an era when

princes and potentates vied with each other to curry the favor of sculptors and painters, musicians and writers, none was a more liberal patron of the arts than this Bavarian princeling, and certainly none entered into more grandiose schemes of city planning. It has been said of him that "he can boast of having done more for the arts than any other living monarch, and if he had accomplished it all without oppressing his people, he would deserve an immortality of fame." Long before he ascended the Bavarian throne in 1826, while he was still Crown Prince, Ludwig had surrounded himself with famous German artists, sculptors, and architects so that preparations could be made and plans laid for transforming this drab capital city into the cultural center of the continent when he should become king. The famous architects Klenze, Gartner, and Ohlmuller were chosen to carry out his building program, while the sculptor Schwanthaler was to provide the plastic embellishments. The renowned artist Cornelius and his many pupils drawn from the four corners of the world enlivened the walls of the buildings with paintings of a monumental character.

The modern magnificence of the new center, surrounded by the historical beauty of the old city, the quaint dialect of the Bavarian burghers that contrasted so strangely with the "high" German of the newly arrived intellectuals, the sudden accumulation of the richest art treasures in all of Germany in a city that had for centuries been known principally for its breweries and its cattle market, brought to Munich an unplanned, synthetic cosmopolitanism. And, as word of the new era that had come to Munich spread throughout Europe, an influx of new settlers began to arrive, soon assuming the proportions of a major boom. Munich, at the turn of the century, had been a community of scarcely seventy-five thousand souls. Now, in 1831, it could boast of well over one hundred and fifty thousand inhabitants, with more coming in every day. While the cost of living was still probably the lowest of any capital city on the continent, luxury and wealth were to increase by leaps and bounds until Munich had as large a proportion of wealthy residents as any city in Germany.

But there was, in the midst of all this splendor and wealth, one corner of Munich of which Ludwig could not very well have been proud, a region as old as any other in the city and that, from a historical point of view, was of far more interest than the glittering new section. This was the Jew's City—a few blocks of narrow, dark alleys into which sunlight seldom reached; streets lined with booths cluttered with all sorts of second-hand articles; crowded, stuffy quarters contrasting strangely with the wide spaciousness and the clean, healthy appearance of the new city. The several hundred Jews of Munich were crowded into this small area, living in tenement buildings built so close together that there was not even a walk between them, with three or four families living on each floor. In this gloomy, miserable atmosphere Jews were destined to spend their lives, for they could not leave their ghetto, even for recreation. The rest of the city was "out of bounds" to them except in rare instances, and only those who had business outside, for which they had been issued a special pass, could leave the Jew's City and go out into the Christian world.

The Jewish community of this Bavarian capital had been little noted for outstanding or unusual contributions to either world Jewry or to world history in the nine hundred years of its existence. Few great scholars or Talmudists had emerged from the long list of rabbis who had held sway over the congregation during the centuries, and few, if any, scientists, writers, poets, or statesmen had come out of the ghetto of Munich to bring honor and fame to the community. The Jewish community of Munich, as is true of the Jewries of so many of the smaller cities of Europe, had always been commonplace and of little importance. Its history is a repetition of the long, dreary centuries of persecution to which Jews were subjected in almost every Christian country, and to the trials and tribulations that beset them in their struggle for survival in a hostile world—to the role they played as victims of a conspiracy on the part of church, state, and society as a whole to force them into baptism or extinction. The ever-recurring cycle of persecution, special disabilities, burdensome taxation, ritual murder charges, forced baptisms, and anti-Jewish riots culminating in expulsion, has been the lot of the Jews of Munich as it has been the fate of all of Europe's Jews ever since the Roman Empire adopted Christianity as its official religion.

Except in the Germanic kingdoms, which in 1831 were still a long way from granting Jews that complete equality of citizenship which the Jews of France had enjoyed since Napoleon's Great Sanhedrin of Jewish notables in 1808, the position of the Jews throughout most of Europe had been materially improved in the fifty years preceding the year in which Moritz Von Hirsch was born. The last quarter of the eighteenth century had seen the dawn of a new era in the Western world—the modern concept of the "dignity of man" had gradually seeped into the consciousness of the peoples of the oppressed countries of Europe, giving rise to a new social order that was to bring political liberty and social equality to vast multitudes who had hitherto been merely pawns of a landed aristocracy. The age-long struggle against the tyranny of a state and church that had steadily sought to bar man's way to freedom and enlightenment was at last bearing fruit. The "Age of Reason" had arrived, and with it came a new concept of the Jew and of his place in society. "What is the great task of our time?" Heine asked. "It is emancipation. Not only that of the Irish, Greeks, Frankfort Jews, West Indian Blacks, and such oppressed races, but the emancipation of the whole world, especially of Europe that has come of age and is now wresting itself free from the leading-strings of the privileged classes, the aristocracy."

There were economic reasons, too, for the sudden acceptance of the Jew as a useful member of society. Feudalism was passing from the European scene, with capitalism fast replacing it as the economic force that was needed to spark the industrial revolution. And for this new form of economic control, the feudal barons were by temperament, inclination, and ability certainly not suited. But the Jews were. For centuries they had been denied the right to engage in agricultural pursuits or to take up any of the handicrafts; they had been unable to hold land and at no time did they have a clear right to settle anywhere permanently; they could be uprooted and scattered to the farthest corners of the earth on the slightest pretext, or on no pretext at all. History has recorded how often, and in what drastic forms, these expulsions came. There was not much left for them, then, but money-changing, and so, besides being the second-hand dealers, the old clothes peddlers, and the petty traders of the continent, they became the pawnbrokers of Europe. Now, however, their money-lending experience and the intercommunication they had always maintained with the ghettos of other commnuities were to stand them in good stead, giving Jews a decided advantage in the field of international finance. With the Talmud serving as a ready-made code of international law, the participation of Jewish bankers in the commercial life of any nation that expected to take part in the ever-widening industrial revolution was not only desirable but almost mandatory.

Austrian Emperor Maximilian Joseph II (1747-1790), titular head of the so-called South German Confederation, was probably the first of the autocratic rulers to recognize this fact and to encourage Jews to enter into the business life of the country. His "Toleranzpatent" of January 2, 1782, said: "The only reason for the expulsion of the Jews is that they are not Christians. To me they are human beings, consumers, and taxpayers, and consequently useful, if properly kept in check." He called for the gradual removal of many of the restrictions and disabilities that had heretofore been imposed on the Jews of that country. He encouraged Jews to adapt themselves to agricultural life and to learn trades and handicrafts. Not only did he establish a number of Jewish schools throughout the country in which secular courses of instruction were given to children who had hitherto been denied anything but a Talmudic education, but he also opened the Austrian school system to them. In 1787 Maximilian Joseph enacted a law that made the Jews of his empire subject to compulsory military service, the first time in European history that Jews had been granted the right to bear arms in defense of the country of their birth. Most of the more irksome disabilities under which Jews labored, however, remained in effect for many years and it was not until the latter days of the nineteenth century that Jews were able to achieve complete equality in all the provinces of the

Austro-Hungarian empire. The ghetto, the restrictions against Jewish marriages, the inability to hold public office, the "Leibzoll," or Jew's poll tax, and many other discriminatory regulations were to linger on for almost a century in many sections of the country, often creating embarrassing situations. The story is told of the dilemma the city fathers of Vienna found themselves in when it was learned that Meyerbeer, the great composer who had been invited to conduct the Vienna Symphony Orchestra in 1847, was a Jew. Jews were not allowed to visit Vienna without paying the Leibzoll, or Jew's tax, but how could they embarrass so great a musician, a guest of the city, by asking him to pay the Leibzoll for staying overnight in Vienna. A way out was found when it was decided that, because Meyerbeer had been made a Chevalier of France, it would be better to bill him as a famous French composer.

Owing in part to the new spirit of religious tolerance displayed by the Austrian Emperor, but more likely because of the unfavorable financial condition of the country, the treatment meted out to the Jews of Bavaria, too, took a turn for the better and a series of decrees enacted between the years 1800 and 1825 reflected a changed attitude on the part of the government. Jews who possessed business ability were granted permission to engage in commercial activities. The infamous "Leibzoll" was repealed and Jews could travel the length and breadth of the land without being humiliated at every city gate by having to pay a Jew's tax in order to pass through into the city itself. Many municipalities canceled or repealed long-standing expulsion orders, while others ignored laws that prohibited Jewish residence within their walls, or made these laws inoperative. In 1804 Jewish children were admitted to the schools of Bavaria, and in 1809 Jews were given the right to bear arms in the service of their fatherland. The ghettos, though, remained, as did many other restrictions and special disabilities. With the exception of those engaged in agriculture, manufacture, or the handicrafts, Jews were placed under a marriage registration law that required them to obtain a special license in order to marry. The number of licenses to be issued was set by law and, once all licenses were distributed, no Jew could marry except in the event of the death of another Jew who had held a license. "The path to the wedding canopy led only over the coffin of one who already had been registered," was the macabre tale of ghetto romance.

At the beginning of the nineteenth century some thirty Jewish families had taken up residence in the Munich ghetto. By the year 1818 the community had grown large enough to obtain a grant for a cemetery. But Bavarian law required fifty families to constitute a congregation large enough to build a synagogue and it was not until 1824 that the Jews of Munich, under the leadership of Israel Hirsch Pappenheim, who had long taken the lead in the fight for Jewish emancipation, were finally able to obtain a permit to build a synagogue. In that year a medal was struck commemorating the laying of the cornerstone for the new structure and in 1826 another medal appeared on which was engraved a replica of the completed synagogue.

Pappenheim, as president of the congregation, assembled a "Meeting of Bavarian Jewish Notables" in Munich in 1827, which laid before the Bavarian ministry a plan for organizing a consistorial system similar to that which had been so successful in France, but this came to nothing. In refusing to take action on this and other Jewish questions, Bavaria was merely following the lead of the other Germanic States that were so slow to accept the new age of enlightenment that was sweeping the world. Independence had been granted to all peoples of all faiths in the United States in 1783. France had accorded Jews complete equality before the law in 1791 and had introduced the same laws into Holland when it conquered that country in 1796. England had long ago established equality, and the Italian States were not far behind. Of all the large countries in Europe, with the exception of Russia and Poland, where serfdom was still being practised and where Jewish emancipation was not even remotely thought of, only Germany persisted in treating the Jews as somewhat less than citizens.

It was of little avail for Jews to proclaim their patriotism and devotion to the country of their birth because the Germans could only say, "Jew, convert! If you want to be a German, accept Jesus." But Gabriel Riesser, a leader in the fight of the German Jews for emancipation, answered: "The songs of the German poets have kindled and nourished the sacred fire of German freedom in our breasts. We want to belong to the German fatherland, we will belong to it in all respects. It can and may demand of us everything that it is justified in demanding of its citizens. We will sacrifice everything to it willingly—only not religion and faith and truth and honor: for Germany's heroes and Germany's scholars have not taught us that one becomes a German through a sacrifice of this kind."

Freedom for the Jews of Germany came hard. Where they succeeded in obtaining concessions from kings and potentates, they were set back by the Church, and where the Church accepted Jewish emancipation, the people opposed it. When reactionaries were won over to the cause of the Jews, the liberals would take up cudgels against them.

In trying to explain why Germany's liberals would actively oppose so fundamental a principle as the total enfranchisement of all groups, the Jewish historian Karpeles says: "Various causes contributed to the fact—the narrow-mindedness of the learned, factiousness, the inflexibility of public opinion, blind adherence to principles, political orthodoxy, and much else. Science—including, it must be stated, theology as well as history—politics, and the press were equally powerful factors in retarding the progress of liberalism. Such is the only explanation that throws light upon the determined stand taken against the emancipation of the Jews in the period between 1815 and 1840 by the most learned historians and the most open-minded politicians." What could be expected of the people at large, whose humanitarian standards were extremely low, and who were for the most part illiterate, if the intellectuals of Germany not only did not lend support to Jewish emancipation, but actually opposed it?

The latest French rationalistic philosophy spreading over the intellectual circles of Europe could not have failed to excite the Jews of the continent, inspiring new hope for that complete emancipation which was so widely enjoyed by the Jews of France. Morley Sachar in his book *The Course of Modern Jewish History*, says "By 1810 Jewish integration into French life was so much a matter of public notice that the Metz Town Council, in special session, proclaimed that many followers of the law of Moses each day make laudable efforts to draw closer to our customs, usages, our civilization, our special practices, to escape at last from the state of abjection to which our old laws and perhaps our prejudices condemned them."

Looking about them, seeing in all its ugliness the stilted, degraded lives they were forced to live, comparing the disabilities under which they labored with the freedom enjoyed by the Jewries of the liberated countries, the Jews of Munich and of all Southern Germany began to bestir themselves. Viewing the hopelessness of their situation under the paternal despotism of the Germanic kingdoms, and realizing the utter futility of trying to attain equality under such regimes, their thoughts turned to emigration and to the new world. Spurred on by the desire for marriage and family life still denied to so many of them, thousands of young, ambitious Jews left their Bavarian homes and sought their fortunes in America.

The impact of the changes the works of Moses Mendelssohn had brought to Jewish religious and intellectual life had begun to reach Munich, too, by the year in which Moritz de Hirsch was born, bringing to the Jews there the freedom of expression and thought that the new age of enlightenment had brought to the Christian world when it drew a sharp distinction between theology and secular knowledge. The ghetto had taken away from Jews the only means by which they could participate in the intellectual activities of the outside world—a common language. This Mendelssohn recognized as being a major stumbling-block in the path of Jewish assimilation. His translation of the Pentateuch into German was to be the opening wedge in the movement that was to see the Jews of Germany adopt the German language as their mother tongue, his German Torah becoming the inspiration for them to learn to speak and write the German language to prepare themselves for participation in German life. His close friend and colleague, David Friedlander, established a Jewish free school in Berlin in 1778, the first Jewish school in all of Germany in which nothing but the German tongue was used. The idea took hold and it was not long before secular education became the educational fare of Jewish children throughout Germany. In 1783 a periodical, *Der Sammler*, made its appearance. It was designed to impart general information and current world news to adult Jews in the hope that it would stimulate a desire to take up the study of German.

In Bavaria, Alexander Beer, the famous religious teacher and author, brother of the composer Meyerbeer, had, in 1826, written a catechism in the German vernacular. An abridged form of this catechism was published at the expense of the state under the endorsement of King Ludwig, with a view to promoting systematic religious instruction among the Jews in modern form. By the year 1831 there was scarcely a Jew in Munich who was not thoroughly literate in the German tongue.

The Reform Judaism Movement, too, had made some headway in Munich. The fifty or more families who made up the community were about equally divided on this question and, had it not been for the diplomatic maneuverings of Rabbi Hirsch Aub, the congregation would probably have split into several factions. Hirsch Aub proved to be so adept at handling this issue wherever it appeared that he was to become known throughout all of Southern Germany as "ba'al Sholom" (peace-maker). He held to a middle course, accepting some of the moderations that Reform Judaism advocated but adhering closely to the orthodox form in the synagogue. Rabbi Hirsch Aub in later years was to gain fame for his leadership in the fight for Jewish emancipation, and for his ceaseless agitation for the abolition of the law under which the number of married Jews who could reside in each of the Bavarian towns was legally limited.

Those were the years, too, that were to provide the test of whether or not Jews could break away from the narrow, binding traditions of the ghetto and become assimilated into the social and cultural life of the peoples among whom they lived, and whether or not Judaism could withstand the impact of this assimilation and the new religious freedoms. Cutting themselves off suddenly from the strict religious observances of the ghetto, not prepared for sudden release from the restrictive influences of orthodoxy, many Jews were unable to find a middle ground on which they could rest and soon drifted to Christianity. A veritable mania for baptism began to make itself evident in the larger cities. The historian Karpeles says, "In the first quarter of the nineteenth century a large part of the Jewish community of Berlin, in the opinion of some authorities fully half its members, were converted to Christianity. The same happened in Konigsberg, Frankfort, Breslau and other large cities."

In the meantime, though, the work of Leopold Zunz, Edward Gans, Moses Moser, Solomon Judah Rapoport of Lemberg, and Samuel David Luzzato of Trieste, was establishing and disseminating the "science of Judaism," which was to find many adherents for the new Reform movement. The object of this new science was "the presentation of Judaism first from the historical point of view, its gradual development and growth, and then from the philosophic point of view, its essential meaning and thought; but before all, a knowledge of Jewish literature must be arrived at through philological channels." The literary investigations of scholars of such stature brought a renaissance of Judaism as a living religion that continues to this day. They lifted the works of the ancient Hebrew scholars from the stagnation of the ghetto and brought to the Jews a new respect for Judaism as an adaptable, modern religion that they could live with in an assimilated world. In the words of Karpeles "The rise of the science of Judaism marked the end of the time in which the young found salvation only in one-sided negation, or sought salvation only beyond the limits of their religious community, in regions in which the Jew was ashamed to be a Jew, was ashamed to call himself a Jew."

The Reform synagogue ritual, introduced in 1815, enabled the assimilated Jew to eliminate the unwieldly customs so restrictive to free life in an emancipated society and still remain a Jew. It put a stop to the headlong rush to conversion.

2

FAMILY

Not much is known of the origin of the Hirsch family, although the name seems to have been quite common throughout southern Germany for hundreds of years, appearing in the records of ghetto communities all over Bavaria as far back as the first entries in the Nuremberg Memor-Buch. The earliest of Moritz von Hirsch's ancestors of whom we have any record was his great-grandfather, Moses Hirsch von Gau-Konigshofen, the founder of the family fortune. Under the firm name of Moses & Sohne he was given the first permit issued to a Jew to own real estate in Bavaria. His son Jacob, who started life as a Talmud "Bahur," rose from a Handelsmann, (a Jew who had been granted the right to move freely throughout the country) to the position of Hofbankier or Court Banker to the Bavarian Crown, and finally, in 1818, to knighthood under the title of Baron von Hirsch auf Gereuth.

Born at Konigshofen near Wurzburg in the year 1764, Jacob Hirsch's early years were much the same as those of any other Jewish youth of this small community. Brought up and educated for the Rabbinate in the typical ghetto manner, with a thorough training in Talmudic lore but with little or no secular education of any kind, he grew to manhood as one of the most devoted "bahurim" of the community, spending all his spare hours poring over the weighty tomes of the Talmud and studying the teachings of the ancient scholars. Throughout his lifetime he carried with him an abiding faith in Judaism, never for a moment allowing himself to relax his observance of the rituals of the religion, no matter how demanding, even while holding the highest position in the country to which a Jew could aspire.

Although the city of Wurzburg still permitted no Jews to settle within its confines, many of the surrounding towns no longer restricted Jewish residence, the neighboring town of Konigshofen among them. The Konigshofen ghetto, while not large, was an important trading center for Wurzburg, whose burghers would travel to Konigshofen to do business with the Jews. Many of the Jews, too, had special permits that allowed them, after paying the Leibzoll or Jew's poll-tax, to enter the forbidden city of Wurzburg for business purposes, spending the daytime in the city taking care of their trading activities, but returning each night before dark to be locked up in the Konigshofen ghetto.

Jacob Hirsch must have been one of the more successful of these traders. Succeeding to his father's business, which he moved to a house in a narrow lane behind the Cathedral of Wurzburg, he did a large traffic in all sorts of merchandise, laying the foundation for the gigantic fortune he and his descendants were to accumulate. His unusual ability in matters of finance and the acumen he displayed in manipulating several large transactions, soon brought him to the attention of Maxmilian Joseph, who raised him to the position of Court Banker to the Bavarian Crown, a position he was to hold for many years. When the capital was transferred to Munich he took up residence there. During the War of Liberation (1813-1815), which saw the coalition of European states desert Napoleon and turn against the French conqueror, Jacob Hirsch organized and equipped at his own expense an entire regiment of soldiers, which joined forces with Bavaria's allies and pursued the French armies right to the gates of Paris. For this display of patriotism, he was raised to the nobility by royal proclamation on August 13, 1818, thus becoming the first Jew in Bavaria to be allowed to engage in agricultural pursuits. Besides his large estate at Gereuth, he acquired several other agricultural tracts, on one of which he established a fish-hatchery and on another a sugar refinery. On his estate at Planegg near Munich he established a brewery.

The position of "Hof-Jude," or Court Jew, placed him under the protection of the Crown and made him an important member of the Court, enjoying the privileges and honors that went with the rank of court functionary. He was relieved of all the medieval disabilities that still bound his coreligionists: he could travel without encumbrance; he was permitted to trade in any merchandise he wished; he could employ servants, Christian or Jewish, and the rights he possessed were also enjoyed by them; and he dressed as did the Christian members of the community, without the customary Jew-badge or any other humiliating distinctions of dress.

The functions of the Court Jew were many and varied. He was to furnish loans to the monarch and handle the direction of his personal finances. He was the purveyor of jewelry, furnishings, art objects, and all the trappings so necessary to court life. He supervised the handling of supplies to the army. Sometimes his services to the Crown were of an unusual or personal nature and there have been many stories told of romantic intrigues in which Court Jews acted as the intermediaries in royal romances.

The lot of the Court Jew, though, was not always a happy one. His position, precarious at best, was dependent on retaining the good will of the monarch he served, who, only too often, was uneducated and could neither read nor write. The Court Jew had to be ready to supply whatever the monarch asked for, no matter how impossible of attainment, while still handling the financial affairs of the Crown efficiently and profitably. And always he was subject to immediate dismissal, or even imprisonment, if he failed in any of these duties. He was exposed, too, to humiliation and insult from the other members of the court entourage, even though he was under the protection of the Crown. He was still a Jew, not acceptable socially to the Christian members of the court, most of whom were descended from long lines of nobility. Just as Jews on the whole were second-rate citizens of the country, Court Jews were second-rate courtiers.

But, although they could call no man "friend," the salons of the Court Jews were always well attended. The Court hangers-on, the perennial favor seekers, the intellectuals who looked to the nobility for patronage, the teachers and professors whose salary the Hof-Jude paid from the royal treasury, all attended the particularly brilliant soirées and salons for which the Court Jews were noted. But each was there for a selfish motive, and few were there because of their regard for the man himself.

The position of the Court Jew in the Jewish communities, too, was one of strained coolness. Accepted as a leader because of the money he donated to the synagogue and to the charitable organizations of the ghetto, he had to be consulted in all matters affecting Jewry as a whole, and he imposed his will almost as a benevolent dictator. Often he would go so far as to install one of his own relatives, usually a son-in-law, as rabbi of the congregation, whether qualified or not. He was virtually a dictator in Judaism, but he was the object of suspicion and distrust on the part of his coreligionists who had to tolerate his interference in their affairs.

Joseph von Hirsch, the father of Moritz, was born in 1805, the second of the two sons of Jacob Hirsch. Brought up in the home of the most prominent Jew in Bavaria, he received a thorough Jewish training, but without the long tedious hours of Talmudic study that his father had undergone, and a well-rounded secular education that would fit him for modern life in the emancipated world that lay ahead. One of his religious teachers was Isaac Bernays who, after graduating from the University of Wurzburg, came to live in the Hirsch home as a private tutor. Bernays, who was later to become widely known as the progressive "hakam" or "clerical functionary" of Hamburg (he considered the title Rabbi as not being in high enough esteem to be held by the spiritual leader of a modern congregation) was possessed of a rare knowledge of the Bible and the Talmud, and held wide philosophical views. He was the first of the orthodox rabbis to attempt to interpret Judaism in modern form and to try to preserve the ancestral creed, even in cultured circles. His teachings undoubtedly influenced Joseph von Hirsch, for he remained a loyal and religious Jew all his life, passing on to his children an abiding faith in Judaism.

Joseph von Hirsch entered his father's banking establishment at the age of eighteen. Where his brother Joel, sixteen years his senior, was the ultra-conservative banker, Joseph was inclined to indulge in highly speculative ventures, often in direct opposition to the wishes of his father. His investments were usually successful though, and, young as he was, his willingness to go into unusual deals brought the firm many opportunities for profitable investments that were denied others. Before his twenty-fifth birthday he had become prominently identified with many agricultural enterprises, so much so that he was better known as an agriculturalist and cattle dealer than as a banker. His first public appointment was to the Central Committee for the Promotion of Forest Culture, a position he was to hold for many years. It was only in his later years that he was to become identified with the building of railroads as the chief constructor of the Bavarian Ostbahn. His record of service to the Bavarian Kingdom was a long one and in 1869 he was raised to the hereditary baronage by King Ludwig II in recognition of "his fidelity to the throne and in acknowledgment of his many useful works."

Joseph von Hirsch in 1828 married Caroline Wertheimer, daughter of the banker Wolf Wertheimer of Frankfort-on-the-Main, a descendant of Samson Wertheimer (1658-1724), the distinguished Austrian Court Jew, financier, and rabbi, whose important career has engaged the attention of so many historians. Many of the descendants of Samson Wertheimer were to become influential personages in Jewish life and in European financial circles, among them his grandsons, Bernard Eskeles of Vienna, whose firm, Arnstein and Eskeles, was one of the leading banking firms of Europe during the first half of the nineteenth century, and Joseph Ritter von Wertheimer, banker, philanthropist, author and educator, and

long head of the Jewish community of Vienna. Thus, to
the already great resources of the von Hirsch firm, Joseph
brought added prestige and power in the person of a
daughter of the illustrious Wertheimer family, greatly
increasing his influence in financial circles throughout
Southern Germany.

Caroline Wertheimer had been raised in a family long
known for its interest in the preservation of Judaism as a
dynamic, living religion. She leaned to the orthodox tradition and, despite her high social position, she observed
in her home and in her everyday life every ritual that her
religion prescribed. Deeply concerned with the plight of
those Jews less fortunate than she, Caroline von Hirsch
devoted most of her life to charitable activities as a leading spirit in any group working to relieve distress or to
improve the depressing life of the Jews of the ghetto. She
imbued her children with her religious fervor and an
understanding of the responsibility toward their fellow
men that the possession of great riches entailed.

Of this union Moritz von Hirsch was born on December 9, 1831, the third child in a family that was to grow
to nine children.

3

CHILDHOOD

The winter dawn came through the trees as the first light of the December morning caught the windows of the castle, reflecting bright rays of sunlight on the garden below. Beyond the barren fields from which every last particle of grain had been harvested but a month or so before, the gleaming river flowed on toward the nearby city of Munich, which was beginning to stir although the streets and squares were still in the shadows. The ghetto was slowly coming to life, the pious Jews wending their way to the synagogue for morning prayers. But it was broad daylight before the husky cries of the newborn baby boy were first heard and Moritz von Hirsch, destined to become one of the richest men in the world, renowned as an empire builder and marked for greatness as the savior of countless thousands of his fellow Jews, saw the light of day.

The ghetto, by this time, was all astir. Small clusters of Jews could be seen gathering together, excitedly passing on the happy news that a son had been born to Joseph von Hirsch and his wife Caroline, the favorite daughter of the wealthy Wertheimer family. This was an occasion for rejoicing and merry-making, for the Baron and his father, the "Old Baron," as Jacob was called by the Jewish community, were both fine Jews. They had done much to lighten the burden of the Jewish people of Munich because of the high esteem in which they were held by the Christian aristocracy and by the King himself. And their generous charity and giving of huge sums for the synagogue was legendary.

Jacob, the old Baron, had been no ordinary Court Jew. He had never forsaken Judaism as had Baron von Eichtal, who had converted to Christianity, nor had he forgotten a Jew's duty toward his fellow men. No one had been more charitable than he, and no one had been more devout in his adherence to the religion of his forefathers. His son Joseph, too, had proved worthy to carry on the Hirsch name, and Caroline, who had come to the community but a short time before, had won the hearts of all. Her happy disposition, her sympathetic nature, and her inability to resist her charitable impulses had soon won her a lasting place in the affections of the community.

Seldom, if ever, did a Jewish child come into the world under so bright a star as did Moritz von Hirsch. Grandson and heir to two of the greatest German banking families, bearer of a name already famous in the world of finance, a life of luxury and ease stretched out ahead of him. His future could be of his own choosing. He could become a rabbi, a physician, a scholar, a banker, or he could enter any of the new fields that had been closed to his father and to his grandfather but that now were open to Jews. Emancipation was on the march. Already Jews in England and France were holding public office, and who could tell but what Jews might some day occupy the highest positions their countries could offer. Even Germany, more nationalistic, more anti-Jewish, more Catholic than the other countries of western Europe, could not long deny Jews their rightful place in the community. The march of progress would see to that. The nineteenth century was on its way.

While the record that has come down to us of the boyhood years of Moritz von Hirsch is, as with most famous men, completely barren of all but the barest details, enough is known of the family from which he came, of the city in which he spent his most impressionable years, and of the history of its Jewish community to determine the influences that went into shaping the character of the man who was to become the great Baron de Hirsch.

His early years were spent in the seclusion of the great castle on the rural estate at Planegg or in the baronial summer home at Baiersdorff. He did not play in the streets and squares as did ordinary children, and he saw little, if anything, of the ghetto. Among the children with whom he spent his childhood years were the children of the wealthier members of the community. It was a closely bound clique, which permitted of no association with the children of the ghetto. There were the Seligmann children, whose father had for many years been a Bavarian Court Banker along with Jacob Hirsch, and who had converted when he was created Baron von Eichtal for his many services to the Crown; Elise Henle, a year older than Moritz, who was to become the famous German novelist and dramatist; her older brother, Sigmund, later Bavaria's most famous lawyer, legal representative of King Ludwig, and a member of the Bavarian Diet; Henriette Mendel, the great beauty and world-famous actress who married Duke Ludwig Wilhelm, son of Duke Maximilian Joseph of Bavaria, after being converted to the Catholic Church; Louis Neustatter, the famous portrait painter on whom both King Ludwig II and Franz Joseph of Austria conferred high honors; and David and William Ritter von Gutmann, who, under the firm name of Gutmann Brothers, were to become the largest coal miners in all of Europe. It is interesting that in later life David Von Gutmann became President of the Baron de Hirsch School Fund for Galicia.

Moritz von Hirsch's early years were the years during which all the dreams of King Ludwig were being brought to fruition, with building going on on all sides on an unprecedented scale. There were the new buildings being added to th University of Munich; the Ludwigskirche; the Church of St. Louis; the Blind Asylum; the Gates of Victory; the Odeon, built in the modern style for public balls and concerts; the improvements and alterations to the royal palace; the Festaalbau with its festive halls; the magnificent new post office on Max-Joseph Platz; the Royal Chapel; and the Church of St. Boniface; all were under construction during the thirteen years Moritz von Hirsch was to spend in Munich as a child. The city was a hodge-podge of contrasts between the old and the new; between the cosmopolitan intellectuals who thronged its art centers and the provincial burghers who peopled the beer gardens in their colorful Bavarian costumes; between the medieval splendor of the old town and the enchantment of the glittering new city of stone and marble. Munich had become, under the paternalism of Ludwig I, a truly enchanted city. In glowing terms Bayard Taylor, the renowned traveler and author, describes the city in his book *Views Afoot*, published in 1845:

I have been walking in a dream where the fairy tales of boyhood were realized, and the golden and jewelled

halls of the Eastern genii rose glittering around me—
a vision of the brain no more. All I had conceived of oriental magnificence, all descriptions of the splendor of
kingly halls and palaces, fall short of what I here see.
Where shall I begin to describe the crowd of splendid
edifices that line its streets, or how give an idea of the
profusion of paintings and statutes—of marble, jasper
and gold?

If a well-traveled globe-trotter, who had seen all the
magnificence of the ancient cities of Europe, could be
roused to such heights of poetic fervor by what he saw in
Munich, it is not difficult to imagine the effect the city
must have had on an impressionable Jewish boy who was
exposed to all this grandeur during the hey-day of its
development. All his life he was to be imbued with daring
ideas, for what he saw going on all around him was a
living example of the value of laying large plans. Ludwig
planned on a large scale and big things were done. Those
whose vision was not large enough to conceive mammoth
undertakings accomplished little. If one was to be more
than just an idle dreamer one had to dream big dreams,
for Ludwig had demonstrated that, with imagination and
nerve, it was no more difficult to bring to completion an
ambitious undertaking than it was an insignificant, medio-
cre enterprise.

Perhaps it was this that gave Moritz von Hirsch his
flair for the spectacular undertakings that were to make
him the most talked-about banker of the nineteenth century, leading the older, more conservative bankers to consider him wild and irresponsible. Perhaps his bent for
large-scale promotions, for business ventures breathtaking
in scope, for building a railroad across half a continent,
can be traced to the large-scale program of city beautifi-

cation he had seen Ludwig bring to fruition in a few short years. Ludwig had demonstrated that he had the fortitude to undertake a program of such huge scope that it staggered the imagination of the scoffers who called him a fool for thinking he could create a city of splendor out of the dull, drab, ancient town of Munich, and make cosmopolitan art lovers of its beer-drinking burghers. But now that his plans were nearing completion and Munich was turning into one of the most glorious cities in all of Europe, these same scoffers called Ludwig a genius.

The world in which Moritz von Hirsch spent his youth was far from a harmonious one. It was an age of confusion. The religious orthodoxy of his parents and grandparents clashed with the rationalism of the new Reform Movement, which was creating a great many problems for religious leaders everywhere. The high social position his family had attained as outstanding, wealthy bankers contrasted with the degradation of the ghetto Jew and the condescension with which Jews were treated by the landed gentry and even by their associates in the business world. But probably the most confusing paradox of all was that, although the ghetto continued and Jews still had no civil status in Bavaria, Jewish intellectuals were admitted to the universities. And with the influx of students and intellectuals from all over Europe into Munich came many Jewish students and scholars to attend classes at the University of Munich.

Isaac Lowie, one of the early leaders of the Reform Movement, was one of the first Jews to study at the University of Munich, where he obtained a Doctor of Philosophy degree in 1828. He was elected District Rabbi of Furth in 1830 but the opposition of the orthodox community of Furth was so vehement that the government had to interfere and a "Decree of Installation" was issued by King Ludwig I on March 10, 1831. The following year, the orthodox community, led by Lowie's former teacher, Rabbi Wolf Hamburger, petitioned the government to "depose him for irreligious doctrine, and for introducing reform into divine services without regard for the ancient law." The case dragged on for eight years and in 1838 the government issued an order to Rabbi Lowie to "be more careful in his words and actions and have more regard for those who conformed to the true Mosaic ceremonials and did not adhere to pernicious neology." Rabbi Lowie was ordered to pay one-third of the cost of the law suit.

Many of the nineteenth century's outstanding rabbinical scholars and leaders, some of whom were to become famous in America, received their education at the University of Munich—men like Elias Grunebaum, who in 1836 became Rabbi of the Landau district after receiving a degree from the University of Munich. It was due to his unremitting efforts that the Jew's Oath was finally abolished in Bavaria in 1862. There was Henry Hochheimer, who attended the University from 1839 to 1844 and who, because of his political writings, was forced to flee to the United States, where he became famous as a rabbi in Baltimore. David Einhorn, too, studied at the University of Munich. It was he who, while spiritual leader of a Baltimore congregation during the Civil War, had the temerity to denounce slavery and, on April 22, 1861, was forced to flee the city at night, guarded and secreted from the mob by friends. He later became rabbi of the Adath Yeshurun congregation in New York. There was Bernhard Felsenthal, who became the first rabbi of Sinai Congregation in Chicago. And Isaac Nordheimer, who

received a Ph.D. from the University of Munich in 1834
and left immediately for New York, where he was to become widely known as a professor of Arabic and Oriental
languages at New York University, and later as an in-
structor at the Union Theological Seminary. Max Lilien-
thal, whose stormy career in Russia is well known, received a Ph.D. degree from Munich in1837. He too found
his way to America, after his attempt to introduce secular
education into the Jewish communities of Russia led him
into many difficulties. For twenty-seven years he was to
occupy a pulpit in Cincinnati.

The great Heine himself went to Munich in 1827 with
the idea of taking a chair as professor at the University
of Munich, where his brother Maximilian was a medical
student. He applied for the post and asked the editor of
the paper for which he wrote occasionally to personally
present his petition to the King. "It would also benefit me
greatly," he said, "if you could indicate to him that the
author is now quite a different person from the writer of
his earlier works. I think the King is wise enough to judge
the blade by its edge and not by any good or bad use that
has already been made of it." The appointment was about
to be made and nothing was lacking but the royal signa-
ture, when Heine changed his mind and went to Italy.
Unable to find employment there, he moved to France,
where he found that his Jewish birth proved to be an
advantage rather than otherwise. His brother Maximilian
joined the Russian Army as a surgeon and settled in St.
Petersburg, where he spent most of his life.

Many of these students, while attending their studies,
earned their living by taking positions as tutors to the
children of the wealthier families of Munich, and some of
them must have been employed as tutors to Moritz von

Hirsch. His mother, who remained a devout Jewess all the days of her life, saw to it that her children were given a thorough, if not an intensive, education in Judaism and in the Hebrew language. She employed the best available teachers, especially young student rabbis. Some of these may have had an adverse effect on the young, impressionistic von Hirsch heir, for he often referred in later life to the fact that his lack of interest in religion was due to the hypocrisy of some of his teachers, whose actions, often, were far different from their religious teachings. He particularly commented on the difference between precept and practice on the part of an early teacher whose name he never mentioned, which alienated him so much from the dogma of creed and religion that he never, as an adult, entered a house of worship.

Despite the fact that he did not observe any religious practices, he refused to become baptized as had so many prominent Jews of the period, who found it easy to rid themselves of many of the disabilities that made life difficult for Jews by going through a ritual that took but a few minutes and could be forgotten about once the ritual had been performed. The majority of conversions that took place during this period were for reasons of convenience and not as a result of religious conviction. The ulterior motives behind most of the conversions soon became apparent even to the Christian missionaries, who, in their zeal for converts, did not ask too many questions. Typical of the "high-pressure" conversions is the story told by the Protestant court preacher at Berlin, Dr. Rudolph Kogel, in his *Reminiscences*. "With all signs of impatient haste, a Jewish banker entered my room: 'I wish to be baptized,' he said. 'May I ask you to state your motives for the step?' I replied. 'Motives! Suffice it to say that I have given serious thought to the matter!' 'But as a clergy-man I must be acquainted with the motives for your re-solve; I have no desire to add one more to the number of those who are Christians only in name; as it is, there are more than enough of them!' 'Very well,' said the Jew, aggrieved, and rising from his seat, 'I shall apply to some other clergyman who takes his vocation less seriously!' "

In his novel *Ilona,* Hans Haber tells a story, too, that could have happened anywhere in Europe during this period, a story of the conversion mania that extended to the poorest of ghetto dwellings, to a man like Shlomko, whose son "didn't want to be a Jew any more. He decided he'd go over to the Orthodox Church. That was a misery to poor Shlomko. He had always been a wizened little man; now he seemed even more shrunken, and his wife wept, but it was no use. Simon had himself baptized. Now in the village there was another Jew, a devout one, al-most a rabbi. He had always got on well with the priest, but one day he met him and didn't greet him; he turned his head away. The priest stopped him and asked the reason. Then the devout Jew reproached the priest be-cause he had baptized Shlomko's son and so helped him give up his religion. The priest looked at the Jew for a minute and then he said: 'We've got the worst of the bargain. You Jews have lost a lump of dirt and we Chris-tians have picked it up.' "

Rabbi Hirsch Aub was probably as responsible as any-one else for the almost complete absence of baptisms among the Jews of Munich. While throughout all of Germany the venomous diatribes that passed for discus-sion between the opposing factions in Judaism had caused many Jews to leave the fold because they felt that they had no place in this sharply divided contest, the Jews of

Munich, almost to a man, remained loyal to the faith of their fathers. Under the leadership of Hirsch Aub they reached a common ground of understanding. Compromise took the place of bitter acrimony, with a wise realization that survival of the whole was far more important than survival of the ancient rituals or the acceptance of modern customs. They agreed to let the matter rest with individual consciences. Those who wished to retain orthodox Judaism in their homes were free to do so. Those who felt that the restraints that the old order placed against them in the modern world were too difficult could retain whatever rituals they wished to maintain in their own homes, or they could abolish those they no longer felt were important. The Synagogue, under Hirsch Aub, retained the ancient rituals but incorporated many of the innovations that reform Judaism had brought into being. With this arrangement everybody was satisfied. Nobody felt that his wishes were disregarded or that there was nothing left for him but baptism.

The literary efforts of Rabbi Lazarus Adler, too, had a great deal of influence on the Jews of Bavaria because of the periodical, *The Synagogue,* that he published. Rabbi Adler, who had received his doctorate at the University of Munich, started publication of his journal in Wurzburg in 1837, moving to Munich in 1839, where it met with instant success. Following a middle-of-the-road course on the controvers⸱ ⸱⸱⸱ ⸱⸱⸱⸱m Judaism, *The Synagogue* went a long way toward establishing a liberalized orthodoxy. Many of the editorials that dealt wisely with this subject had the effect of calming the atmosphere and of making Jews realize that nothing would be gained by bickering and squabbling among themselves when there was so much more work to be done toward gaining that full equality before the law which they all hoped would eventually be granted to them.

The failure of the Jewish community to make any headway in its struggle for emancipation, and the refusal of the Bavarian authorities to accord to them even the barest of human rights also made a great impression on young von Hirsch. The conference called by the government in 1836, when it summoned Jewish scholars and communal representatives from all over Bavaria to meet with government representatives in Munich to discuss the complete emancipation of Bavaria's Jewry, had come to nought. Seligman Baer Hamberger, a successful businessman of Wurzburg who had become an outstanding Talmudist, represented the community of Wurzburg and uttered an impassioned plea for justice. Israel Hirsch Pappenheim, now the patriarch of the community, had also lent a voice to the proceedings. Isaac Lowie, the rabbi at Furth, who had been for some time bitterly opposed by the older members of the community because of his reform teachings, was also one of the outstanding Jews present at this assembly. Nothing came of this, however, and Munich's Jews continued to be classless citizens with no civil rights before the law.

At almost every succeeding session of the Bavarian Diet the question of Jewish emancipation would come up for discussion, only to be dropped again without any definite action taken. As year followed year, with no improvement in sight for the alleviation of Jewish disabilities, more and more the realization was brought home to the Jewish community that for a full enjoyment of the newly discovered rights of man, they would have to look elsewhere. Thousands upon thousands of young Jews and Jewesses, unable to marry and found a family because of the restrictions on Jewish marriages, unwilling to face a future such as that which confronted them in the ghettos of Bavaria, migrated to the more enlightened countries, and especially to the New World. It is from here that most of the large influx of German Jews who arrived in America between the years 1845 and 1875 originated.

The continual struggle of Munich's Jewry for that equality and justice which had been granted to the Jews of France, Holland, and England so long ago must have impressed young von Hirsch with the injustice of the treatment accorded the Bavarian Jews and with the utter disregard for human rights displayed by all of the Germanic peoples. All around him he could see an acceptance of authoritarian government by the German burghers, with never a protest, with never a momentary doubt of the divine right of kings, and with never a glimmer of the democratic dream. And all around him he could see a handful of Jews battering their heads against the wall of German stubbornness in an attempt to gain for their people the most elementary rights of a human being, to be able to live their lives free from unwarranted molestation and to worship God in their own way. Certain it is that young von Hirsch developed a dislike for Germans that was to remain with him all the days of his life. He distrusted them and he had no wish to live among them. It is significant that he entered the business world, not in Munich where his family had been for so long established and where the Hirsch name was so widely known and respected, but in Brussels. It is significant, too, that during his lifetime he maintained residences in Paris, London, Brussels, and Hungary, but never in Germany itself.

This, then, was the social and political condition of the Jewish community of Munich in which Moritz von Hirsch lived until his fourteenth birthday. Accepted into the business world of the city but ostracized socially, the Jews of Munich were still a long way removed from the equality that the Jews of the northern countries of Europe enjoyed. While the Jews of England and the United States enjoyed full equality with all other subjects and had even been granted the franchise, the Jews of Germany were still subject to the humiliating "More Judaico" or Jew's Oath. While the French Jews had been accorded the status of Frenchmen under the consistory system, the Jews of Bavaria were still unable to marry without the coveted "Matrikel." And while the new kingdoms of Belgium and Holland had placed no restrictions against Jews in their constitutions, the Jews of Munich were still confined to the ghetto. While the fight for emancipation was going on relentlessly, it was making little progress. Freedom came hard for the Jews of Bavaria.

Despite the prominent position the family held, Joseph von Hirsch began to question his son's future in the Bavarian capital. He realized only too well the precarious position of the Court Banker, dependent at all times on the whims of a monarch who had never been too friendly to the Jews. He began to think that perhaps his son would be better off in one of the more enlightened countries, such as France or England or the Netherlands. Many were the conversations he and Caroline held together to decide Moritz's future. Although his mind was bright and alert, Moritz was not a brilliant student. He had no genius for any particular subject. His father had hoped that he would take up the legal profession, but he had no talents in that direction. He showed a precocious interest in speculative transactions, though, and at an early age it was obvious that he was cut out for a business career. It was natural that he should follow the family tradition of banking. With many doubts and misgivings they reached the difficult decision that it would be best to send their son away to complete his education; Brussels was selected as the city in which he was to continue his schooling. Here Joseph von Hirsch's good friend, Senator Raphael Bischoffsheim, enjoyed an exceptionally profitable banking business and a prominent position in the community, and he had promised to make a place in his establishment for the young von Hirsch heir when he was ready to enter the business world.

4

BELGIUM

The Brussels to which Moritz von Hirsch, who was now to take the French form of his name, Maurice de Hirsch, came in 1844 was an enlightened community in which there were few, if any, restrictions against the Jews living there. It was a community that in no way resembled the Jewish community he had left behind in Munich. Until 1794, when Belgium was occupied by French troops, the Jews had been subject to some of the same disabilities as had been placed against them in Germany. With the coming of the French occupation, however, all restrictions against Jews were cast aside. They could enter the country and settle as citizens, enjoying the same rights as Napoleon had granted the Jews of France.

Under an Imperial edict issued by Napoleon on March 17, 1808, the Jews of Belgium were divided into consistories, similar to the French system. Brussels was included in the consistory of Crefeld. When Napoleon was overthrown, Belgium was united with Holland, and the Jewish community of Brussels became the fourteenth religious district of Holland. After the revolution of 1830, when Belgium won its freedom from Holland, Brussels

73

became the center of the Belgian consistory system, and a Chief Rabbi was named.

The Jews Maurice met here were vastly different from the Jews he had left behind in Munich. Made up of not more than fifty or sixty families, the Jewish community of Brussels was far advanced along the road toward emancipation, so much so that, as in France, the government contributed largely to the support of Belgium's Jewish religious institutions. Synagogues, as a result, were subsidized by the state in exactly the same manner as were the Catholic and the Protestant churches. Ghetto walls that separated Jews from the rest of the people had been broken down, and Jews had ventured forth into a world in which they were as one with their neighbors, subject to the same economic forces and influences. No longer did they spend interminable hours wrangling over the Talmud. The silk hat had replaced the skullcap and the stylishly tailored suit had taken the place of the "caftan." The sacred had yielded slowly to the secular, and the religious fanatic of old was rapidly disappearing from the scene. The scholar of yesterday, whose word on Talmudic discussions was considered authentic and final, now became the philosophic visionary.

Many honored positions were held by the Jews of Brussels by the time young de Hirsch arrived there in 1844. Under the stimulus of the tolerant regime of Leopold I, many Jews had achieved distinction in the field of higher learning. The King's physician, Gottlieb Gluge, not only was considered the best medical practitioner in the country, but was professor of physiology at the University of Brussels as well, earning the distinction in 1837 of being the first of his profession to have described influenza. Charles Narcisse Oulif, the first Jew to receive a law degree at

Strasbourg, had held the chair of law at the University of Brussels since 1834, and was to occupy this position almost to the time of his death in 1867. He had been made a member of the Legion of Honor in 1837, and was decorated with the "Order of Leopold of Belgium." There were, too, the wealthy bankers who had moved to Brussels from Germany—the Landaus, the Furths, the Simons, his cousins the Hirsches and the great banking families who made up the firm of Bischoffsheim & Goldschmidt.

It was a vastly different Christian world, too, from that in which he had spent his childhood, and the free air of the low countries was a refreshing change to the boy who had been brought up in the narrow, provincial atmosphere of a small Bavarian principality that had never known anything other than a paternalistic despotism. Belgium, it is true, had for many centuries been the battleground of Europe—a pawn in the game of power politics that had gone on endlessly, generation after generation and dynasty after dynasty. Ever since she had broken away from Holland, however, Belgium had progressed steadily on the road toward political freedom, holding her position as one of the few constitutional monarchies on the continent. Small but independent, her freedom guaranteed by international treaties and by the power of Great Britain, she had, under the strong influence of neighboring France, adopted many of the ideas that the French Revolution had unloosed.

The diverse character of the city of Brussels, divided as it was into the ancient town in the valley, largely given over to those whose customs, sympathies, and language were Flemish, and the new court quarter built high on the Montagne de la Cour, inhabited generally by those who were French in speech and manner, led to a tolerance and

understanding rarely to be found anywhere else in Europe.
The atmosphere was pervaded with the spirit of the new
Age of Reason itself.

There was, however, an outstanding tourist attraction,
which continued to be an embarrassing thorn in the side
of the Jews of Brussels. The magnificent Cathedral of
Ste. Gude continued to draw large numbers of visitors to
the Sacrament des Miracles, famed for its beautiful
stained glass windows with portraits of King John III of
Portugal, Louis of Hungary, Francis I of France, Ferdinand of Austria, and their wives and patron saints. One
window commemorates the events that followed the steal-
ing by a Jew of some wafers of the Host. A guide book
of the period, (1855-1860), describes this event:

> The legend of the Miraculous Wafers is probably
> one of quite a number of similar stories invented by
> the monks and priests for the purpose of influencing
> the superstitious, and may very possibly also have its
> origin in the hatred and contempt for the Jews which
> existed at that period. Any accusation which would
> enable the populace to find an excuse to attack the latter
> and confiscate their goods was eagerly seized upon.
>
> The story goes that a Jew of the name of Jonathan,
> residing in the little town of Enghein in the year 1369,
> prevailed upon one of his fellow Jews, named John of
> Louvain, who was a sham convert to Christianity, to
> steal for him some of the consecrated wafers used in
> the service of the Mass. At first, we are told, John of
> Louvain refused to be a party to this crime, but the
> promise of sixty gold angels appears to have ultimately
> overcome his fears and scruples, with the result that one
> dark night in the month of October of the year we have
> named he broke into the Church of Ste. Catherine, Brus-
> sels, and stole the ciborium containing the wafers, the

number of which is variously stated to have been from
three to sixteen.

Soon afterwards it appears the instigator of this
sacrilege was murdered in his own garden, and his wife
removed to Brussels, carrying with her the stolen
wafers. On Good Friday a number of Jews gathered together in their synagogue, which then stood near the
Hotel Dieu, and the wafers having been produced,
they were thrown upon the table and were subject to
all the insults the Jewish mind could conceive. Finally
some of those present stabbed them with their knives
when they were horrified to see drops of blood oozing
from them. Many of the impious Jews, we are told, fell
to the floor in fits brought about by this extraordinary
miracle. The perpetrators of this sacrilege were ulti-
mately discovered by means of a second miracle, and
on being confronted by witnesses confessed what they
had done. Another version of the story, however, states
that they were cruelly tortured to extort a confession,
and afterwards were burned alive and their goods con-
fiscated, and all the Jews in Brussels banished outside
the Province of Brabant. This gruesome medieval legend is illustrated in the large stained glass windows of
the chapel.

And so, at the age of fourteen, Maurice de Hirsch entered into the last phase of his academic education. For
four years he attended the Ecole Centrale des Arts et
Manufactures in Brussels, spending en months of each
year there, going home to Munich ly during the summer recesses. He was not a particu rly good student,
although he had an alert mind and w s quick to learn.
It was just that he was not interested. Brought up in a
family of bankers and businessmen, he si unned the dangerous and unsettling revolutionary philosophical ideas

that were sweeping the world. His childhood, spent in close association with his father and grandfather, had given him but one interest and one ambition. He wanted to be a banker and he was impatient of the years he had to spend in school. Why should he, at an age at which most boys were already working at trades or in their father's stores, have to spend so many years at studies that would never be of any use to him in the work he intended taking up as his life's activity? He applied himself diligently to the study of languages. With German as his native tongue, he rapidly became fluent in French, which was used by the upper classes of Brussels almost exclusively. And, at the same time, he included the study of English as one of the most important subjects in his curriculum.

He learned to ride and to follow the hounds. He learned to dance the popular dances of the day. He acquired a smattering of knowledge of the arts, so as to be able to converse with the entrepreneurs in the salons of the wealthy and the influential he knew he would frequent. And he acquired a degree of refinement that was to remain with him all his life as one of his outstanding characteristics. All in all, by the time he was ready to leave school and go out into the world, he stood out from his Jewish brethren as a person of distinction and refinement.

Among the youths with whom he associated during his school years in Brussels were the scions of the wealthy and aristocratic families of Europe who had made the Belgian capital the fashionable center for the finishing touches to their education. Here they could acquire a touch of French influence without being exposed to the libertine life of Paris, which, in those days of hectic finance and quick money, had already earned a reputation as a city of free

and easy living and of low moral values. Maurice was
thrown into contact with English and French aristocracy
at an early age but, while most of the groups accepted
him, he did not feel completely at ease in their company.
Always there was present the knowledge that he was accepted on sufferance only because he was a "different"
kind of Jew. He did not belong among Jews of the skullcap and the caftan. He was a modern Jew.

He grew to be increasingly resentful of those Jews who
persisted in retaining the customs of the ghetto in a city
that had no ghetto. Why could not those Jews realize that
their insistence on wearing their unkempt beards and their
caftans merely kept alive the flame of Jew hatred? Surely,
if the Christians were willing to remove the Jew's badge,
the Jew himself should be more than glad to remove the
identifying characteristics that for centuries had marked
him as being different from those among whom he lived.
Many were the times when he was out walking with his
Christian friends and one of these "typical" Jews would
come into sight. Instantly an embarrassed hush would
come over the group, a silence more telling of what was
passing through each of their minds than any spoken remark. The young baron felt these incidents keenly. It was
not fair for those Jews who were not ready for assimilation to stand in the way of younger Jews for whom the
new era of freedom held out so much promise. They must
be made to see that Judaism belonged in the synagogue
and in the home and that it was not necessary to carry it
into the streets and market places.

Emancipation, he felt, would come to the Jews only
after they had themselves become emancipated from the
ancient customs of the medieval ghetto, which had no
place in the modern world. When the Jew dressed, spoke,

and conducted himself in the same manner as those among whom he lived, restrictive laws would be removed or would be allowed to remain inactive. If Jews learned trades and skills, ghetto walls would have to crumble because educated, skilled workmen could not be impounded behind walls or segregated from the rest of the community.

This was to remain de Hirsch's attitude toward the assimilation of the Jews all his life. Emancipation, he insisted, required complete surrender of all the ethnic differences that had barred Jews from full participation in the life of the western world. It was the old-fashioned Jew, the ghetto Jew, who was impeding the acceptance of the Jew as a man. One half of Jewry still had to beg for its existence from a civilization intent on wiping it out completely, while the other half, the emancipated half, had to exist in a world in which emancipation had been declared an accomplished legal fact, but in which the environment was still charged with danger. In many instances firm promises of freedom for the Jews had produced a net result of almost nothing. Legally the Jews had attained certain prescribed rights. In the eyes of the law they were judged to be the equal of the Christians. But to the people among whom they lived they were still the "stranger within the gates." And in this, according to the assimilationists, the Gentiles were not altogether to blame. The Jews had not met them half way. They still persisted in clinging to their age-old customs. They insisted on carrying into the new era the habits of the ghetto.

De Hirsch became increasingly annoyed, too, with the intellectual Jews, those who wrote and spoke in demanding tones, calling on the Christians "to do justice to the people they had held in subjugation for so many centuries." Incapable of fathoming the intellectual mind, he could not understand this attitude. What right had they to demand anything? Was not this a gentile world? Since when had Jews, who had been locked up in ghettos but a few years earlier, the right to demand anything? Surely this was not the way to gain concessions from the Christians. Were not the anti-Semites already saying "Give the Jews an inch and they ask for a mile?" Were they not already complaining because too many Jews were flocking to the universities, acquiring educations from the Gentiles, and then using their new-found knowledge to write polemics against their benefactors? And were not too many Jews taking to the professions instead of being satisfied with learning trades? Already the medical profession was becoming crowded with Jews, and the anti-Semites were bemoaning the fact that Jews were forcing Christians from this field altogether.

Karl Marx, who had settled in Brussels in 1845 with his wife Jenny, the daughter of Baron von Westphal, was to young de Hirsch an outstanding example of the intellectual Jews who were completely insensitive to the harm they might do to their own people. True, Marx's father had had him baptized in 1824, but in the eyes of the world he was a Jew; and Jews felt the consequences of his radical foolishness. Taking advantage of the liberal policies of the country that had given him a haven, he had almost immediately repaid the hospitality of the Belgians by organizing a branch of the "Kommunistenbund" there in 1847. This was more than the Belgian government had bargained for and he was summarily expelled from the country. Men such as this, in the eyes of the young capitalist, were doubly irresponsible. Not only were they spreading dangerous doctrines of the most revolutionary nature, but they were causing a cloud of suspicion to be raised against Jews everywhere. Anti-Semites were not slow in labeling all Jews as radicals because of Karl Marx and men of his stripe.

It was during these years that de Hirsch was to adopt the attitude toward Judaism that was to remain with him all his life—"Unto Caesar render that which is Caesar's and unto God render that which is God's." He disassociated Judaism from his everyday world and, as a result, he saw no need for conversion. Why accept a new religion when religion had no place in the business world, or in the everyday life of a nation? He could be a Jew and be a good citizen of his country at the same time. Napoleon had recognized this. The French government recognized this. King Leopold of Belgium recognized this. The consistory system itself was based on the conception that a Jew was merely a Frenchman or a German or a Dutchman who practiced Judaism, and many of the influences that surrounded him helped to confirm this belief. The Revue Orientale, Belgium's first Jewish publication, which had made its appearance in 1841, continually dwelt on this theme, and the many prominent Jews in Brussels who lived outwardly as ordinary Belgians were proof that this attitude was the right one. The Jews of Germany were flocking to baptism because there was no alternative for them. Either they remained content to spend their lives under the restrictive laws that still obtained in the Germanic kingdoms or they would have to accept baptism. There was no middle course for them. Here it was different. Jews were already emancipated and their progress under their newly found freedoms was up to them and to them alone. They had but to make the most of their opportunities to achieve equality and social standing.

The four years that de Hirsch spent in school were the years in which unbridled speculation was reaching its highest peak, sparked by the railway mania that, starting in England in 1837, had quickly spread to France and the western countries of Europe, bringing into being a revolutionary age of movement. The ancient highways and roads were emptied of their stagecoaches as locomotives puffed their way along miles of track. Horses no longer stamped outside posting-houses, for the Tally-ho was removed to the museum. Country peasants moved into the towns and became city burghers. All the world was moving faster now on wheels propelled by steam, that new master of power. Capitalists replaced dukes and princelings as a new hierarchy took the place of the landed aristocracy— manufacturers, shippers, the industrialists, and the bankers. "Where the railroads led," says Paul H. Emden,

> ... material prosperity followed, and the golden age of speculation set in. And with it came an era of peace to Europe, for nothing was permitted to interfere with the growth of the new wealth which was found. And, as the boom rolled on, it spread wider and wider, in a wild, uncontrollable rush toward disaster. Morning, noon and night the banks were besieged by clamorous crowds, the streets leading to the stockbrokers were filled with the carriages of ladies and gentlemen of rank, and each train brought a new load of country people to town. In every capital and among all classes there was but one purpose—to purchase shares from the stockbrokers. The soundness of the shares was of little concern.

So hectic did speculation in railroading become that the wildest ideas were advanced and people were found who were willing to support and invest in these ideas. It was even proposed to span the Bering Straits and connect

North America with Asia and Europe by an international railway. In a book published in 1890, *History of Railroads in the United States,* there is this comment on the idea of a railroad from North America to Europe:

> This line, if constructed, would be simply an extension of the proposed Pan-American Railroad and would follow the Western Coast of the United States as far as Bering Strait, then cross over into Asia, traverse Siberia and finally reach London via St. Petersburg, Berlin and Paris. It is questionable whether such a line is feasible either from a technical or financial point of view, but the time will probably come when railroad tracks will connect New York and London.

Wealth was being created faster than it could be spent and everybody wanted a share of it. Stock in the most fantastic schemes rose to unheard of prices, some as much as 1500 percent above par. Bribery and corruption kept pace with material prosperity, and fraud was rampant. In France, where the boom reached its highest peak, money and the pleasures it could buy became the god and in Paris immorality existed as never before. Luxury and vice were the order of the day. No theatre could remain open long which did not feature an indelicate play, and the more the play ran to outright indecency, the more success it enjoyed. Historians have estimated that during this decade almost one third of the children born in Paris were the children of illicit romances.

It is not surprising that even school children were infected with this craze for speculation. "Following the market" became the popular pastime. Forgotten were the usual activities of college youth—the athletic field, the debating society, the historical club. A new interest had made all that seem adolescent and superfluous. Discussions that might have dealt with social questions or with the rise of socialism and communism now knew but one subject—the boom. And in all this young de Hirsch took a leading part. With a family background so solidly placed in the banking world, he was looked upon as an authority by his school-mates. On the history of the banks and of the companies whose shares they jobbed, and of new schemes and spectacular promotions, even before they were floated on the market, he had been uncanny in his predictions of the shares that would boom. He was an expert on the subject of high finance long before he was ready to leave school for a career in the business world.

Ten years of unbridled speculation such as the world had never before seen could have but one result. Sooner or later the bubble was bound to burst and when it did wide unrest and revolution followed. The year 1848 was scarcely more than a few days old when unrest made itself felt, gaining in momentum until by early spring a simultaneous impulse to revolt swept over Rome, South Germany, Milan, Vienna, Venice, and Berlin. Riots swept through almost every country west of the Russian border, with streets and squares filled with shouting mobs against whom the frightened police were ineffective and impotent. Widespread as were these outbreaks, there was little unity about the general uproar and each country had its revolution based on local problems. Mazzini led the Italians in their fight to be rid of the Austrian yoke. The Austrians were determined to be free of Metternich. Czechs, Hungarians, and Croats demanded self-government. Germans sought a stronger, more substantial union than that provided by the Germanic Confederation, which held the thirty-eight constituent states loosely together.

New constitutions were the order of the day and a rededication to the principle of the inalienable "rights of man" swept through the continent. And, as is true in every troubled age, the "lunatic fringe" was widely active, with scarcely a country in Europe that did not come forth with its quota of hair-brained schemes. In the words of a historian of the period, "Rival European prophets, each more inspired than his competitors, emitted their divergent teachings in a carnival of contradiction. Nationalism was the order of the day. The Germans were taught the blessings of being German. The Slavs, Magyars and Poles each had their reasons for exalting their own nationalities without the least regard for other peoples."

It was during this confusing period in European history that Maurice de Hirsch embarked on his business career. Unwilling to serve an apprenticeship as was customary for young men who intended to follow a banking career, he refused to enter his father's bank or any of the conservative banking institutions that were, as a result of the turbulent times through which they had just passed, wary of promotional schemes that did not promise the utmost in the way of security. Willful and headstrong, he felt that he did not need this experience. He had been watching the investment field all during his school years and he had made almost a perfect record in forecasting to his schoolmates those shares which were most likely to rise. True, he had not foreseen the crash, but neither had the experts. Almost every banker in Europe, men whose investments ran into the millions, had been fooled into believing that the boom was here to stay, that the millennium had arrived.

He was young, but his father had entered the business world as a cattle dealer at a youthful age and he had been

successful, amassing a fortune before he was twenty-five
years of age and earning a reputation as one of the leading cattlemen in all of Bavaria. Other men, too, had made
their mark in the business world in what should have been
their tender years. Louis Raphael Bischoffsheim had
started his banking business in Belgium when he was but
twenty years of age, and he had been highly successful.

It was inevitable that young de Hirsch would lose the
better part of his inheritance in a few years of wild speculation in a market that was in almost continuous upheaval,
fluctuating up and down following the fortunes of war and
revolution. Wiser and older heads found themselves unable to navigate in this difficult world of secret diplomacy
and high finance, and it was a foregone conclusion that a
youth of apprentice age, attempting to compete in the
money market with some of the shrewdest manipulators
in the financial world, simply had no chance.

He had just turned seventeen when he rashly undertook his first speculation. Using his family's name to establish credit, he bought up all the sugar, coffee, and cotton
he could lay his hands on and actually found himself in a
position to control the output of some of the biggest factories in Bavaria. The collapse of Europe's economy in
the unrest following the abortive revolutions of 1848
turned his speculative ventures into disaster. Considerably
chastened after this disastrous experience in the field of
international finance, Baron Maurice de Hirsch auf
Gereuth joined the great banking firm of Bischoffsheim
and Goldschmidt in Brussels, whose prestige was never
higher. Conservative in all their dealings, highly respected
because of a long record of successful enterprises, the
partners were reluctant to take into their fold a young
man who had so well proved to be "the proverbial fool

who was soon parted from his money." Senator Bisschoffs-
heim, however, had the greatest respect and admiration
for his friend Baron Joseph de Hirsch, who had a few
years before been appointed Court Banker to the King of
Bavaria, and he probably felt that some of the financial
genius the Baron and his father had displayed in their
many business ventures in Bavaria must have rubbed off
on the young man. Perhaps he had good possibilities if
he could be brought to a realization that he had much to
learn and that his headstrong nature would have to be
brooked. And, then again, perhaps the Senator's daughter
Clara influenced his decision.

5

BISCHOFFSHEIM FAMILY

Jewish banking families have been so interrelated with
each other that they have often been accused of ar-
ranging marriages to further their banking interests or to
strengthen their position in financial circles, much as royalty has made use of the marriage ceremony to form military alliances or to bolster weak dynasties. In the case of
the Jewish bankers, though, there may have been other
reasons. Set so far above the ordinary people of their
faith whose way of life was, to say the least, vastly different from that of the wealthy bankers, there was little else
Court Jews could do but marry their own kind. Many of
the women, it is true, married intellectuals—rabbis,
writers, scholars, and physicians. The sons of bankers,
though, could look for suitable mates only among the
marriageable daughters of other bankers, often marrying
first cousins and in some instances their own nieces. Whatever the reason, intermarriage among the banking families created a network of interrelated banking houses that
extended the influence of Jewish banking interests over the
continent and beyond to the Americas and the farthest
corners of the world.

The history of the Bischoffsheim family presents a

typical study of the complicated interrelationships that were developed through well-planned marriages by many of the Jewish banking houses, for it is almost as difficult to follow the complicated interwoven genealogy and family connections of the Bischoffsheims as it is to follow the family relationships developed by the reigning families of Europe during the nineteenth century.

Originating in the obscure town of Bischoffsheim-on-the-Tauber in southern Germany, the family first came into prominence when the founder of its fortune, Raphael Nathan Bischoffsheim, achieved a local reputation as a merchant. During the French revolution he went to Mayence and, starting business as a small merchant, he expanded rapidly and soon became a purveyor to Napoleon's army.

His eldest son, Louis Raphael, must have left Germany a few years after his father's death in 1814, for we find him in Antwerp in 1820 where, at the age of twenty, he founded a banking business. Two years later he married Amalia Goldschmidt, a sister of the wealthy and highly respected banker of Frankfort, Benedict H. Goldschmidt. After many successful years as a banker in Belgium and Holland, he moved his operations to Paris, where he became involved in almost all the great enterprises of his time. He financed the great southern railway, the Chemin de Fer du Midi, and he was the founder of Société Generale, the Banque des Pays-bas, Credit Foncier Colonial, and the Franco-Egyptian Bank.

A second son of Raphael Nathan Bischoffsheim, Raphael Jonathan, moved from Antwerp to the new capital at Brussels when Belgium was granted its independence from Holland in 1830. In 1832 he married Henriette Goldschmidt, the sister of his brother's wife, second daughter of Frankfort banker Goldschmidt. Thus the two Bischoffsheim brothers married two of the wealthiest sisters in Europe.

A sister, Clara Bischoffsheim, became the wife of L. Cahen of Antwerp (d'Anvers) who, although a produce dealer at the time of their marriage, later became one of the leading French bankers when he moved to Paris in 1849. To make sure that he would not be confused with a man named Cahen who had a reputation for not paying his bills, L. Cahen began signing his name Cahen d'Anvers and then just C. d'Anvers. This became the source of many jokes. One story that went around was that a member of the Oppenheimer family, the famous Cologne bankers, once had to sign his name immediately below that of L. Cahen who had signed C. d'Anvers. Oppenheimer signed merely "O. de Cologne."

Another sister, Amalia, married the banker August Bamberger of Maintz. A son born of this marriage, Ludwig Bamberger, was to become famous as the founder of Germany's Reichbank and the originator of the German gold standard. He married his first cousin, the oldest daughter of Jonathan Bischoffsheim and Henriette Goldschmidt. When Maurice de Hirsch married her sister Clara, Ludwig Bamberger, who was already firmly established as a partner in the firm of Bischoffsheim and Goldschmidt, became his brother-in-law. Maurice was already related to Ludwig Bamberger, however, because his father's sister Amalie had married Heinrich, a brother of Ludwig Bamberger's father, administrator of the Banque de Paris et des Pays Bas. As with the Rothschilds, cousins married cousins and uncles married nieces. Each marriage, however, strengthened the family's position in the financial world.

Jonathan Bischoffsheim started construction of the railways of Belgium in 1834. Both King William I of Holland and Leopold I of Belgium were quick to see the advantages of railways to supplement the waterway systems that were so effective in both countries, and rivalry quickly developed between the two to build the first railroads that would link up with France and Germany so as to attract commerce to and from these countries through their ports. Jonathan Bischoffsheim was to play an important part in giving Belgium the lead by cleverly building railway lines interlaced with the country's waterway system instead of following the usual method of constructing railways independently from existing transportation systems. As a result, trade and commerce were attracted to Belgium that might otherwise have gone elsewhere.

At the same time he was an active participant in the formation of Société Cockerill at Seraing, one of the largest iron works in Europe, in which King William I of Holland was a heavy investor. Jonathan Bischoffsheim was to achieve recognition as one of Europe's outstanding bankers and economists when he worked out the fundamental plan for the establishment of the Banque Nationale de Belgique, a feat that brought him wide acclaim as the founder of Belgian currency. From that time on he held the unique position of confidential adviser to King Leopold I, enjoying a close personal friendship with the monarch, who placed complete confidence in his judgment.

For his services, Jonathan was awarded the Cross of the Order of Leopold. He became a member of the Communal Council of Brussels and for twenty years was a senator representing the arrondissement of Brussels in the Belgian Senate. At his death on February 6, 1883, the name of the street on which he lived, Boulevard de l'Observatoire, was changed to Boulevard Bischoffsheim. His daughter Clara was to become one of the most famous women in the world as Baroness Clara de Hirsch.

Although Clara and Maurice had known each other from the time he first came to Brussels as a boy of fourteen to attend school, neither had shown much interest in the other. When he returned after his financial debacle in Munich, however, they began to see a lot of each other. Clara felt sorry for the young man. Her sympathetic nature was aroused by the quiet dignity of his bearing and by the sincerity with which he applied himself to his work. He had been deeply hurt, and he showed it. Gone was the bravado and the devil-may-care attitude with which he had tackled the business world when he first left school. Now he was just a minor clerk in one of the most important banking firms in Europe, surrounded by men of mature financial experience who could point to many successful business ventures. Young de Hirsch felt his position keenly. Tolerated only for his patent of nobility and because the prominence of the de Hirsch name in Southern Germany lent some prestige to the bank, he was not at any time taken into the confidence of the senior partners. His opinions on financial matters were always taken with a grain of salt, and his suggestions were looked at askance, for had he not already squandered a fortune? Were his plans based on sound reasoning, or was he day-dreaming again? Clara was the only one who paid serious attention to his ideas, and perhaps because of her Senator Bischoffscheim went out of his way to be kind to him.

Smarting under the knowledge that he had made a fool of himself and that everybody knew it, chagrined that his dreams of quick success had crashed to earth and that the chances of his ever becoming a boy wonder in the financial world seemed gone forever, Maurice was nevertheless undaunted. He had been unlucky, that was all, and he was not going to let this one failure discourage him from trying again. All he needed was new capital and the right opportunity. In the meantime he would work hard at his new job and try to regain his father's confidence. And he would prove to Senator Bischoffsheim that he had not been mistaken in taking him into his bank.

More and more he took to spending his spare time in the company of Clara. She understood him because she, too, was a dreamer with big ideas. Hour after hour they would walk through the parks that lined the banks of the River Seine, discussing the wonderful promise of the new world of capitalism, which saw millions of people everywhere pouring their money into banks, a few pennies here and a few dollars there, creating huge funds of capital running into millions of dollars to be used to build railroads and mills and factories that would do so much for the people. To the young dreamers it seemed that a full flowering of capitalism would bring the millennium.

Although she was raised in the era of crinoline and old lace, Clara's advice and help were not to be taken lightly, for she was recognized as a business expert. No sewing circles or women's auxiliaries for her! At an early age she had shown a keen interest in banking and Senator Bischoffsheim had let her come to work in his office instead of going to one of the fashionable finishing schools that her friends attended. She soon came to be his very efficient private secretary, fluent in French, English, German, and Italian, and he learned to lean on her for assistance more than he did on many of the bright young juniors in the firm. She had a level head on her shoulders and he felt that she was more capable of mature judgment in matters involving huge sums of money than many of the juniors and even some of the senior partners in the firm. No one was surprised by Clara's presence in her father's office, and rarely did he ask her to leave the room when he was in a meeting with anyone and then only when a matter involving some personal details of his visitor's life was being discussed. She was regarded as an established factor in the firm and her position was unchallenged.

Clara studied the history of Bischoffsheim & Goldschmidt's business connections from the very beginning, and she began to understand the value of an interrelated system of family-linked banks such as they had put together almost accidentally over the years, creating a powerful instrument for taking advantage of the many profitable deals that were developing in the headlong rush into the industrial revolution and the capitalistic era. She studied the history of banking in the seventeenth and eighteenth centuries and saw how a mastery of financing techniques brought Jews into contact with monarchs and potentates, with statesmen and generals, with men of importance throughout the entire world. Even sooner than Maurice, Clara saw that the coming of the railroads would bring an era of change in the ways and habits of people everywhere, revolutionizing commercial activity and changing the map of the world, ushering in an age of movement—of canals replacing wagons and of railroads challenging canals, of locomotives puffing their way along hundreds of miles of rails, of excited speculators lending, promoting, borrowing, and giving their souls to push the railroads thousands of miles more.

Already railroads were being built in every corner of the continent. Stagecoaches disappeared and the tally-ho became a picturesque antique. All the world was moving faster now, opening up vast new worlds to education and enlightenment and the new concept of things to come. And, as the new enlightenment reached into the dark corners of Europe on the wheels of the railways, feudalism would vanish forever and with it would go all the evils of the past.

It did not take long for militarists, however, to see the vital importance of railroads to national defense or for offensive tactics against an enemy. While in the western hemisphere railroading was used as a means of colonizing new countries, the great railway systems of Europe, Asia, and Africa were built principally for political or strategic purposes. The German Government did not construct its great east-west lines primarily to carry passengers or freight, or even to make money. The ability to rush troops to the frontiers of their traditional enemies, Russia and France, superseded any other motives. Kings and potentates, rulers and despots soon saw the political and military advantages of railroads and they offered state aid in ever-increasing amounts in land grants, loans, or guarantees of interest payments and dividends to private concessionaires, construction firms, banks, and railroad operators.

Louis Napoleon, recognizing the great need for railroads in a country as decentralized as France, was handing out concessions right and left, furnishing the right-of-way and preparing the roadbed while the concessionaire or railway company laid the track, supplied the equipment, and operated the railway. Concessions were established for as long as forty years, with the French government guaranteeing payment of principal and interest on the securities issued by the operating companies. Many other countries were equally as generous in their anxiety to get into the railway race. Strangely enough, there were not too many takers to pick up these concessions. The older, well-established conservative banks for the most part passed up these opportunities, allowing the small banks, the newcomers, and the entrepreneurs to capture this field.

Paul H. Emden, in his *Money Powers of Europe in the 19th and 20th Centuries,* chides the conservative English bankers for not seeing the part railroads would play in revolutionizing trade and commerce throughout the world. "When the railway days dawned," he said, "they (the English bankers) were found sadly wanting. Hidebound in their all too rigid conservatism, they refused to be convinced that the construction of railroads meant the most gigantic enterprise of modern times—perhaps of any times. They neglected to take their share in the development which was to transform the ideas of mankind, conceptions of time and space far beyond the political and financial situation, and to an extent far greater than was achieved in our day by the airship and the aeroplane. They held to the view that a railway could not enter into successful competition with a canal; even with the best locomotive engine the average rate would not be but $3\frac{1}{2}$ miles an hour which was slower than canal conveyance,— a prophecy which was negatived in the most convincing manner in practice when in 1830 Stephenson's engine attained a speed of 36 miles in 60 minutes."

The established banks might well have pointed out that a great deal of capital was needed to start a railroad. Rights-of-way had to be purchased, often without benefit of government backing; roadbeds had to be leveled on which rails could be laid; bridges and tunnels, rolling-stock, stations, and coaling stations had to be constructed; and all had to be paid for. European countries were autocracies, and governments of this kind do not generally stimulate the private investor because properties were often seized on the sudden whim of a monarch. Revolution, too, presented a constant threat that might at any time overthrow an existing government because so many European countries were impoverished from almost continual warfare, and their regimes were shaky. As a result, railways were constructed for the most part by entrepreneurs who provided private capital, financiers willing to incur great risks in the hope that the railroads they built would open up vast new areas of undeveloped hinterland, creating untold wealth for those who controlled the operation of the railroads. In this, Jews played a prominent, though little known, part.

An interesting chapter in the history of railroading will be written when the great contribution made by these pioneer Jewish railroad builders in the development of early European railway systems comes to light. The Rothschilds, whose railroad from Vienna to Bochnia in Galicia in 1835 started the Austrians on a program of penetration into the most important trade areas of the Balkans; the Pereiras, whose Credit Mobilier financed the construction of so many railroads in Italy, France, and Austria; the de Hirsch family—the grandfather and father in Bavaria and the son in Turkey and the Balkans; the Poliakoffs, who built almost all of the Russian railroads; the Bischoffsheims and the Goldschmidts, who were responsible for the creation of the railroads throughout the Low Countries; and the many others who built railroads in the remotest sections of Europe—Rodriguez David, the Bleichroeder family, Solomon Heine (uncle of the great poet), the Foulds, the Oppenheimers, the Sterns, the Eichtals who, like the de Hirsch family, were Court Bankers in Munich, and L. von Steiger and Company, successors to the Buifus Brother firm, which finally was forced into liquidation in 1895 after having been in business for nearly 200 years—all were among the pioneers in the building of railroads, those great agencies of commerce which not only revolutionized trade and commerce but which changed man's entire scheme of living. Clara and Maurice felt that railroad building offered the best opportunity for a relatively unknown Jewish banker to get started, and they resolved to wait for the right railroad enterprise to come along before undertaking another venture. They were to wait almost fifteen years.

Gradually Clara and Maurice began to talk of marriage. It had been an unromantic, matter-of-fact courtship. They had just fallen into the habit of "going steady," and before long it came to be an accepted fact between them that they would get married. The parents on both sides were slow to accept the idea of marriage, however, especially Clara's father and mother, who professed great surprise when they learned of the couple's intentions.

In later life, Clara was fond of repeating the story of how her father was finally prevailed upon to give his consent to her marriage to young de Hirsch. She said that one evening when Maurice was sitting in the upstairs living room with her, they overheard a discussion of an intricate business matter between her father and one of his partners as they were walking under the porte-cochère of the house. When they reentered the room, Maurice explained that they had overheard the conversation and he asked if they would like to have his opinion in the matter. Somewhat condescendingly, they agreed to hear what he had to say and, surprisingly, his ingenious suggestion seemed to offer the solution they were looking for. They adopted his idea, which proved to be extremely successful. Senator Bischoffsheim, feeling that he may have been a little too harsh on the young man and that, perhaps, the poor judgment he had shown in his early business ventures might have been because he was too young to be involved in such large projects, consented to the marriage and gave the young couple his blessing and a very handsome dowry reputed to be somewhere between twenty and thirty million francs, giving Maurice the capital he needed to start financing his own ventures again.

Maurice's father was similarly not too taken with the marriage. He could not understand why his son wanted Clara instead of her younger sister, who was a tall, beautiful girl. Clara said she could "clearly see the father's disappointment when he discovered that his son had chosen the ugly duckling." Her father-in-law told her many years later that when he saw her open the package containing the gift he had brought from Munich, carefully unknotting the string instead of cutting it and neatly folding the paper and tying the string around it, he realized that anyone so frugal would be a good wife for his son, countering his extravagance and carelessness about money matters.

Throughout her entire lifetime, Clara made it a practice not to waste or destroy anything that could be put to further use, no matter how much money she had. One of her eccentricities was that she always saved the blank pages of letters she received and sent them to the Baron de Hirsch schools to be used as scribbling paper for the children. Maurice, too, probably owing to Clara's influence, acquired a reputation for being careful about money.

Although he spent millions on pleasure and charity, he was never known to have wasted a penny. He even cut words out of telegrams announcing donations of millions to charity, in order to save a few cents on the cost of the wire.

To any other girl, the months between the engagement and the wedding would have been the most exciting time of her life, with all the dinner parties and balls given in her honor by the most famous hostesses in Brussels. To Clara, however, the preparations for the wedding, the fittings that had to be arranged with dressmakers, furriers, shoemakers, and designers of worldwide reputation were just so much interference with the work in her father's office in which she was so interested. The Senator, realizing that his daughter would soon be leaving him, began to train other people to take over and handle her work. Clara helped in this, pouring out her knowledge of the business to the young man her father had picked as her successor. Logically, Maurice should have taken over most of Clara's work, but Maurice felt that he would like to step out on his own, using the money he would get as a dowry to capitalize his new ventures. And, because he thought he might be able to pick up a railway concession in Germany, he and Clara decided to live in Munich after their wedding.

6
WEDDING

And so, on June 28, 1855, Clara Bischoffsheim and Maurice de Hirsch were married, in the mellow late afternoon sunshine of a perfect summer day; the Bischoffsheim home was a veritable palace set in a beautifully landscaped garden. The wedding, uniting two great fortunes, was a brilliant affair, probably the most spectacular Jewish wedding that had ever taken place in Belgium, attended as it was by representatives of most of the Jewish banking houses of Europe as well as by the Christian aristocracy and members of the royal families of Bavaria and the Low Countries. King Leopold of Belgium and King William of Holland were represented by Court attachés who came bearing handsome gifts sent by their monarchs. The young couple could not have wished for a more impressive wedding party, with so many prominent people from all over Europe assembled to do homage to bride and groom.

Almost one hundred and fifty persons sat down to the wedding dinner at a great oval table on which ornate vases and silver bowls alternately filled with flowers and fruit rose between the tall candelabra on either side of a miniature-fountain centerpiece. The dinner plates and cutlery were of silver gilt and the delicate crystal goblets edged with gold were filled with pale wine with a fine bouquet.

The question of protocol was a difficult one. Who should be "above the salt" and who below? How satisfy the mixed group, half Jewish and half Gentile, and keep everyone happy? How serve a kosher meal for the orthodox Jews while presenting the kind of table the Christian dignitaries were used to? All this Henrietta Bischoffsheim handled with good taste and extreme delicacy, turning the wedding party into a huge success, rated as one of the outstanding social events of the year in the Belgian capital.

As the two stood under the wedding canopy, Clara, just turned twenty-two several weeks before, petite and slender, with her shining black eyes lighting up her usually placid, almost expressionless face, and Maurice, tall and handsome, well-groomed and distinguished, his haughty bearing giving an impression almost of disdain, the wedding guests wondered about them. What manner of person was this arrogant lad from Munich who, at twenty-three, was already an old hand at the game of international finance, who had already gone through a large fortune by his willful plunging into rash undertakings? And what about Clara, quiet and self-effacing, coming from a family of the best-known financiers in all of Europe, renowned for their conservative policies and the prudence with which they approached business ventures. Would two such completely different personalities get along together?

The assembled guests saw only a handsome young couple on whom all the gods had smiled. They could not foresee that the happy bridegroom was destined to become one of the greatest figures in the world, achieving renown both as an empire builder and as a philanthropist. And little did they guess that this typically spoiled rich man's son would one day be worshipped as a modern-day Moses by the Jews of the Pale of Settlement, his picture adorning the walls of almost every ghetto home. Maurice himself had little thought of the direction in which his destiny lay. Only Clara might have guessed, for she knew that the boy she was marrying was no ordinary youth. She knew he was different, and she knew that he would be successful. And perhaps she felt too, that underneath his pose of being the haughty, stern businessman lay a heart that was deeply hurt by the injustices his people had endured for so many centuries in the despotic countries of eastern Europe.

Because he was a Hirsch he was a capitalist. Because of the teachings of his mother, Caroline Wertheimer, he could not abandon Judaism entirely. Because he was a grandson of Jacob Hirsch, the first Jew in Bavaria to be permitted to own land for agricultural purposes, he was to donate most of his money to Jewish agricultural colonies. Because his father had been the head of the Bavarian Ostbahn and had constructed many of the railways in that country, he was to become one of the outstanding railroad builders in Europe. And, because he married Clara Bischoffsheim, he was to become the greatest philanthropist of the nineteenth century, for Clara was one of the first practical sociologists who believed that the giving of money indiscriminately merely perpetuated the need for charity and that true philanthropy meant helping people to become self-supporting. Even before her marriage she had helped to start a small-loan society to advance capital without interest to people who were too proud to accept charity but who felt they could earn enough to support their families if they could find the capital to establish a small business of some kind.

Clara and Maurice left immediately after the wedding for a leisurely honeymoon trip through Europe on their way to Munich, where they were to make their home. At 8 o'clock the next morning they were on one of the railway trains her father had built that crawled along for twelve hours or so and, with frequent stops, finally reached Paris. Intending to spend several months in Paris, they settled down in a luxurious suite in one of the beautiful hotels in Fauberg St. Germain. The ribald, licentious night life for which the French capital was noted throughout the world was a new experience to them and they enjoyed it to the fullest—theater and late supper and dancing to the early morning hours each day of their stay.

The trip from Paris to Munich was a long one. The trains were hot and dirty and the connections between trains were badly scheduled, sometimes as long as a day or two apart. Constant packing and unpacking was wearisome and the provincial inns at which they stopped were uncomfortable and dingy, even in the larger towns. To the young couple, fresh from their stay in one of the finest Parisian hotels, their accommodations along the way were depressing. The scenery, however, was startling. To the girl looking out the window, the landscape became stranger and stranger as the train progressed into the heart of southeastern Europe. Until now, she was familiar only with the neat countryside of the Low Countries and the flat, uninteresting scenery one saw on the train ride from Brussels to Paris. Now she was going through unfamiliar country where everything was new to her. As the train moved on into huge valleys, mountains and hills towered on both sides as if they were trying to crowd in on the tracks. Evergreen trees, which appeared in Belgium during the Christmas season, stood on mountain slopes by the thousands, a huge dark green fragrant forest of pines and firs. And the farther the train penetrated into the mountains, the colder the air became and the darker the night. In the valleys there was no twilight. First there was sunlight and then, all of a sudden, complete darkness as the sun disappeared over the rim of the mountains. For hours on end she saw no sign of life. Castles and villages and little stations along the way were solitary milestones, almost as though they had been put there as markers for the railway system.

And so, almost three months after their wedding, the young couple arrived in Munich and took up residence in an apartment set aside for them in the family castle. Here Clara met, for the first time, the members of Maurice's family who had been unable to travel the long distance to Brussels—his younger brothers and sisters, and his many cousins. The family was a large one. Kurt Grunwald, in his book *Turkenhirsch*, tells us that when Maurice's grandfather Jacob died in 1841, he left "twenty-six grandchildren by his two sons alone, not counting those by his two daughters."

All the Hirsch men were good looking—tall, well above average height, well proportioned and well-groomed, almost aristocratic in appearance. They were never careless in their dress or in their movements, nor did they ever lose their sense of dignity or display temper in the presence of others. While they thought rapidly, they talked slowly, and they never monopolized the conversation. Grandfather, father, uncles, and cousins all possessed the same characteristics, as though they were cut from the same mold.

The Hirsch women were not beautiful but they, too, were well-groomed and aristocratic. They did not take to

Clara. They could not understand a young girl who dressed so plainly and who would sooner talk about banking and finance than about the newest styles and the latest coiffures. A girl who appeared to have no interest whatsoever in clothes was a strange one indeed.

Clara had never understood Maurice's love for diamonds and jewelry, which she considered ostentatious, nor why the diamond that he wore on his left hand—a stone weighing 18 carats and worth a king's ransom—was never off his finger. To Clara, precious stones were merely a commodity on which to earn a profit. Trading in stones was a tradition among Jews. Having one's fortune invested in diamonds and other precious stones gave a sense of security because, should disaster strike, the stones could be easily concealed and carried away. If the Jews were ever again to flee the Germanic kingdoms, there was nothing better in which to have money invested, because they held their value no matter to what corner of the world one traveled, and they could quickly be converted into cash. Now she found that Maurice's family loved diamonds for their own sake and that all the men had large collections of precious stones. One collected sapphires, another rubies, another semi-precious stones, amethysts and topazes. Maurice's father collected emeralds of rare color or rare cut, some with histories that could be traced back for centuries.

Clara enjoyed driving around Munich with its strange contrasts of the new with the old—the Church of the Theatines, built in 1675, the last of the old religious houses; and public buildings: the Odeon Concert Hall, the Royal Library, the Blind Asylum, and the University of Munich, which had been transferred in 1826 from Landshut. She was particularly fascinated by the music center in Kaiser Ludwig Platz, crisscrossed by the streets so quaintly named after the great composers—Schubert-strasse, Beethovenstrasse, Haydnstrasse, and Mozart-strasse. But her favorite drive was through the Maximil-ian-Platz because it reminded her so much of the parks in Brussels. Waving treetops, green lawns dotted with flow-ers, and the soft splash of the fountains almost made one forget that this was the center of a great city. Officers drove through the park, handsome in their faultlessly fitted jackets, their colorful uniforms contrasting strangely with the blonde, blue-aproned beer girls who carried as many as eight and ten steins of beer in one hand, rarely, if ever, spilling a drop. The burghers, too, enjoyed the pure air of the Bavarian plateau. In the beer garden, they could listen to the songs of a popular troupe of folk sing-ers, songs that were a mixture of sentimentality and licen-tiousness. Ending every concert was the Munich city hymn, "As long as old Peter shall stand on his hill, As long as green Isar shall run at its will, so long will good fellowship in Munich hold sway."

Clara was the object of much speculation by the aristo-cratic social arbiters of Munich. She was so different from the other Jewesses, even the wealthy ones! When she walked down the Ludwig-Strasse she often noticed that people on both sides of the street would turn to look at her as she went by. When she and Maurice appeared at the Hof-Theater—imposing indeed with its five balconies in white and gold and the old rose curtain on which the letter "L" for King Ludwig was inscribed at intervals—opera glasses were turned on their box almost throughout the entire performance. Society accepted her, but with many reservations. All the important drawing rooms of Munich were open to her, but she never felt comfortable in any of them.

Their son Lucien was born a year after their marriage. Fifteen months later Clara gave birth prematurely to a daughter who lived but a few days. She became despondent after this and longed to go back to Brussels. She was not happy in Munich. She did not get along too well with Maurice's family, especially the women. She did not like their stilted, provincial outlook and she wanted once again to live in the free world of the Low Countries. Maurice had been unsuccessful in his business ventures, too, and once again had lost a fortune. Her father had said that he would take Maurice into the firm again if they came back. Therefore, in June of 1859, they left Munich permanently and returned to Clara's home in Brussels. Here Maurice was to make the first of many changes in citizenship. He became a citizen of Belgium.

Two failures in less than ten years had considerably dimmed young de Hirsch's light. He returned to Belgium crestfallen and beaten. Holding a minor post in his father-in-law's firm for several years, he contented himself with fulfilling the ordinary functions of a clerk in a large banking institution. It was not long, however, before he was again undertaking risky ventures on his own. In 1862 he started his own bank with Clara's brother Ferdinand, doing business under the name Bischoffsheim and de Hirsch. The firm must have done well. Grunwald in *Turkenhirsch* quotes the wife of the Dutch diplomat, Baroness Ainis de Wilmar, in her reminiscences of Brussels in 1862, as remembering Baron de Hirsch "as a very rich man and a real gentleman."

But it was not until 1865 that an opportunity came along that placed him in the center of a diplomatic maneuver that was to earn him a reputation as a shrewd and unscrupulous negotiator, which stayed with him all his life. Bischoffsheim and Goldschmidt had become heavily involved financially in the Wilhelm-Luxembourg Railway, which, although an independent company, was being operated in connection with a French line. When the French railroad did not renew the operating agreement in 1865, the Wilhelm-Luxembourg Railway was faced with ruin, placing the Bishoffscheim and Goldschmidt investment in extreme jeopardy. Maurice, mostly because of the prestige of the name Baron de Hirsch, was given the assignment of seeing what could be done to revive French interest in continuing operation of the almost defunct railroad. Studying the situation carefully, taking into account the possible future military importance of Luxembourg, and especially the diplomatic designs on her openly displayed by both France and Prussia, he shrewdly decided to approach Germany first. He traveled to Berlin, where he spent weeks desperately trying to get an appointment with Prince Bismarck. When he finally did get an interview he called Bismarck's attention to the military advantage Germany would gain by entering into the traffic agreement with the Wilhelm-Luxembourg Railway, because the strategic location of the railroad line would almost certainly give Prussia control over the entire region in the event of war with France. Bismarck recognized the truth of this. He quickly took up de Hirsch's proposition and asked him to present formal papers within thirty days. Maurice, however, had other intentions. He lost no time in letting it be known in the right circles that he had reached an understanding with Bismarck and that he was about to enter into an agreement with the Prussian government to take over operation of the railroad. It was not long before the French authorities were made aware of these negotiations and, after allowing time to let the import of what he was about to do sink in, he

called on them and disclosed the terms of the agreement
he had reached with Prussia. The French were quick to
see the danger in which France would be placed if Germany controlled access to the Wilhelm-Luxembourg Railway. The government brought great pressure to bear on
the French railway line, which promptly entered into a
new traffic agreement with the Wilhelm-Luxembourg Railway on far better terms than the former agreement it had
refused to renew. It is one of those ironies of fate that
Germany, at the end of the Franco-Prussian War, assumed control of this very railroad as one of the terms of
the Treaty of Peace. Bismarck, of course, was furious at
what he considered a blatant double-cross, and he was to
have several opportunities in later years to repay de
Hirsch when occasions arose in which his cooperation and
goodwill were sorely needed.

Maurice de Hirsch, as a result of his disastrous early
ventures, was no longer interested in stock market speculations nor in commodity manipulations. Unlike the Rothschilds, he was unable or unwilling to go into ventures that
required so much gambling of fortunes, won or lost in a
single day. His interest lay in finding constructive enterprises that offered large possibilities for profit over a long
period of time. The more he watched the success of the
Jewish bankers who were making fortunes in railway
financing, the more he felt that this was his field. He resolved to wait for the right opportunity to get into railroad finance and construction. The opportunity was not
long in coming.

7

TURKISH RAILROADS

From time immemorial, nations have fought bloody wars to seize and maintain control of the avenues over which commerce travels—the highways over land or the canals and waterways that lead to the wide open seas. The ancient Phoenicians were able to establish complete domination of the seas only because they made themselves masters of the routes leading to the best harbors in the Mediterranean and the Arabian Gulf. Once they captured and took control of these harbors, they were able to establish a regular intercourse of trade with the countries bordering on the Mediterranean, as well as with India and the eastern coast of Africa, and for many years they enjoyed a monopoly over trade with this part of the world. For centuries rivers and lakes, streams and oceans, and the boats that ply them offered the easiest and most logical mode of travel, for nature had placed them there, while trails and highways had to be built.

George Stephenson's invention of the steam-coach, however, ushered in a new avenue of commerce that was to create untold riches for those with foresight enough to see the effect this new method of travel would have on the economy of the world. Those countries that were first to install railroad systems soon became wealthy and powerful, while those nations that were not progressive enough to join the network of railroad tracks that began to honeycomb Europe saw industry and commerce leave their borders because there were no well-developed railway transportation systems.

The first railroad in England was opened for traffic in 1825 while the first American railroad started operations in 1829. Although capital to build the American railway lines was provided by private parties, the government, recognizing the value of railroads in opening up for settlement new sections of a new continent, made large grants of land and paid many subsidies to have the roads constructed. In Europe, however, because of the good roads that had been in use for centuries throughout the continent, the need for railroads was not so urgent as in America and European railroads were much slower in being developed. The first German railroad was constructed between Nuremberg and Furth in 1832. The first railroad in Belgium was built by the state from Brussels to Malines in 1835. In Austria a line was established in 1837 from Vienna to Galicia, followed by a railroad from Vienna through Prague to Bodenbach on the Saxon frontier, and another from Vienna to Trieste on the Adriatic. Russia lagged far behind the more progressive European countries. The first railroad in Russia, built in 1840 especially for the Czar's use, connected the Czar's palace at Tzarskoe Selo with St. Petersburg and Moscow. But for the next twenty years there was not a single railroad line built in Russia. When, in 1860, it was realized that the great natural resources of the country could best be exploited by railroad, both private and public funds were used to build roads for commercial purposes, with the Jewish banker

Poliakoff taking the lead as the foremost builder and operator of Russian railways.

For years the power politics of the Near East turned upon the railroad question. While the history of the events leading to the outbreak of the first World War has shed much light on the struggle for control of the Berlin-Bagdad Railway, events during the last quarter of the nineteenth century, when this struggle actually started, remain largely shrouded in mystery. Herbert Adams Gibbons in *The Reconstruction of Poland and the Near East,* refers to

the greed of European statesmen in their effort to solve the Eastern question in ways that they thought in favor of their country and adverse to their rivals, which has not hesitated to play armies and navies on the diplomatic chess board, to excite ill-feeling among peoples who had no reason to be enemies of one another, and to use cynically forces behind them for the purpose of keeping in slavery the small Christian races of the Balkans and Asiatic Turkey.

Into this struggle, with all its intrigue and political complications, Baron de Hirsch found himself suddenly precipitated. He had become interested in an Eastern European railroad venture in 1868, when he organized the East Hungarian Railway Company under the firm name of Bischoffsheim & de Hirsch. Believing that the approach to financing any project dealing with the Balkan countries should logically be made through Vienna, the gateway to the Near East, he looked first to the Viennese banks for assistance, spending months of valuable time in the Austrian capital, attending meeting after meeting, and interviewing banker after banker, all to no avail. The glowing words he used in depicting the untapped riches hidden in the Balkan countries and the Near East, the minerals and the grain and the vast trade that lay ready for the plucking, fell on deaf ears. The large banks simply could not see the possibility of profits through opening up the Near East to exploitation, while the thought of having to deal with the petty intrigues of the small Balkan states was enough to frighten off the most daring of independent financiers.

As a representative of Bischoffsheim and Goldschmidt, however, de Hirsch had learned how to deal with difficult governments in the course of negotiating for the building of railways in Belgium, France, and Luxembourg. His natural ease of manner, his innate shrewdness, his ability to deal with people, and his carefully cultivated friendships with the aristocracy of many nations stood him in good stead. In the days when financiers entered into more matters of state and secret diplomacy than did many of the actual rulers of Europe, he had earned an unusual reputation as a diplomat of no mean ability. Ludwig Bamberger once said that "the Baron's unusual qualities fitted him for statesmanship and, had he been born other than a Jew, he might have been a great foreign minister."

There was one bank in Vienna that finally did listen to him. Glyn, Mills & Company, an English bank that had been influential in European financial matters since 1740, had organized a syndicate of English private bankers who felt that Austria offered a good field for profitable investment of their tremendous capital reserves. They had organized the Anglo-Austrian Bank, which opened its doors on January 4, 1864, "for the purpose of facilitating and promoting financial and commercial relations between England and Austria." They found, however, that the

Austrian investment field was not nearly so lucrative as they had anticipated because there was not enough potential industry to absorb all their capital. Baron de Hirsch's railroad deal, which looked as though it would open the door to exploitation possibilities, came along at the right time and they were induced to participate in his venture, financing the construction of a short line connecting two already existing railroads.

At about this same time Turkey became interested in opening up for development the vast territories over which it had held sway for so many centuries. Ali Pasha, the Turkish Grand Vizier, was convinced that the one way to expose the Ottoman Empire to the revolutionary ideas of nineteenth-century capitalism and industrial expansion was by means of a railway. He had tried to interest many European and English bankers in projects to construct railways through the Turkish Balkans, but he had been unsuccessful in attracting the needed capital. No one wanted to become involved in any venture that would be subject to the well-known erratic tendencies of the "sick man of Europe." But international events were playing into his hands. The rapidly approaching completion of the Suez Canal threatened to deprive Austria-Hungary and Germany, neither of whom had the ships with which to rival the western maritime powers, of the lucrative trade with the East that had been carried on for centuries over an all-land route through Austria and the Balkans. Furthermore, Austrian policy was changing. Although Turkey had long been regarded as the hereditary foe of the Austro-Hungarian Empire, Austria now publicly proclaimed that it might be interested in a sound project for the economic development of the Turkish dominions. As a first step in this direction, Count Beust, the Austrian

Foreign Minister, proposed construction of a railway from Vienna to Constantinople with the assistance of the Austrian government. While this plan seemed to offer the benefits that a railroad would bring to Turkey, it was not lost on the Turkish government that such a railway would not only give Austria a valuable military advantage but it might also serve to perpetuate a natural trade monopoly for Austria. Count Beust's plan could very well make Vienna the transportation center of Europe.

As a first step in a campaign to cultivate friendly relations with Turkey after so many centuries of hostility and suspicion, Sultan Abdul Aziz was invited to visit Austria and, in 1867, accompanied by his able Grand Vizier Ali Pasha, he was given a royal reception in Vienna.

Some eighteen months later, Austrian Emperor Franz Joseph, traveling to Egypt for the ceremonies at the opening of the Suez Canal in November, 1869, paid a visit to Constantinople, accompanied by Count Beust and a royal entourage. Here it was pointed out to the Sultan that the absence of good railroads throughout his domains had been largely responsible for his defeats in recent wars. He was shown that the strategically needed railways would cement his hold over his Balkan dominions and protect them from Russian penetration. His liberal anti-Russian ministers, Ali Pasha and Fuad Pasha, induced him to go along with the Austrian proposals and on May 31, 1868, he granted right-of-way concessions for the proposed railroad to Van der Elst and Company, representatives for Count Langrand-Dumonceau, a Belgian financier who had recently begun operating throughout Europe under a Papal rescript that was based, as Sir Henry Drummond Wolff in his *Rambling Recollections* says, "upon the Christianization of capital, which meant that Roman Catholics shall entrust their money only to Catholics and not to Protestants or Jews."

Langrand-Dumonceau had embarked on a wild spree of quick deals, buying up land all over Europe. He floated thirty-two companies, using the capital of one company to buy shares and debentures in the other companies, and in this way all the companies were closely linked together. The whole combine was under the jurisdiction of a syndicate, the International Land Credit Company, in whose varied operations many scores of millions were invested, much of it belonging to the crowned heads and nobility of Belgium and Austria, and to Church figures all over Europe. It counted many prominent political lights among its directors. Count Beust, Austria's Finance Minister, was personally interested in some of its affairs, and Lord Salisbury, who was later to become Prime Minister of England, was Chairman of the Board of the company.

After three years of the most desperate efforts to keep this "house of cards" solvent, Langrand-Dumonceau's financial empire collapsed and in 1871 his Roman Catholic bank-like organization went into bankruptcy. On the surface it appeared that the firm had gone under because it had overreached itself by undertaking so many varied activities that no one was able properly to keep track of the vast holdings. Investigation, however, soon uncovered more serious matters. The most flagrant frauds had been committed by Count Langrand-Dumonceau and he was charged with fraudulent bankruptcy. The Board of Directors, anxious to protect him from prosecution to avoid a scandal, used every technicality and device to delay the proceedings. This the small investors greatly resented, and riots broke out throughout Austria and Belgium, reaching serious proportions in Brussels, whose citizens had been heavy investors in the company. When, however, the matter was finally ready for trial, Langrand-Dumonceau had fled the country and was safely ensconced in Brazil.

Not all of the projects Langrand-Dumonceau had entered into were worthless, however, and some proved to be quite valuable assets, among them the concession from the Turkish government to build railways connecting the Ottoman Empire with the rest of Europe. It is one of the ironies of fate that this concession from a Mohammedan Sultan to a Catholic bank was next to go to a relatively unimportant Jewish financier when Baron de Hirsch took the project over from the estate of the bankrupt Langrand-Dumonceau.

It caused general surprise throughout European financial circles when the award was made. The Turkish Minister of Public Works, Fuad Pasha, was known to have been negotiating for some time with Austrian interests, the Rothschilds and the Austrian Land Credit Institution in particular, and it was not even known that de Hirsch was being considered. Baron de Hirsch, however, recognized that the large banking interests had been playing one Turkish politician against another, with the Rothschilds having one group lined up on their side while the Austrian Land Credit Union had an equal number of politicians who favored granting the concession to them. It looked like a deadlock; he rightly figured that in a situation like this a completely unknown entry, a "dark horse" that had no commitments from either side, might very well carry the day. He suddenly intervened in the matter in his own behalf when preliminary negotiations through a young Belgian entrepreneur named Lavely produced no results. He enlisted the support of the Belgian Minister at Vienna and many other influential Austrian politicians, and he was awarded the contract. After the award was made, the Austrian authorities threw their support to him because of their great interest in the strategic value of the railways, exerting strong diplomatic pressures in his favor wherever he needed influence.

For centuries the only means of reaching the Orient, unless one wished to undertake the long sea voyage around the Cape, was by undertaking a hazardous journey overland through the wild mountainous regions of the Balkans. The Suez Canal, however, had outmoded that method of travel and commerce now moved from Europe to Asia by water, bypassing that great fertile region lying between western Europe and Turkey. Baron de Hirsch proposed to build his railroad through this region, again linking Europe overland with the Near East, thus reopening the old historic highway that united Europe to Asia.

Perhaps de Hirsch's flair for the dramatic had drawn him into this project which assumed a romantic aspect because of the centuries-old struggle for control of the mystic lands of the Near East that had sparked the ambition of all the great empires of ancient and mediaeval times. It is doubtful that he could have foreseen the historical role his railway was to take as an important link in what was to become the Bagdad Railway, which gives his project a political import far transcending its financial aspect as one of the great commercial enterprises of the nineteenth century. If he did, he was years ahead of the German geopoliticians and the German Kaiser, for it was not until the turn of the century that they adopted the slogan "drang noch Osten" as the cornerstone of German diplomacy. Whatever the reason, he found himself in the center of the greatest power struggle of the late nineteenth century, a stuggle that was to lead to two world wars in the twentieth century.

Not more than a few miles of track had been laid by the Langrand-Dumonceau interests when Baron de Hirsch picked up Turkish concessions, the time limit having almost run out. He had numerous consultations with Fuad Pasha, the Turkish Minister of Finance, with a view to obtaining a badly needed time extension on the concession. Clara was to tell Oscar Straus, the American Minister to Turkey, many lears later, "I came to Paris with my husband while these negotiations were being conducted. Maurice gave a dinner at the Le Croyan Restaurant and invited a number of prominent gentlemen to meet Fuad Pasha and discuss the matter. The Pasha came quite late. When he came he produced a dispatch from Sultan Abdul Azia confirming his right to extend the concession. Strange to say, while the dinner was in progress, a dispatch came to the Pasha recalling him. It seems this latter telegram was sent before the former one, recalling him because he had failed in completing arrangements about the railroad. The telegram that arrived first had really been sent later, making the Pasha the official head of the delegation and giving him authority to extend the concession." Naturally the undertaking did not grow more promising to investors after the Langrand-Dumonceau financial crash, nor did the Sultan become more enthusiastic over Austrian official cooperation. Sir Henry Drummond Wolff represents Fuad Pasha himself as having jokingly predicted a crash for Turkish concessions when he said: "Tout le monde ici demande une concession, l'un demande une banque, l'autre une route. Ça finira mal—banque et route—banqueroute!"

The undertaking was so hazardous that the firm of Bischoffsheim & Goldschmidt declined to participate,

Senator Bischoffsheim remarking that "such a venture would result in making its undertaker either a beggar or a multi-millionaire; it is very doubtful which." European bankers were unable to foresee what the threatened Franco-Prussian war would do to European banking conditions. Having seen Austria defeated in 1866 by the same Prussian armies that had since overrun Denmark, and fearful of Prussian expansionist ideas in Europe and of Russian designs on the territories of the Near East, the bankers were wary. They would not listen to the appeals of a young, relatively inexperienced banker, whose ideas they considered foolhardy and visionary. Clara, writing to Maurice's sister in Munich, explaining why he was so determined to go ahead with this project despite these discouraging rejections, said, "All Maurice needed to drive him forward was opposition. To put obstacles in his way or to oppose him was to fire up all his energy. Any success he achieves will be won that way."

Baron de Hirsch's plan was to extend farther eastward the Austro-Hungarian lines he had already constructed and to connect them with the railways he had contracted to build within Turkey. With this thought in mind he went to Vienna in search of assistance. In vain did he point out to the bankers there the tremendous possibilities for trade and expansion that would be made accessible to Austrian business and banking through his plan. Turkey and the Near East offered untold riches to those who would uncover them. The vast territories the railroad would open up to exploitation would yield huge returns to the banks and to the railroad company. Vienna's financial circles, however, were unsettled in their policies and undetermined as to the course of future events. They turned him down.

After three years of dealing with difficult governments in constructing his East Hungarian railroads, the forty-year-old Baron felt equal to tackling the almost insurmountable problems he knew he would have to face if he were to make use of the concession he had acquired from the bankrupt Langrand-Dumonceau concern. The thought of having to deal with the Sublime Porte and its intrigues, which was enough to frighten off the most seasoned and battle-scarred financiers, did not deter him. Impatient at the delay, and disgusted with the dilatory practices of the Vienna financiers, de Hirsch decided to look for assistance in Turkey itself. There he found a ready and willing ally. Ali Pasha, the Grand Vizier of Turkey, had for years been trying to induce foreign capital into the Empire. Everywhere he had met with refusals. In vain did he protest that conditions in Turkey had changed for the better, that there was now an enlightened leadership in the government, a leadership that deplored the frivolities of former grand viziers. When de Hirsch approached the Porte with his plans, therefore, he found ready assistance and the utmost cooperation from Ali Pasha, who did everything possible to ease the way for him. De Hirsch carried out the preliminary negotiations himself, remaining in Constantinople until all the arrangements had been completed. His diplomatic ability stood him in good stand, and he was able, with the help of Ali Pasha, to change a number of the conditions in the concession to his advantage. His alert and penetrating vision, his almost uncanny ability to make friends where it would do him the most good, his intuitive quickness to grasp a situation and wring from it the utmost concession for himself, won him many advantages in the renegotiated contract. Untrained in diplomatic procedure, he was nevertheless able to win from the Sultan, alone and unaided, concessions far greater than the Langrand-Dumonceau interests had been able to obtain with all the help they had had from powerful governments' interceding on their behalf.

The concession called for the organization of a construction company to build the road which, when finished, was to be operated by the Austrian Sudbahn, a railroad under the control of the Rothschilds. A general meeting of stockholders of that company authorized the Austrian Sudbahn board to enter into the proposed contracts with de Hirsch, but a few weeks later it declined to execute the agreement, ostensibly for political reasons, but more likely because the Rothschilds were fearful of the difficulties of dealing with erratic Turkish authorities. From that time on the enmity between the Rothschilds and Baron de Hirsch was to become legendary. As a result of this setback Baron de Hirsch was compelled to secure a modification of the agreement with the Turkish Government, allowing him to organize an operating company as well as a construction company. Each operation was to be capitalized at fifty million francs.

Realizing the need for people with practical experience in construction work, Baron de Hirsch surrounded himself with the best technicians and engineers he could find. His genius for large undertakings made itself evident almost immediately, for the organization he built up became widely known as the most efficient railroad construction company ever to be assembled in Europe. He had no compunction, either, about hiring Wilhelm von Bressel, Rothschild's chief engineer in charge of construction work on the Austrian Sudbahn, to become his chief engineer.

Baron de Hirsch was quick to see that consolidation of many connecting railway lines would eventually have to take place so that the myriad little railroads covering the Balkans would be transformed into one large through route that would carry commerce all the way from Constantinople to Vienna quickly and efficiently, without frequent trans-shipment from one line to another. Consolidation was the answer. He visualized the completed railroad with its many connecting links as running about 660 miles in a southeasterly direction from Belgrade to Constantinople, with 212 miles in Servia, 110 miles in Bulgaria, 116 miles in Eastern Rumelia, and 222 miles in Turkey. Shortly after construction was begun, as disinterested and discriminating an observer as Wayne MacVeagh, United States Minister at Constantinople, advised the American State Department under date of May 26, 1871, that "the general increase of the stability as well as of the resources of Turkey that would result from this railway system would exert an almost magical influence in the development and improvement of the entire Ottoman Empire."

The international character of the project is indicated by the personnel of the board of directors de Hirsch selected for his companies. The construction company, "Société Impériale des Chemins de fer de la Turquie d'Europe," had on its board Messrs. Seidler, Mayer, and Springer (representing the Anglo-Austrian Bank), de Hayendorf of the Netherland R. R. Co., and M. Cezannve, a French engineer, as director general. On the board of the operating company, "Compagnie Générale pour l'Exploitation des Chemins de fer de la Turquie d'Europe," were M. Paulin Talabot, Edward Hentsch, Count Kinsky, and Edward Blount, the English financier who built France's first railroad and who became President of the Société Générale, one of France's largest banks.

About 2,000 kilometers of railway track were to be

laid. The main line was to run from Constantinople through Adrianople, Philippoli, Sofia, Nisch, Pristina, and Serajevo, and end at the Austrian frontier near the Same, where it was to connect with the Austrian Sudbahn line. Four connecting branch lines were to be built, one from Adrianople to the Aegean Sea, the second from Philippoli to Bourgos and the Black Sea, the third from Pristina to Salonica, and the fourth from Nisch to the Serbian frontier. All this was to be fully completed in from five to seven years.

An operating franchise for 99 years was granted under which the Turkish Government was to pay a subsidy of 14,000 franks per kilometer annually to the construction company. The operating company was to pay the construction company 8,000 francs per kilometer annually in addition. The Turkish Government was to provide the right-of-way. Receipts of operation in excess of 22,000 francs per kilometer were to be divided among Turkey, the construction company, and the operating company. A guarantee fund of 65 million francs was to be deposited by the Turkish Government with the Société Générale de Paris and the Anglo-Austrian Bank in semi-annual instalments of three-and-a-quarter million francs each for ten years to meet the 8,000 francs per kilometer annual governmental subsidies. Because construction of the section through Bosnia leading to the Austrian frontier presented almost insurmountable physical difficulties, the Turkish Government agreed to pay three-fourths of the cost of construction in excess of 250,000 francs per kilometer. Baron de Hirsch's construction company was to furnish the equivalent of one million dollars as a performance bond to be held by the Turkish authorities. The construction company also acquired rights to the minerals and forests along the right-of-way, paying a royalty to the Sultan for every dollar's worth of lumber or minerals it took out. Turkish bonds were to be issued to raise the money with which to cover the Turkish subsidy, but there was little or no assurance that the bonds could be sold or that Turkey could raise the money for its share of the investment.

Turkish finances had long been in a deplorable state. The "sick man of Europe" had been on the verge of financial collapse for many years. Military action and wars had been frequent and costly. Political pressure from the outside was almost overpowering and only the jealousies and antagonisms of the European powers toward each other had prevented the complete dismemberment of the Ottoman Empire. Bond issue after bond issue had been floated in European markets, each of which had resulted in disaster for the hapless investors. Defaults had become so common an occurrence that there was scarcely a bank in Europe that would handle Turkish bond issues. Business ventures in the Ottoman Empire, too, had invariably resulted in disaster. The difficulty of dealing with an allpowerful Sultan hidden away behind a dilatory Sublime Porte and a cunning Grand Vizier made it virtually impossible to negotiate business transactions with any degree of assurance that the terms would be carried out. Added to this, English stockholders in small railroads in the Balkans were publicly complaining about this time that Turkey had not made interest payments under her guarantees for several years. Turkish 5 percent Government bonds were being quoted at less than 40 percent of par value, with few takers even at this low price.

Rarely did a venture look less promising. Only to a visionary like Maurice de Hirsch did there seem a chance of pushing the railroad through to completion. Even though he was not assured of the necessary financing, he was ready to take the chance, knowing, too, that he would find himself involved in the crossfire of intrigue and secret diplomacy that pervaded the European political scene. His projected railroad was certain to lead him into the area that was the key to domination of the Continent, because whichever nation controlled the Balkans might easily become the most powerful nation in the world.

Baron de Hirsch resorted to an ingenious device. He issued 1,980,000 Turkish "lottery bonds" with a par value of 400 francs each, bearing a low 3 percent interest rate. Seven hundred fifty thousand of these bonds were offered for sale immediately at 100 francs each. Although the bonds were redeemable only in 104 years, each bond entitled the purchaser to a draw in a gigantic lottery. Six times a year a drawing was held for lottery prizes, three of which were for 600,000 francs each. The most spectacular and alluring advertising campaigns were developed to advance the lottery bond sale. News space was even purchased in the Austrian press without indicating that it was paid advertising matter. Even Bismarck's organ, the semi-official North German Gazette, stated on March 15, 1873, that Count Beust had "shown statesmanlike patriotism in calling the attention of the ministry of the dual empire to the political necessity of not opposing these railway plans of Turkey, and that the loan was favored not by reason of sympathy for Turkey, but because it offered a natural assist to the dream of 'drang nach osten.' "

Even with all this help, only about 300,000 of the 750,000 bonds offered for sale were subscribed for by the public, and the remaining 450,000 had to be taken up by the de Hirsch syndicate as underwriters, at a fixed price of 155 francs each. When the remaining bonds were issued two years later, the prices realized were still lower. These figures are interesting in view of the popular belief that Baron de Hirsch had made enormous profits on the bond issue, which would probably have been true if all the bonds had been disposed of at the maximum price.

Austrian governmental authorities made frequent appeals for the lottery-bond idea on the grounds of national interest and patriotism. Count Beust's vehement advocacy of the lottery created suspicions of conflict of interest and aroused much public comment. A distinguished Austrian historian even records the circumstance "that Beust used his influence to secure the appointment of the new Potocki cabinet to replace a former one, in order to secure approval of this bond issue."

The highly speculative character of the lottery bonds was realized from the start and purchasers were well aware of the risky nature of their investment. Nevertheless, when Turkey defaulted on these bonds along with all her other interest-paying obligations in 1875, de Hirsch was blamed for the substantial losses the bondholders suffered.

Germany and Austria were both deeply interested in having the connecting railroads completed and the entire system in operation as soon as possible because it would serve as an important agency of international commerce for shipping profitable produce from Central Europe to the East. Russia, on the other hand, was interested in preventing this penetration into what she considered her special preserves, while England, France, and Holland were anxious to slow down the completion of Baron de Hirsch's railway so as to give them time to solidify the advantages they had obtained since the opening of the Suez Canal. As far as the German Central Powers were concerned, each day of delay in completing the Austrian railway connection injured their chances of competing for this trade and commerce and left their rivals in unchallenged control.

At once a serious question of policy arose for Baron de Hirsch. Should he start building at the Hungarian frontier or at Constantinople? It was obvious that if he elected to start at Constantinople and build westward, he would play directly into the hands of England and the western group, giving to their trade and commerce the first entrance into the new territories his railway was opening up. England had long been a sea power, with a commercial fleet second to none. She had carefully fostered and developed trade with the Orient and her vessels were a familiar sight in the harbors of Turkey, Greece, and the Levant. If the railway were to be in operation from Constantinople to Salonika several years before connecting Austria with Salonika, the products of the vast hinterland that was now opening up would come to the ports at which British ships were regular callers. Austria, on the other hand, had no commercial fleet to speak of and her businessmen would have to wait for the connecting link to be made between her railroads and the new lines before they could hope to exploit any of the new markets.

An interesting work entitled *The Memoirs of a Balkan Diplomatist* (London, 1917) by Count Mijatovich, Servian Minister at London, Constantinople, and other points, throws much light on the diplomatic pressures under which de Hirsch had to make his decision. The author relates that his maiden diplomatic mission on behalf of his government was to confer with Austria's

Count Beust to try to have Servia substituted for the practically impenetrable Bosnia, through which it was planned
to make the Austrian connection with de Hirsch's railway. Naturally, there was intense rivalry between the
various Balkan states for this railway connection, and
Servia coveted it for herself. Mijatovich was informed
by Count Beust that Russian diplomacy, after having
failed in its efforts to prevent the granting of the railway
concessions to de Hirsch, had induced Turkey to fix upon
Bosnia as the connection point. A further factor in Turkey's selection of Bosnia, according to the Austrians, was
that the Sublime Porte felt that, in the event of war, the
railway would be strategically less dangerous to Turkey
if it fell into enemy hands. Count Mijatovich informed
Count Beust that "if construction would be attempted in
Bosnia, Servian bands would destroy every night what had
been built during the day!" Beust answered that "Count
Mijatovich should inform his chiefs that diplomacy never
uses such menacing language unless the country it represents is ready to declare war in 48 hours!" He counseled
patience, promising that the matter would be discussed
with the Sublime Porte and that Austria's influence would
be exerted to have the plans modified so as to eliminate
the Bosnian junction.

The Bosnian route, in any event, was found to be too
expensive and Baron de Hirsch made use of the chance
thus offered of becoming a party to a new agreement,
which materially modified the earlier contract to his decided advantage. Turkey was now to pay 22,000 francs
per kilometer annually to the construction company during
the term of an operating franchise reduced from 99 years
to 50 years. Instead of being obligated to lay about 2,000
kilometers of track in Bosnia, he was required to build

only 1,280 kilometers. Turkey assumed the burden of
making a modified connection with Austria and building
other sections, including one connecting with the Russo-
Rumanian Ruschek-Varnu line, and agreed to build various connecting quays, roads, and harbors to serve as
feeders for the railway. Baron de Hirsch's construction
company became merely an agent, surrendering all participation in receipts of operation as well as the mineral and
forest rights it had acquired under the earlier contract.
The specific provision for a guarantee by Turkey was
omitted, a major change that later led to much controversy.

Even though he found himself involved in an undertaking with important political and international impli-
cations, de Hirsch felt that his primary obligations were
to the corporations he had put together and to Turkey;
he had no right to prejudice these pecuniary interests in
order to advance Austro-German foreign commerce. He
based his decision to start at Constantinople and build
westward on simple economics. Because of the configura-
tion of the country, the section of the prospective railway
adjacent to Constantinople was much easier and cheaper
to build than the physically difficult Austro-Hungarian
section, and it was much less difficult to bring in supplies
by water to Constantinople than to attempt to drag them
overland through Central Europe. Considerable traffic,
too, would become available from Constantinople as soon
as some sections of the railway were in operation, and the
subsidies per kilometer would become payable much
sooner.

It was apparent to Baron de Hirsch that the many
small unconnected railroads in Eastern Austria and the
Balkans should be merged together so as to establish one

major railroad, which would run from Vienna to Constantinople. Through traffic, especially freight, should be handled in one shipment because frequent transshipment from one line to another was an unnecessary expense to the shipper as well as a burden to the railroad. By starting at Constantinople he could hold off making a decision as to where he would connect at the Austrian border and with what line, so as to make the best deal possible. He wanted to stall for time because he felt that the longer he waited, the better the deal he would be able to make on the hook-up with the railroad running from Vienna eastward. By playing one destination point against another, he was able to keep those railroads that were anxious to make the connection with him on tenterhooks, and he did this to great advantage.

Taking all these facts into consideration, he made the decision that any sensible business man would have made, much to the satisfaction of his engineering people, who felt that an attempt to build eastward from the Austrian border would have wrecked the project at the start, as had happened to so many frustrated Balkan railway schemes. The decision to start in the East and build westward nevertheless played into the hands of the Western powers, for it gave England and the other maritime nations whose ships were in control of the Mediterranean maritime route the opportunity of "getting there first," an advantage Austria was never able to overcome. When de Hirsch hired Ralph Earle, a former member of the British Parliament who had at one time been Disraeli's private secretary, to head the construction company, it added fuel to the fire and gave substance to the Austrian and German claims that Baron de Hirsch was a tool of English imperialism.

To many, it looked as though he were constructing the lowest cost spurs of the railroad first in order to cash in quickly on the mileage payments he was to collect for each kilometer completed. As a practical matter, however, military expediency rather than financial considerations dictated the route the railway was to take. Turkey was more interested in railroads that could be easily defended and that had strategic military value than in their commercial usefulness, and Turkish authorities carefully scrutinized and approved all construction plans from this standpoint. Events were to prove that Turkey was justified in this stand when, in the Russo-Turkish war of 1877-78, its railways proved to be of great military value in transporting men and supplies. The absence of existing lines into Turkey at first hampered Russian military strategy, but she rapidly built military railways into Turkey under the supervision of her great Jewish railway constructor, Samuel Poliakoff (whose daughter later married Baron de Hirsch's brother James), so that the curious, but not unusual spectacle was here presented of finding Jewish enterprise arrayed on two opposing sides.

German and Austrian trade, as was to be expected, suffered greatly in competition with that of the maritime powers, especially as the railroad connection with Austria was unexpectedly delayed for many years.

Baron de Hirsch was severely criticized in Austria, the press being unusually venomous in attacks on him. Overlooking the fact that he had given the Austrian bankers the first opportunity, which they, in their short-sightedness, had turned down, newspapers heaped abuse on his head from then on. Even after his death, obituary notices in the Vienna papers made vicious anti-Semitic remarks about him because of the harm he had done to Austrian interests in Turkey and the Balkans.

The two able, liberal-minded Turkish Viziers who had been Baron de Hirsch's strongest supporters, Ali Pasha and Fuad Pasha, both died soon after construction of the railroad was begun. They were succeeded by a pro-Russian Vizier, Mahmoud Nedim Pasha, who owed his appointment to Ignatieff, the intriguing Russian ambassador at Constantinople. Sir Horace Rumbold, British Secretary of Legation at Constantinople from 1871 to 1873, in his *Recollections of a Diplomatist,* while characterizing this new Vizier as "reputed to be honest and trustworthy in his dealings, though others charged him with freely accepting large bribes," says that Mahmoud Nedim was "so subservient to Russian influence as to earn the Russianized nickname of 'Mahmudoff.'" Russia's policy was to discourage trade relations between Austria and Turkey by delaying Turkish railroad building. She was herself erecting a more northerly railroad running through her own dominions toward Persia, and she desired to connect the Turkish railway system with her own and Roumanian lines. Accordingly, all sorts of intrigues were started by the new Turkish administration to prevent completion of de Hirsch's Austrian railroad connection.

Despite the fact that large revenues would become payable to Turkey under the railway construction contracts when the roads were completed and in operation, Mahmoud Nedim, under various pretexts, began a long-drawn-out course of attempted frustration of all operations and even the suspension of the building of some sections. Added to this, many small localized wars had begun to appear on the horizon and Turkey's financial plight was becoming more serious day by day.

There were many other problems to overcome. Baron de Hirsch once described the difficulties of trying to establish fixed train schedules. "Turks count their hours from each day's sunset," he said, "giving night and day twelve hours each from that moment. It follows that any given Turkish hour never happens at exactly the same time any two days together, and that a Turkish watch, being regulated only once each week, is never exactly right. However, the arrangement seems to have the merit of getting the Turk up by sunrise; after that he can afford a little unpunctuality through the day." Thus 12 o'clock, whether noon or midnight came at a different time each day and was heralded by the firing of cannons from ships in the harbor or in the Upper Bosporus. While local affairs were arranged on Turkish time, most Europeans preferred to set their watches by western time, creating a state of constant confusion for people who were attending meetings or had to be at certain places at a certain time. What time? Turkish or Western? This, too, created untold problems for Hirsch in trying to operate his railroad. Should he establish train departure time on western schedules, or on Turkish time, with trains leaving at a different time each day?

Labor presented many difficulties, too. In discussing some of the unusual difficulties of trying to operate any venture in the Near East, de Hirsch said: "Sometimes one gets the impression that every day is Sunday in Turkey. There is Friday for the Mussulman, Saturday for the Jews and Sunday for the Christians. Each religiously rests on his own holy day, which makes it almost impossible to figure on a full work week for anyone. One of the major problems in building the railroad developed around this. We first sought to hire only Turks so that we could get a full work week. We soon found, however, that their qualifications were limited and we had to hire Christians and Jews as well. Chaos ensued until we were able to work out schedules so that we had a full work force on hand all the time." He brought workmen from all over Europe, uniting them into one large group made up of English, Irish, Scots, French, German, Dutch, Italian, Polish, until, in fact, almost every known nationality in Europe was represented on the project.

Baron de Hirsch was probably one of the first of the employers who believed that the conditions under which a man labored determined, in large measure, his efficiency. If workers were fed properly they would work that much harder. If they were housed in pleasant, clean, and sanitary surroundings, they would not be susceptible to colds and other illnesses. If they were paid fairly they would be satisfied workmen and the quality of their workmanship would improve. His liberal policies toward his workers, however, brought him nothing but condemnation from employers along the right-of-way of his railway line, because he was making their workers dissatisfied.

Despite all these difficulties, five different sections of the railway were opened to traffic between August, 1872, and December, 1874. On June 17, 1873, as reported at length in the London Times, "there was a gala celebration at Adrianople, attended by the Turkish Grand Vizier, at which Baron James de Hirsch, as his brother's representative, was decorated by the Sultan in honor of the completion of the Constantinople-Adrianople-Philippoli-Bellora section."

Turkey suspended payment of interest on its railway bonds in 1875, and Baron de Hirsch was sued by a group of bondholders in a Vienna court. Judgment was rendered in his favor, however, vindicating him and his company. He then took over the roads himself, setting up an operating company without Turkish governmental participation, which gave him the opportunity to establish a really independent operation. For years he ran the railway system in this fashion, impounding the gross receipts in full, notwithstanding the Sultan's indignation.

Trouble was brewing, however, and it became apparent that he might find himself involved in serious difficulties if his controversies with Turkey worsened, and he might need outside help. He deemed it advisable to reorganize the operating company in order to secure strong diplomatic protection that would come to his aid in the event his problems with Turkey had to be arbitrated. His company had been organized under French law and he was a French citizen, but France had lost its old-time prestige in the Near East when she was so soundly defeated in the Franco-Prussian War. Austria, on the other hand, was keenly interested in using the railroads the Baron was building in the development of trade with the Near East, and Austrian protection would be truly valuable in the event of trouble. The Sultan, backed by Count de Vogue, the French Ambassador, objected vehemently to the proposed transformation of the de Hirsch operation from a French to an Austrian company, and diplomatic relations between Austria and Turkey became somewhat strained over this issue. The Sultan is said to have written a personal letter to the Emperor of Austria, objecting to any diplomatic consideration of Baron de Hirsch's rights, stating that Turkey could not see that the interests of the Austrian Government were identical with those of Baron de Hirsch!

Nevertheless, Baron de Hirsch reorganized the company under Austrian law in 1880, and became an Austrian citizen, thus placing himself in a position to call on Austria to intercede if it became necessary to protect the

company's rights under its contracts with the Sublime
Porte, or to prevent forceful Turkish seizure of his railroad. The wisdom of this move was borne out when, on
one occasion, the Sultan sought to seize Baron de Hirsch
and have him executed, and he was able to take refuge on
an Austrian vessel lying in the harbor. As an Austrian
subject, he was clearly entitled to that country's official
support and the benefit of the Turkish extraterritorial
agreement with Austria.

The Treaty of Berlin in 1878 contained a number of
references to Baron de Hirsch's railways. Each of the new
states that had been carved out of the Ottoman Empire
and was not independent of Turkey obligated itself to
complete the section of the railroad that lay within its
own territory, while the settlement of accounts was reserved for a future understanding between Austria, Turkey, the new Balkan states, and the railroad company.
The inclusion of these clauses in so important an international treaty was regarded as one of the most important advantages gained by Austria at this Congress. Certainly it was a triumph for Baron de Hirsch.

Under the new agreement, which was negotiated as a
result of Servian protests, two routes from Vienna to
Constantinople were to be constructed, one via Servia and
Bulgaria, and the other through Salonica, across Servia
and Macedonia. Servia in 1881 awarded the contract for
constructing her section to Eugene Bontoux of Paris and
his "Union Générale." Gross bribery attended the award;
Count Mijatovich, the Servian Minister of Finance,
charged that he had on one occasion rejected a bribe of
two million francs. Evidence directly connecting the Servian king himself with acceptance of large "douceurs"
was subsequently produced in court. Scarcely had work on

the railway commenced, when the "Union Générale" failed in January, 1882, with many millions of liabilities, and Bontoux found himself under arrest, thus adding another chapter to the history of failures in Balkan railway construction. What made Bontoux's enterprise of particular concern to the Jewish community in Austria was its curious anti-Semitic overtones—the beginning of a trend to place the blame for every economic disaster on Jewish bankers. Eugene Bontoux had organized his "Union Générale" in Paris under Jesuit influence, with the slogan "Christian money for Christian investment only!" The ostensibly sectarian character of the undertaking lent much color to the baseless, but widely current charge that he had fallen victim to a Jewish conspiracy headed up by his rival, Baron de Hirsch. Dr. Joseph S. Bloch, in his *Reminiscences,* narrates that Austrian Archduchess Maria Theresa is supposed to have lent so much credence to this charge that she gave liberally to the Austrian anti-Semitic cause.

On April 9, 1882, a Dr. Budde, Constantinople correspondent of the *Kolnische Zeitung,* contributed a vehement attack on the Baron entitled "Turkey and Baron Hirsch," in the course of which he advocated that Turkey simply seize the railway system and ignore the arbitration clauses in the contracts of 1869 and 1872. The Baron answered this letter at length in the same paper's issue of April 15, 1882, departing from his usual custom of bearing abuse in silence. Budde's attack on de Hirsch, however, was adopted wholesale by the anti-Semitic writer Dehn in a book he published the next year under the title *Deutschland und die Orientbahmen.* Some months after Budde's articles appeared, Bismarck avenged himself publicly for de Hirsch's actions in the old matter of the

Luxembourg railways by publishing a vitriolic article in the *Deutsches Tageblatt,* in which he pointed out that Justegrath Brinker, a Constantinople agent of Baron de Hirsch, "has contrived to make it appear as if he were on the staff of the German Embassy and had the German Government's backing, which would be deeply regretted." He concluded his letter by declaring that "as to the Austrian Government, they have committed themselves too far with Hirsch."

From this unfortunate incident and the severe stock market crashes that began to dot the financial scene for several years, anti-Semitism made its appearance as a political phenomenon, marked by a speech by Edward Lasker in the German Reichstag on February 7, 1883, in which he blamed the stock market crashes on "Jewish swindling schemes." Following a particularly violent election campaign, during which Lasker's party had as its slogan a statement that all of Europe's ills were caused by Jewish bankers, an anti-Semitic political party took seats for the first time in the German Reichstag, and from then on anti-Semitism was to be the slogan of at least one political party at every election in Germany until the Nazis took over the country some fifty years later.

One of many charges brought against Hirsch was that he or his agents distributed "Boksheesh" on an enormous scale. This charge overlooked the fact that in a land in which officials, instead of being paid salaries, were dependent upon what they could extort from those they governed, no extensive railway operations could have been carried on without a liberal sprinkling of graft. Sometimes the bitter resentment against the company and de Hirsch that was prevalent among the inhabitants of the Balkans and Turkey proper was caused by Turkish officials who often pocketed the compensation collected for lands and buildings taken for railway stations and rights of way, which left the unfortunate victims with the impression that Baron de Hirsch and his construction company had refused to pay for the expropriated property.

United States Ambassador Oscar S. Straus is authority for the story that on one occasion it was necessary to locate a station in the center of a little village about ten miles from Constantinople, the first section of the railroad running from Constantinople to Seven Towers having been completed. This necessitated the expropriation and tearing down of a number of houses belonging to poor people, with payment for the land and houses to be made by the Turkish government. The villagers who were about to be dispossessed, knowing how uncertain would be the collection of claims against their government, presented their grievances to Baroness de Hirsch, who was in Constantinople with her husband. Maurice explained to her that the location of the stations was a matter for the Turkish Government and not his concern. She replied that she would make it her concern and that she would not consent to have the railway start out creating misery for poor people. She would advance the money out of her private funds, assuming that the railway would claim it from the Government. She determined the amount involved and, learning that it was over a million francs, sent her agent to the poor people whose houses were destroyed and indemnified each one to the full extent of his loss.

Austria, on her own and Baron de Hirsch's behalf, had entered into a secret treaty with Turkey in 1875, providing that a connecting link would be constructed between de

Hirsch's railway and the Austrian railways before the end
of 1879, but the Russo-Turkish War of 1877-78 intervened. Turkey did not build the desired line, and probably made no serious effort to do so. The diary of King
Charles of Rumania, under date of March 21, 1875, refers to Baron de Hirsch's presence in Constantinople for
months on end to urge the building of the Austrian and
Servian connections. These would have opened the entire
continental carrying business for his railroad, which
presently consisted of three detached sections without
enough business to earn carrying charges.

In 1880 Austria insisted that Turkey and the other
signatories to the Treaty complete the railway system
pursuant to the terms of the Treaty of Berlin. Bulgaria
and the other principalities, however, were weak financially and endeavored to make Turkey bear a larger degree of the cost than she was willing to assume. A new
international railway conference met in 1883 at which a
treaty, known as the "Convention à Quatre," was duly
signed by all the powers concerned. Written consent had
to be secured from Baron de Hirsch, approving the
agreement among Austro-Hungary, Turkey, Serbia, and
Bulgaria under which he was to waive indemnity for
variations from the original agreements that somewhat
modified his concessions. Anti-Semitic writers made much
of the unique spectacle presented by the circumstance that
sovereign states could enter into a treaty only with the
consent of a Jewish financier.

Numerous obstacles kept cropping up to delay completion of the railway in the manner prescribed by the
Treaty of Berlin, and the many political problems that
arose in Turkey's liberated Balkan dependencies delayed
operation far beyond the stipulated dates. However, the

final railroad connection between Sofia in Bulgaria and Nishi in Servia, actually connecting Turkey with Europe for the first time, was completed in April, 1888, and through trains ran from Vienna to Constantinople, operated by Baron de Hirsch's company.

To commemorate the arrival of the first train at the Austrian border, a giant celebration was ordered. A colorful procession, led by a gypsy orchestra, walked around and around the square in the little border town. The air was mild and filled with the tart aroma of wine from the inn, mingled with the sweet smell of acacias. Peasant boys in short jackets and high boots, and girls in peasant costumes—their starched petticoats rustling as they walked while the richly embroidered aprons of the older women flapped in the wind—marched in the almost completely disorganized parade. The baker, the clockmaker, the tailor, standing outside their quaint shops, called out greetings. Aristocrats from the provinces and high-ranking officers and courtiers who had come for the celebration mingled with the peasants and burghers who strolled on the promenade underneath the windows of the hotel. Or they sat in the sunshine on little iron chairs while the military band and the gypsy orchestra played in the pavilion. The procession continued circling the square for hours before going into the hotel for the celebration feast.

The city fathers had decorated the hotel festively. In the large oak-paneled dining room, places were laid for over 200 people. Long serving-tables stood around the walls, laden with food and delicacies—black pudding, warm ham, pork shanks, tasty liver sausage, bacon, and smoked pork. Everywhere there was the smell of Bock beer and sauerkraut. Wine jugs were passed from hand to hand. In the main ballroom, gypsies were striking up a dance and soon the whole party was alive to the vibrations of a lively czardas.

The single-car train bearing Baron and Baroness de Hirsch and the many dignitaries representing the Sultan of Turkey and the Emperor of Austria was scheduled to arrive at the railroad station at 3:45 P.M. But it was 7 P.M. before the train reached the frontier station between the empire of the Sultans and the empire of Hapsburgs. The celebration was at its height. The delay, the Baron explained, was caused by the ceremonies and speech-making at every station along the way.

The railway was an instant success. Paul H. Emden in his *Money Powers of Europe in the 19th Century,* says, "From every point of view, the railways which Baron de Hirsch completed in 1888, were a gigantic success; they were a civilizing influence of the very first rank. A foolhardy promoter had grown into a leader and a predominant money power on the grandest possible scale. It is as impossible to form even an approximate idea of the fortune amassed by Baron de Hirsch as it is to arrive at an accurate estimate of the sums which this most generous of European financiers gave away, but a conservative guess might fix the amount at 20 million pounds at the least."

Suddenly Maurice de Hirsch found himself a figure of importance in the world of finance. Now the mighty wooed him and sought him out. His advice and opinions in financial matters, which but a short time before had been looked upon as visionary and impractical, now became words of wisdom. Emperors and kings, princes and dukes, the rich and the near rich, the famous and the near famous, all were rivals for his good will and attention. Begging letters from "schnorers" and charitable organizations all over the world poured in by the thousands, and the hangers-on who abound where money is plentiful soon made their appearance. Unknown artists and writers, so adept during the nineteenth century at wheedling money out of wealthy patrons, were not long in coming to him for assistance, the surest sign of acknowledged success.

But the financial difficulties with Turkey were not over; toward the end of 1887 Baron de Hirsch went to Constantinople to adjust his financial problems with the Turkish Government, which claimed he owed 132 million francs, a claim growing out of kilometric guarantees and other concessions. Oscar S. Straus, who had been American representative at the Sublime Porte for three terms, twice as Minister Plenipotentiary and once as Ambassador, suddenly found himself involved in this dispute. In his book *The American Spirit,* he recalls his first meeting with the Baron. "One day," he says, "while I was calling on the Grand Vizier Kiamil Pasha, he introduced me to a tall, slender man in his fifties, dark eyes sparkling with spirit and energy, clean-shaven except for a full black mustache, dressed rather dudishly in a cut-away coat, white vest and white spats." A few days after this, the Sultan discussed his claim against Baron de Hirsch with him. The Sultan said that efforts had been made to arrive at a settlement for some time and it was now proposed to go to arbitration. The Baron had first suggested the French and then the Austrian ambassador, but the Sultan refused. The Sultan then suggested Oscar Straus as an arbitrator and Baron de Hirsch had accepted, it being mutually agreed that Straus would receive an honorarium of one million francs, the Turkish Government and Baron de Hirsch each to pay half. Ambassador Straus explained that he would have to consult his government but the

Sultan said that the Turkish Ambassador in Washington had already done this and had been informed by Secretary of State Bayard that there would be no objection. Straus cabled Secretary of State Bayard and was assured that this was true and that the American government had no objection. Despite this, Straus felt it was best to avoid any dealings with the Turkish Government that involved a money settlement and he so advised Secretary of State Bayard. Instead, Straus suggested that rather than act as arbitrator, he would act as mediator without compensation to see if a satisfactory agreement could be reached between Baron de Hirsch and the Grand Vizier. This offer was accepted. Although there were weeks of disagreement and frequent altercations between the parties, Straus was able to smooth them over and an amicable settlement was reached. On one of the legal points, Professor Rudolph von Gneist, the distinguished German publicist who had once acted as arbitrator between Great Britain and the United States in settling a dispute over the Northwestern frontier with Canada, was selected as umpire and on February 25, 1889, he made the final arbitral award, one of the largest international awards on record.

The chief question was the validity of the franchises held by de Hirsch's operating company. Turkey claimed that the fifty-year term of the franchise was fixed so indefinitely by the provision making it operative only one year after the completion of the line, that the franchise was voided entirely under Turkish law. Professor von Gneist rejected this claim absolutely. Turkey also claimed 50 million francs for alleged accrued rentals for one section, 14 million for another, and 15 million francs as reasonable compensation for a third incomplete section.

As an offset to this, Professor von Gneist ruled that Turkey's failure to erect the ports, quays, and other connecting feeders called for under the agreement had caused heavy losses to the operating company. Under the terms of the final adjudication, the Oriental Railways Operating Company was directed to pay 26¾ million francs to Turkey, together with 12 percent interest accrued for about 15 years. Against this, the Company was granted a credit of 12⅓ million francs for the cost of improvements and charges for military transportation.

Thus was settled once and for all the controversy between Baron de Hirsch and the Sublime Porte that had gone on for so many years. The award was generally considered to be a substantial justification of Baron de Hirsch's position. Of particular interest and significance is the paragraph from a letter written by Professor von Gneist to Baron de Hirsch soon after the award was made, in which he said: "I may proceed on the assumption that, in the matter of the greatly complicated affair, the question of honor is of deepest concern to you, for it is a fine trait in the nature of man that, progressively with his acquisition of wealth, his regard for the importance of his good name increases more and more. It became a source of great satisfaction for me that in a matter of great responsibility and in a time of bitter prejudice, I was enabled in my award repeatedly to emphasize the probity (geschaftliche korrectheit) of your course."

In 1899 the Deutsche Bank acquired from the estate of Baron and Baroness de Hirsch controlling interest in the Orient Railway, which owned the track running through Servia to Constantinople.

8

TURKEY

The Ottoman Empire had for four centuries been a major European power, extending all the way from North Africa to the Austro-Hungarian border. The Star and Crescent waved over Rumania in the southeast of the Balkan Peninsula; over Bosnia, and Herzegovina, Servia, Bulgaria, and Albania to the north and west; over North Africa, even to the Atlantic Ocean; and over Syria, the Hejaz, Asia Minor, and the islands of the Mediterranean. It was a land of many nations, creeds, and tongues, but the official language was Turkish. When Baron de Hirsch started to build his railroad, the European population was estimated to be 9,277,040, the Asiatic population 16,174,056, and the total African nations 7,817,265. There are no reliable figures of the number of Jews, but it has been variously estimated that somewhere between one million and a million-and-a-half Jews lived under Turkish domination. Palestine itself was in Turkish hands.

Constantinople, when Maurice and Clara de Hirsch first visited there, had a population of almost a million souls. The seat of the Sublime Porte, the city lay on Seraglio Point between the Sea of Marmara and the

Golden Horn. Across this peninsula, a heavy stone wall, reaching from the Marmara to the Golden Horn, separated the city from the royal grounds, which extended down almost to the sea. Fine groves of plane trees and cypress flourished in the park in which the royal family could enjoy the cool breezes from the upper Bosporus. Great courts opened into each other, each with elaborate palaces built by the old sultans for the imperial household. Within this area sultans were born, reigned, suffered, and died. It was one of the consecrated spots of history. Passing these sacred precincts on horseback was forbidden, nor was one permitted to carry an open umbrella or any other modern contrivance that might be construed as an affront to the past.

Three great men in the long line of thirty-six sultans, Mohammed the Conqueror, Suleiman the Magnificent, and Mahmoud II, had spent lavishly to adorn the capital. The architectural beauty and dignity of the mosques and other public buildings were evidence of this. The reigning Sultan, with whom Baron de Hirsch had to deal, was Sultan Aziz, whose extravagances were notorious throughout the capitals of Europe. One still heard fabulous stories of the reception he accorded Empress Eugenie on her visit to Constantinople in 1867, when he built the palace of Beylerbey especially for her occupancy.

The extravagances of a Sultan were never questioned in Moslem lands and until nearly the end of his reign no restraint hampered the activities of Aziz. He built nine royal palaces. Three of them, Tcherigan, Beylerbey, and Yildiz Kiosk, were centered on Seraglio Point, between the Golden Horn and the Bosporus. From the roofs and balconies of these palaces it was possible to see, over the picturesque waterways, Asia on one side and Europe on

the other. A secluded latticed corner overlooking the
sparkling Bosporus was arranged especially for the harem,
with the fountain of Sultan Achmet, a beautiful specimen
of Oriental art designed by Achmet himself and erected
about a century before, standing near the principal entrance. Everything was done on the grand scale of a fabled
medieval kingdom. Crown jewels were set with large,
rich pearls. Court robes were magnificent fabrics, on
which were embroidered elaborate, intricate designs in
gold. Heavy silk and rich velvet draperies in brilliant
colors bordered with gold provided the background for
gold and silver wall plaques, interspersed with jeweled
daggers decorated with diamonds. Even the visiting cards
of Sultan Aziz were adorned with diamonds and other
precious stones.

No sudden change of regime could be more dramatic
than that which took place in Turkey at the end of the
reign of Sultan Aziz. On the morning of May 30, 1876,
a crier walked through the old-fashioned stone-paved
streets of Scutari at early dawn. He carried a heavy club
and, as he slowly proceeded, struck the rough pavement
and called out, over and over again, "Sultan Aziz is dead.
May Allah have mercy on his soul." His extravagant
reign had proved financially disastrous. He had brought
about a debt of two hundred and fifty millions of pounds
sterling, with no means of paying it.

Murad the Fifth, who succeeded to the throne, was
adjudged to be suffering from idiocy by the Council of
Ministers on August 31, 1876, and was deposed.

Abdul-Hamid II, second son of Abdul Medjid, succeeded his brother to the throne, becoming the 34th Ottoman Sultan. Probably because of the influence of Baron de
Hirsch, Sultan Abdul Hamid instituted a liberalized offi-

cial policy toward the Jews of Turkey, thereby becoming
the first Turkish sovereign to grant equality of the law to
Jews. On ascending the throne he ordered the payment
by the government of salaries to the rabbis of Turkey,
giving them the position of officials of state. He started
the custom of sending to the Chief Rabbi 8,000 francs
every Passover for distribution among the poor in the
Turkish capital. He allowed Jews to become "Rayas," as
the Christian and other non-Mohammedan Turkish subjects were known, giving them political representation at
the Porte. The Jewish representative was proposed by the
Chief Rabbi of the central consistory of the Jews of Constantinople, the nomination being confirmed by the Minister of Public Worship. His function was to accompany
the Chief Rabbi on all his visits to the palace and to
present the official petitions of the Jewish community to
the Grand Vizier. When the Chief Rabbi could not talk
Turkish, the Kapu Kihaya, as he was called, acted as in-
terpreter. Jacob Gabbai held this office at the beginning of
reign of Sultan Hamid II, when Baron de Hirsch was involved in his dispute with Turkey, and he acted as inter-
preter in many of the meetings.

In 1883 Abdul-Hamid conferred the order of Osmanie
on Moses Levi, the Chief Rabbi of Constantinople. In his
presentation, he criticized the Christians of Europe for
their persecution of the Jews. "As for me," he said, "I am
very much satisfied with the Jewish officials for their
activity and zeal; and I will in the future increase their
number. When the Jews were expelled from Spain, a land
which had been the home of their fathers for about 800
years they, the best of the Spanish kingdom, writers and
scientists, physicians and jurists, artisans and farmers
were cast impoverished and plague-ridden, upon the mercy

of foreign nations. Portugal, for a high tax, gave them temporary shelter; the cities of Italy granted them a grudging welcome to the ghettos; Germany admitted them to a share in the persecution of their brethren; England and France spurned them utterly. In all Europe they were welcomed in but one place, in Turkey, the home of the infidel."

During the many trips through the Balkans, which their activities made necessary, Maurice and Clara were able to see at first hand the extreme poverty of the Jews of Eastern Europe. Clara, who always accompanied her husband on these trips to the Orient, was deeply touched by the misery she saw. She spent most of her time in the Jewish quarters of the cities they visited, wandering through the ramshackle, dilapidated, filthy hovels in which Jews were forced to spend their lives, dismayed and despondent because, in the very countries in which she and her husband were amassing immense wealth, their coreligionists lived in abject misery and, worse still, in abysmal ignorance. Unlike the Jews of Western Europe's ghettos, who were at least schooled in Talmudic lore, the Jews of the Near East had little or no education in anything. Few could even read or write. Most of them spent their lives eking out a bare living as unskilled day laborers. While the western Jews, untrained in skills or trades, were able to live precariously as pack-on-the-back peddlers or dealers in old shoes and old clothes, in the countries of the Near East Jews were unable to exist by trade alone, and many of them earned their living as water-carriers and porters, or in the lowest of menial jobs. When, in one of his personal interviews with the Sultan in connection with railway problems, Baron de Hirsch protested against the prevailing rule that the employment of Jews on public telegraph and railway lines in Turkey was forbidden, he was informed that Jews were, in fact, incompetent to fill such posts.

Maurice and Clara de Hirsch became intimately acquainted with the rabbinical and lay leaders of each community they visited, and from them they gained a firsthand knowledge of conditions in almost every Jewish community in the Turkish and Austrian domains. While Clara liked to involve herself in charitable undertakings, dispensing charity herself in a personal way, Maurice, busily engaged in a vast, highly complicated railroad construction enterprise, preferred to carry out his considerable works of charity through organizations and private almoners. Believing strongly that the first need of the Eastern Jews was secular education, and impressed with the excellent educational work and benevolent services of the Alliance Israélite Universelle, Baron de Hirsch placed large sums of money at its disposal to enable the organization to extend its work in European Turkey. At the same time, he engaged Chevalier Emmanuel Felix Veneziani, an Italian Jew born in Leghorn in 1825, who had been manager of the Banque Camondo in Constantinople while also serving as Belgian Consul there, to act as his private almoner. Veneziani moved to Paris, where he was elected to the Central Committee of the Alliance Israélite Universelle. He was to become widely known as a French philanthropist because, as Baron de Hirsch's almoner and an officer of the Alliance, he traveled extensively throughout Turkey and Bulgaria, dispensing large amounts for schools and hospitals. He spent almost a year in Galicia supervising the care and movement of the hordes of Russian Jews who escaped into the border town of Brody during the pogroms of 1882. He was honored by the French government when he was made a Chevalier of France, and by Turkey when he was made a Commander in the Order of Nishan-i-Medjidie. ·

Veneziani, probably more than any one person, was responsible for the belief Baron de Hirsch was known to hold that Palestine had nothing to offer as a place in which to resettle eastern Europe's Jews. He and a group of engineers and technicians made a survey of Palestine at the Baron's request and reported to him that the country was virtually uninhabitable and that the Jewish colonies there could survive only with charitable donations from European Jews. The report recommended that Jewish immigration into Palestine be stopped.

The Alliance Israélite Universelle grew out of the famous Damascus Case of 1840, which saw the Jews of the largest European countries unite for the first time in concerted action to obtain justice for a handful of Jews who were involved in a matter that had always been considered local and not subject to the interference of outsiders. Thirteen Jews of Damascus were imprisoned, accused of ritual murder in the mysterious disappearance of a certain Father Thomas. The case attracted world-wide attention when the Archbishop of Canterbury called a "Mansion House and Guildhall Meeting" in London to protest these charges. The meeting was attended by a large number of prominent Englishmen, Christian leaders as well as Jews, and as a result of their interest in the case, a formal note of protest was lodged with the embassies of all the world's leading powers. The United States government also became interested in the case, and a formal American protest note was sent to the Sultan.

Three of the most prominent Jews of the period decided to intervene. Sir Moses Montefiere, the English philanthropist, Adolphe Isaac Crémieux, the French statesman, and Solomon Munk, the renowned Jewish Orientalist, traveled to Egypt to intercede with Mehemet Ali and to defend the accused Jews. They succeeded in obtaining an acquittal for the nine prisoners who were still alive, the other four having succumbed to the many months of imprisonment and torture.

A new spirit of self-confidence and self-respect was born because Jews for the first time had successfully fought as equals and as free men. They had seized the issue and forced it out into the open instead of cowering behind ghetto walls as they had done so many times in the past when the same charge had been raised—and Christians had come to their assistance. They had seen demonstrated the age-old axiom that those who fight for their legitimate rights command respect. Judaism had taken on a new dignity in the eyes of the world and, of far greater importance, it took on a new dignity in the eyes of the Jew himself. The sense of inferiority that the degradation of the ghetto had bred in Jewry gave way from that date on to a new-found pride in Jewish accomplishment that was to evolve into the Zionist demand for full-fledged nationhood in a Jewish national homeland.

As a result of the success of the Damascus Affair, a group of six public-spirited Jews of Paris, none of whom were especially prominent and none of whom were among the wealthy Jewish bankers, tried to form an organization that would be in a position to defend Jews from injustice wherever unwarranted charges were brought against them. Aristide Astruc, who later became the Chief Rabbi of Belgium; Isidore Cahen, editor of the Archives Israélites; Jules Carvallo, a civil engineer; Narcisse Leven, a lawyer; Professor Eugene Manual; and the well-known merchant Charles Netter launched the new movement, which attracted much interest among Christians. Many prominent Protestant intellectuals lent encouraging support to the group, among them Alexandre Dumas, the younger.

Despite the proven need for Jewish communities throughout the world to be linked together, opposition by Jewish groups everywhere made itself evident almost immediately. The more prominent of the Jewish writers were against the plan because they felt that the best way to cure anti-Semitism was to ignore it and, if it was ignored long enough, it would disappear completely. The wealthy Jewish barons and the Jewish bankers were afraid of the political nature of such an organization and of the connotation of internationalism that it implied. Weren't Jews already accused of being part of an international conspiracy? Many of the leading rabbis, too, were in complete disagreement with the aims and purposes of the Alliance because the Jew was to look only to God for help. The rabbis would watch over their flocks and heal their wounds with prayer. No international political organization was needed.

For two decades the debate went on, until 1858 when a new incident, the Mortara Case, again attracted worldwide attention. Church authorities in the Papal States had refused to return Edgar Mortara, an infant who had been kidnaped from his home and baptized, to his Jewish parents. The furore this case aroused provided the necessary impetus that finally dissolved all opposition, and in 1860 the Alliance Israélite Universelle was founded under the sponsorship of the same six leaders who had carried on the struggle for almost twenty years. It had been originally intended that the Alliance would be an international organization. The Franco-Prussian war, however, changed this concept because of the diverse loyalties of the two largest groups in the Alliance, the French and the Austro-Germans. Austrian Jewry broke away and formed the Israelitish Alliance of Vienna in 1873, declaring the organization's aims to be the same as those of the original Alliance but confining activities to aiding the oppressed Jews of Austria and Galicia. The French Jews carried on with the original objective of aiding Jews wherever help was needed, anywhere in the world. They retained the name Alliance Israélite Universelle for their organization, which was destined to play a leading part in the lives of European and North African Jewry for many years—even to this day. The scope of its charitable and political activities extended all the way from Palestine to the New World, wherever injustice appeared. One of its first official acts, although it was organized specifically to aid Jews, was to raise a fund for the relief of the Christians who were being persecuted by the Moslems in Lebanon. During the Russo-Turkish War of 1877-78, too, the Alliance did the work of humanity on and near the battlefields, establishing and maintaining hospitals for both armies. Baron de Hirsch is reported to have paid all the costs and to have sent the Empress of Russia $200,000 for the rehabilitation of wounded Russian soldiers. The Christian world was greatly impressed by these gestures, which created world-wide sympathy for the work the Alliance had undertaken.

It was at the Congress of Berlin, which settled the problems that had brought on the Russo-Turkish war, that the Alliance Israélite Universelle achieved its first great political victory. The Alliance was officially represented by three delegates, Kann, Netter, and Veneziani, the first time in almost two thousand years that Jews were represented in a conference of world powers. At the request of this delegation, France proposed that in Rumania, Servia, and Bulgaria "differences of religious belief should not be considered as reason for disability in matters pertaining to the enjoyment of civil and political rights." This proposal was incorporated into the treaty of Berlin, opening the way for the eventual enfranchisement of the Jews of Europe's most backward regions.

Dismayed at the lack of even the most elementary educational facilities among the Jewish communities of the Moslem countries, the Alliance embarked on a program of providing schools that would teach secular subjects and trades and skills to young Jews who were barred from the Christian and Mohammedan educational institutions. It opened schools in Morocco, Bagdad, Adrianople, Aleppo, and Beirut, and then ran out of money. It was at this point that Baron de Hirsch stepped in. Anxious to set up schools for the Jews in European Turkey, particularly in Constantinople, he offered the Alliance, in December 1873, one million francs if they would open schools in the area through which his railway would travel. From then on he was to become widely known as the patron saint of the Alliance Israélite Universelle and, although he at no time held office in this organization, he was its guiding spirit for many years. In addition to specific donations amounting to several millions of dollars for educational activities among the Jews of the Near East, year after year he made up the deficit of the Alliance, which usually amounted to well over $100,000 a year, and he paid all the expenses of the trade schools and agricultural colleges the Alliance operated in the Near East. In 1889 he established a permanent trust fund, which brought the

Alliance an income of 400,000 francs a year. Clara, too, took a keen interest in the work of the Alliance. She enjoyed being directly involved in the various projects, however, rather than just remaining in the background as a donor.

The extreme poverty of their co-religionists weighed heavily on her and she soon took measures for their relief on a grand scale. She became her own charitable agency, spending most of her time in the poor districts of the cities and towns, distributing money among the needy families almost without reservation. It was said she gave to Jew, Christian, and Moslem alike, without distinction of creed, but Jews always received a larger share. On this point Maurice once said in an interview with the London Times: "It is just and fair that Jews should assist Jews, leaving it for others to look after their own, considering others do very little for the Jews except in the way of endeavouring to convert them."

Clara's tireless efforts soon made the name "Baroness de Hirsch" a byword in Jewish communities wherever the railroad led. She was the Angel of Mercy wherever Jews were in need, and her deeds of charity were legendary. In a letter to her sister, Clara described a visit with Veneziani to Salonica in connection with a special request for help as a result of a disastrous fire:

We arrived at Salonica on Friday, the 23rd of September, 1888, and attended the synagogue on Sabbath, the 24th, as early as twenty minutes to eight, and already the Sepher was being read. Minchah went on all through the afternoon of Erev Yom Kippur.

Most interesting is the marble flooring in these schools (shuls). The seats are movable benches, and sometimes chairs. Accommodation for the female synagogue-goers was none too abundant. The galleries, or corners reserved for them, are scrupulously trellised or curtained off from the indiscreet gaze of the opposite sex. They were just like the shelters provided for the Harem beauties in the theatre boxes at Constantinople.

At service time the streets were deserted. More than half of Salonica's 150,000 inhabitants are Jews, and three-quarters of the trade is in their hands. All the boatmen of the port are Jews, and on Saturdays no steamer can load or discharge cargo. Porters and shoe-blacks, bricklayers and silk hands, are all Jews.

The great fire here devastated almost half of Salonica. The Talmud Torah is in ruins and I promised the money to rebuild it, about sixty thousand francs. The Alliance gave the same amount. I was surprised, too, when I saw my picture, together with Maurice's picture in several homes in the poorest district of Salonica. When I walked into those homes, no one recognized me from the pictures. When they found out who I was, they made a big fuss about how much I looked like the picture.

9

AUSTRIA

B aron de Hirsch had taken a keen interest in the Jews of Austria from the day he started his railroad-building activities there. The political set-up, however, was entirely different from that in Turkey. The dual monarchy of Austria and Hungary was established on June 8, 1867, when Emperor Franz Joseph I of Austria was crowned King of Hungary, with legislative power established jointly in the King and the Diet, or Reichstag, consisting of an upper and a lower chamber. The House of Magnates, the upper house, included all hereditary peers, forty bishops and other Roman Catholic clericals, eleven Protestant ministers, and a smattering of the nobility. The House of Representatives was elected by popular vote. Austria at that time had about 1,005,000 Jews, which, with the addition of Hungary's 641,000 Jews, gave the Jewish representation 4.1 percent of the population of the combined countries.

In an attempt to do something about the problem of the more than 400,000 Jews of Galicia who could scarcely read or write the language of the country, and who were ignorant of even the most elementary phases of secular life, an assembly of Jewish delegates was called by the

162

new government to a congress to be held in Budapest in November, 1868, "to draft decrees relating to the organization of Jewish communities and schools, with particular reference to the condition of the Jews in Galicia."

Because Baron de Hirsch had shown so much concern over the problem of the Galician Jews, to whom he had already donated a sum equivalent to about 500,000 pounds, Adolf Jellinek, the former Viennese Rabbi who had become a successful businessman as President of the Budapest Grain and Stock Exchange and builder of the Tramway Company, invited the Baron and Baroness de Hirsch to attend this congress. As guests in his home they were surprised to find that, despite his great wealth, he had not given up observing the dietary laws, even though members of the aristocracy and high officials of the government and the Church were frequent visitors.

In the course of his conversations with Dr. Jellinek, the Baron laid down an interesting declaration of faith when he said: "It would afford me the liveliest satisfaction if the Yiddish jargon were to disappear from Galicia, and if the Jews in that province were to become competent artisans and agriculturists, and to abandon all customs, unconnected with religion, which unnecessarily divided them from their Christian fellow countrymen. I have never mixed in religious affairs, either in the east or in the west. All I desire is that the Jews should receive the necessary culture and be so trained as to enable them to earn their living by the work of their hands."

The congress was held in the Hotel Hungaria, facing the Danube and looking toward the hill of Buda on the other side of the river, and dominated by the royal palace high above the old town below.

Budapest was getting ready for Christmas. The lamplighters lit the gas lamps early, turning Gizell Square and Vali Street into a fairyland of shop windows bursting with clothes, jewelry, toys, candies, and sweetmeats of all sorts. The Jewish delegates, rabbis and leaders from the ghettos of eastern Europe, presented an incongruous sight amid all this splendor, with their long caftans and their somber flat black hats.

Berlin's Rabbi Israel Hildesheimer, known affectionately as the "international schnorer," because of his tireless energy in helping the poor of Germany, Austria, Russia, and even Abyssinia, was elected chairman of this Hungarian Jewish Congress.

It was here that Maurice and Clara met Johanna de Heves Bischitz, founder of the Jewish Women's Association of Budapest and Vice-President of the Christian Maria Dorothea Charitable Union. She was on the board of more than a hundred philanthropic societies and had been twice decorated by Emperor Franz Joseph. At Clara's behest Baron de Hirsch founded and gave into her charge a relief bureau in Budapest as a center for his Hungarian charities, placing at her disposal an annual sum of 120,000 gulden for distribution among the poor. During her presidency of this association more than three million gulden of Baron de Hirsch's money was distributed.

All through the years during which his railroad was being constructed, Maurice and Clara gave unstintingly to the many groups that were organized to help the Jews of the Balkan countries, relying on Johanna Bischitz and Adolf Jellinek for guidance. Together with them he worked out a plan for the establishment of a school fund for Galicia's Jews, but it was not until the beginning of 1891 that the Austrian Government agreed to the statutes of Baron de Hirsch's Foundation. In January of that year he paid in the capital of 12,000,000 francs to the Niederoesterreischischen Landes-Hauptcasse.

The objectives of the Foundation, which was intended to commemorate the 40 years' Jubilee of the Emperor Francis Joseph, were:

1. The establishment of primary schools and of children's recreation grounds in Galicia and Bukovina.

2. The granting of subsidies to teachers.

3. The presentation of schoolbooks and other educational requirements, and of clothing and food to poor pupils.

4. The granting of subsidies for the establishment of Jewish schools.

5. The apprenticing of Jewish youths to handicraftsmen and agriculturists.

6. The granting of assistance of every kind to Jewish pupils at commercial and other professional schools.

7. The granting of loans, free of interest, to artisans and agriculturists.

8. The establishment of commercial, technical, and agricultural schools.

News of this donation created a sensation around the world because of its magnitude. The *New York Journal* of February 25, 1891, reported,

> Within the past two or three weeks Baron de Hirsch has presented the Austrian Government with 12,-000,000 francs for the establishment of non-sectarian schools. The first news of this gift, which was announced exclusively in Monday's *Journal,* marked another step in the development of Austria on the part of Baron de Hirsch. The arrangements for establishing this foundation took almost a year-and-a-half to complete.
>
> In August, 1889, Baron de Hirsch had a long conversation with the late Dr. Jellinek, in whose judgment

he placed the utmost confidence, on the subject of the Galician foundation, and a modus vivendi was then arrived at which satisfied all parties.

Once all obstacles had been removed, the Foundation was called into existence without further delay, and the Trustees (partly appointed by Baron de Hirsch and partly by the Government) set to work in right earnest. The first President of the Board of Trustees was Ritter von Furth, who died before he had held that office for any considerable time. He was succeeded early in 1893 by David Ritter von Guttman, President of the Israelitish Alliance in Vienna, who had been a childhood friend of the Baron's in Munich. At the present time the Fund maintains over 40 educational institutions (the evening schools being attended by children and their parents), commercial, trade and kindergarten schools. Instruction is given in these different establishments to some 5,000 pupils, without distinction of creed, and special provision is made for the religious education of Christian scholars.

The work in Galicia by no means exhausted Baron de Hirsch's generosity. He created a fund, with an annual income of 120,000 florins, which is expended in Vienna and Buda Pesth, to assist tradesmen in reduced circumstances in regaining their former position. Among the regulations which the Baron laid down were that Bourse speculators were to be excluded from the benefits of the fund, and no purely charitable gifts were to be made. Similar funds were also established in Cracow and Lemberg. In December, 1892, the Baron created a new foundation of three million florins, the annual income of which (120,000 florins) is distributed among the Hungarian poor, without regard to religion. Frau David Bischitz, a benevolent Jewish lady in Buda Pesth, to whom Baron de Hirsch gave charge of his original foundation, was again entrusted by him with the distribution of the annual amounts. Owing however to the extensive character of the operations, Frau Bischitz is now aided by a Committee in the administration of the Trust. As a characteristic sample of Baron de Hirsch's generosity on occasions of exceptional distress we may mention the following. In 1888 the greater part of the town of Pedhajce (Galicia) was destroyed by fire, and the Baron gave 50,000 francs for the relief of the sufferers. This gift was subsequently increased to 50,000 florins, and after having, through introductions to wealthy persons in Vienna, enabled the Burgomaster of Pedhajce to collect 33,000 florins, Baron de Hirsch crowned his good work by adding the required balance of 27,000 florins. While mentioning his generosity on the occurrence of calamities, we may state that no disaster, such as conflagrations or earthquakes, in the East, became known without the Baron contributing handsome amounts. One instance that occurs to us is the great fire which devastated a considerable part of Salonica a few years ago, and by which Jews, including hundreds of Russian refugees, were the heaviest sufferers. Baron de Hirsch gave a large sum towards building these people new homes, and in recognition of his munificence the quarter in which they reside has been named after him.

The Baron spent a lot of time on the estates he acquired in Austria, entertaining the most important of his business associates and the elite of the nobility of the Continent. For many years he owned Eichorn Castle, built in the twelfth century on a 20,000-acre estate atop a mountain near the town of Brunn in Moravia, which he bought in 1885 for 230,000 pounds. In 1890 he had another castle built at O'Gyalla, near Ersek-Ujvar in Hungary, on an estate of 80,000 acres located on the sandy plains at the foot of the Carpathian Mountains, and transformed it into a fabulous hunting and shooting palace.

The *New York Sun,* on October 9, 1892, describing these estates, said:

The Baron's personal habits are interesting. As the host in his home in Paris, or on his estates in Austria, he is said to be magnificent without ostentation. The best is none too good for his guests, as is evidenced by the fact that the Prince of Wales' set finds it pleasant to visit him. The partridge shooting at Eichorn, or St. Johann, two of his country estates, is said to be the finest in Europe. He is himself a great sportsman, and loves to hunt. His beaters and trainers are well trained, and everything indicates that the host knows how to furnish sport in the field as well as pleasure in the house for his guests. At the same time his habits are almost ascetic. The pleasures of the table have no attraction for him. Sometimes he mingles a little red wine with his water. He does not smoke. He exercises a great deal, and is a tireless pedestrian.

10

FRANCE

It had taken over two years of negotiations in Constantinople and Vienna to establish the railway construction company and to get the project firmly launched. Maurice and Clara had spent most of this time traveling back and forth between these two cities and their home in Brussels and, in 1871, they decided to make Paris, which was fast becoming the railway and financial center of the Continent, their home. They found the cosmopolitan atmosphere of Paris to their liking, refreshing and invigorating after the somewhat confining provincialism of the low countries, and they adjusted quickly to the faster pace of this social capital of the world. Maurice, although he had just passed his fortieth birthday, was the ideal cosmopolitan. He spoke English as an Englishman, French as a Frenchman, and German, his natural tongue. Clara, too, was equally at home in any of these languages, but she was never completely at ease in the international social circles in which she now found herself. She was content to remain in the background, letting her husband lead the way into this new world of complex social and diplomatic maneuvering. She was anxious to settle down in a permanent home after two years of traveling between Vienna and Constantinople.

Preparing to undertake the lavish entertaining their newly won prominence called for, they acquired the magnificent mansion built by Eugenie de Montagie, the Spanish beauty from Andalusia who had become the Empress Eugenie when she married Napoleon III in 1853. Situated on the corner of Rue de l'Elysée and the Rue Gabriel, it it had already become a landmark because of the many articles of historic importance with which the Empress had furnished the palace—the paintings, the statuary, the miscellaneous objects of art that were tastefully scattered through the spacious drawing rooms, and the famous floor tapestries on which were woven the arms of the Kings of France, reputed to have cost almost one million francs. Baron de Hirsch is said to have paid 2,700,000 francs for the mansion, and to have spent almost ten million francs more in enlarging and remodeling it until it became a huge, monumental palace, which the French Government tried to purchase in 1900 for seven million francs to use as a residence for foreign princes and dignitaries visiting the French capital as guests of the government. In describing the mansion some years later when it was about to be auctioned, the Paris edition of the *New York Herald* on January 21st, 1906, said:

For several days public interest has been drawn to the mansion of the Baron de Hirsch on the corner of Rue de l'Elysee and the Rue Gabriel, which will be sold February 10th, owing to the death of two of its joint owners, Mme. Leopold Goldschmidt and Mme. Montefiore, wife of Belgian Senator George Levi Montefiore, both sisters and heirs of Baroness de Hirsch.

Artistic Paris is interested in this sale. There are
sure to be photographic reproductions of all the artistic
and principal objects which still adorn the mansion, pictures among which there is a portrait of Louis XVI,
wood carvings from the château of Berey, a monumental mantel, Renaissance style, from the château of
Montal, but especially those four wonderful tapestries
with the coat of arms of the Kings of France, after
cartoons by Berain, that add to the splendor of the
grand stairway, which alone cost nearly a million francs.

Baron de Hirsch had hardly moved into the house
when he sought to increase his property. It was easy
enough to buy the houses bearing the numbers 4, 6,
and 8 on the Rue de l'Elysée, now belonging to Messrs.
de Forrest, his adoped sons, and to his niece Mme.
Balser. On the Avenue Gabriel, though, the owner, Mr.
Cebriel seemed at first unwilling to listen to any proposition to dispossess him of the property bearing number
24. After repeated requests, he consented to enter into
negotiations with the Baron's agents and wrote a letter,
kept in the archives, where he said that he would only
relent if he were offered so considerable a price that it
would be folly to refuse it. They agreed upon 3,500,000
francs.

The transformation was begun at once. According to
the plans of Emile Peyre, the architect, the Cebriel
property was almost entirely rebuilt and connected with
the old. The masonry and painting amounted to 1,-
633,946 francs, of which one million, as before stated,
was for the stairway.

On the ground floor, a marble vestibule leads to this
magnificent stairway. There is the dining room with its
wainscoting of carved oak of Louis XV's time, decorated with medallions and friezes painted by Mon-
noyer. It cost 80,000 francs and came from the chateau
of Berey. Next, there is a white drawing room with
white wainscoting, where the famous collection of
Dresden china was kept and which leads to the Ballroom that would hold two thousand people, with its

famous floor composed of exquisite inlaid woodwork or parquetrie. The walls are carved with different colored marble, with pillars surmounted by chiseled gold and bronze. The doors are covered with mirrors as in the great gallery at Versailles.

Opposite the Ballroom, separated by a gallery in which formerly stood two splendid Boulle cabinets, for each of which the Baron had paid 500,000 francs, the monumental stairway is situated. It was designed by Emile Peyre. On each side of this stairway there are two magnificent vases of Spanish marble supported by cupids of white carrara marble suggested by the famous baptismal font of St. Peter in Rome. The bannisters of marble and chiselled bronze lead up to the three balconies of the loggia. The ceilings with their mythological subjects are signed by Chevalier. The walls are covered with decorative paintings by Puyter and Van der Lenlen. The decoration of this stairway cost a million francs.

On the first floor there is a great Renaissance reception hall with a monumental stone mantel and fire place, brought from the Chateau of Montal. This mantel of the 16th century is ornamented along the border with armorial escutcheons, surrounded by wreaths. It is surmounted by an enormous recumbent deer to which Baron de Hirsch had enormous ten-forked antlers of gilt bronze added to serve as an emblem of his name, Hirsch. This room is adjoining the conservatories from which the magnificent floor, which adorned the entire center like an immense bed of tropical flowers, has been removed. These conservatories were taken care of by the gardeners who looked after the Baroness's greenhouses.

One day we inquired of a famous horticulturer and gardener what it would cost to keep this garden well stocked and cared for. He asked 50,000 francs a year. This great garden, now bereft of all its tropical vegetation, is surrounded by four marvelous Beauvais Tapestries with the coat of arms of Louis of Bourbon, Count of Toulouse and Admiral of France. They were executed by Behague from Beram's designs about the end of the 17th or the beginning of the 18th century, and are woven entirely of silk, gold and silver. They respectively represent Amphitrite, Venus and Adonis, Enrus, and Thetis.

On the same floor there is a drawing room in the style of Louis XVI with a very fine portrait of this kind by Callet.

And last of all, in another wing in the older part of the mansion is the Baroness de Hirsch's blue drawing room, decorated by four panels painted by Jourdain in the style of certain pastoral scenes of the 18th century, not in the least like Watteau, but like Winterhalter at best.

In the middle of one of them, gaily dancing around with other children, the Prince Imperial was to be seen. Many years later Empress Eugenie wanted to see the house she had built and which formed the center of Baron de Hirsch's mansion. She was much moved at sight of her son's picture and expressed her thanks to Baroness de Hirsch for preserving it.

The Empress had a great liking for this house which she considered her own private house. We seem to remember that she lent it for several months to the Princess Anna Murat, who had become Duchess of Mouchy, while their mansion of the Avenue de Courselles was being built. The house was decorated with the utmost care, and in spite of the absence of any particular style at that period, several rooms could remain in their original state after the complete transformation.

Several attempts have been made to dispose of the property. In 1905 the Ministry of Colonial Affairs tried to interest government circles in acquiring the De Hirsch mansion for its use. About the same time a Franco-English group proposed to turn the De Hirsch mansion into an international club. Aside from the money question, the restrictive conditions imposed on the use of the former Cibiel property were enough to nip these plans in the bud, as well as all the propositions of Americans coming from New York for the express purpose of buying it. The prohibition against shows, kitchens or restaurants has always raised difficulties when any sale has been contemplated. The death of two of the co-heirs of the estate has led Mr. Ferdinand Bischoffsheim, a brother of the Baroness, to demand the legal sale of the group of buildings. Whether the two parts are to be sold separately or together will be seen a month from now.

Almost from the moment of their arrival in Paris there were controversy and mixed feelings over the acceptance of the couple in exclusive social circles. But, because of their great wealth and prominence, they were taken up by the leading political figures and it was not long before they were able to choose from among the most distinguished members of the French aristocracy in making up their guest lists—princes, archdukes, counts, and barons, the pinnacles of French as well as foreign aristocracy. And, in later years the presence of the heir to the British throne as a frequent visitor made invitations to the Baron de Hirsch receptions the most sought-after invitations in the French capital for a dozen years. In his book *The Edwardian Era,* André Maurois says, "This was a pleasure loving society, and it was easily accessible to any who put amusement or riches in its way. Many businessmen attained a peerage. In 1905 the House of Lords could show thirty-five bankers. The King approved of the social rise of the financiers who had taken his fancy. His greatest intimates, along with diplomats like Soneral and Nieusdorff, were financiers like Sir Ernest Cassel and Baron de Hirsch."

Their frequent dinner parties, too, were delightful

affairs. The setting was elegant, the cuisine superlative, the conversation brilliant, the guests distinguished writers, musicians, artists, political figures, and foreign diplomats, as many as a hundred at a sitting. Often one would find Georges Clemenceau, the doctor who had turned radical politician and journalist and who was to become the "Tiger" Clemenceau of World War I; Sadi Carnot, the eminent engineer who was to become President of France; Gambetta, who ruled the Third Republic, the terror of the royalists; and Victor Hugo, probably France's greatest poet, playwright, essayist, novelist, and political hero. Or one might find the great sculptor Rodin or the artists Dégas, Henley, Renoir, and Cézanne, the scholarly composer César Franck and his protegés, Vincent D'Indy and Jules Massenet. And among the writers and people of the theater, Sarah Bernhardt, Anatole France, Antonin Proust, Victorien Sardou, and the great Emile Zola, who had recently become one of the first writers of the Third Republic.

One of the more frequent visitors was Adolph Crémieux, France's most illustrious Jew, who had been responsible for the famous Crémieux Decree which bestowed French citizenship on all Algerians and which, at the same time, accomplished the legal assimilation of the Algerian Jews. Under this law, Judaism was officially recognized as a religion by the state and, as in France itself, the salaries of the Jewish clergy were paid by the government. No longer were Algerian Jews to be considered a separate nationality. Henceforth they were to be treated as French citizens who followed the Jewish faith. Crémieux had been honored, too, by being chosen, with Baron de Rothschild, to negotiate the peace treaty with Bismarck after the French defeat in the Franco-

Prussian War. He was particularly distressed with the unjust terms imposed by the victorious Germans, which placed France at so great an economic disadvantage for the next half-century, and he offered part of his wealth to help pay the millions demanded by Bismarck. French officialdom, however, would not listen to any plan that called for private subscription to pay the reparations demanded by the Germans. Because of this generous gesture and his long service to France, Adolph Crémieux was made a life senator in 1871. Baron de Hirsch's friendship with Crémieux stemmed from their common interest in the Alliance Israélite Universelle during the many years when Crémieux served as President of that organization. The Jewish agricultural colony of Crémieux, which was started in 1882 in South Dakota, and which lasted only until 1885, was named after Adolph Crémieux.

It was only to be expected that anyone as powerful and as active in political and diplomatic circles as Baron de Hisch would create as many enemies as friends. Europeans of that period looked with suspicion on those who made a practice of dealing in money. The money-lenders "who were to be chased from the Temple," were scorned and feared by decent people everywhere. All international bankers were suspect, especially Jewish bankers. Baron de Hirsch, one of the most spectacular of all Jewish bankers, became a favorite target of anti-Semites the world over. His arrogant bearing and his "pushiness" in his too-obvious attempts to develop close relationships with people who could help him with his railway projects or who would further his social aspirations, exposed him to scurrilous attacks from the European press for over two decades. Paul H. Emden makes an interesting observation on this facet of de Hirsch's character when he says,

Great as he had become, he had not been able to get rid of many human weaknesses, one of the strongest of which was his enormous, almost morbid, ambition to shine in society, which detracted from his inner worth and at times made him look petty and comical. In accordance with his circumstances he lived on a princely scale, had vast estates in Moravia and Hungary, often leased country houses in England and entertained in great style at Newmarket and at Bath House. The Prince of Wales (Edward VII), attracted by the Baron's enthusiasm for the Turf, his philanthropic ardour and his wide knowledge of men and things, was frequently his guest, especially in Hungary, and Hirsch's satisfaction at being allowed to have the heir to the British throne staying with him consoled him for the many snubs from strait-laced circles to which he quite unnecessarily again and again exposed himself.

One example of this, which brought worldwide condemnation to de Hirsch, was his support of the monarchist restoration movements in France and Spain, even though he was opposed to this in principle. Kurt Grunwald, in his book *Turkenhirsch*, says:

According to Dennis Brogan "the great Austrian Jewish banker, Baron de Hirsch, subscribed handsomely to a cause dear to the leaders of Paris society, (i.e., the movement led by General Boulanger). Who knew? It might open doors hitherto closed to him, though he was a friend of the Prince of Wales." Hirsch's behaviour becomes even clearer in Walter Frank's story—based on unpublished documents in the Political Archives of the German Foreign Ministry— that the Count of Paris contributed 800,000 francs to Boulanger's election fund, 500,000 of which were given by De Hirsch, who in return for this gift was promised entry into High Society. On November 20,

1888 Count Munster, the German Ambassador to Paris, reported home that Rothschild remained cool to the Orleans entreaties to come to terms with Boulanger, but that Hirsch was not averse to putting a few millions on this card. And there is the more recent version by Guy Chapman, according to which De Hirsch contributed 2.5 out of the four million francs in the hands of the Royalist Committee in 1888, in return for which gift he was to be elected to the Club of the rue Royale. . . . Baron de Hirsch cultivated members of the High Society and of the Diplomatic Corps and entertained them lavishly. This seems to have been due primarily to a desire to satisfy his 'ego,' without the expectation of an early return on this heavy investment. And it is noteworthy that this investment was particularly heavy after De Hirsch had practically retired from business, when he used his connections, if at all, primarily to further his humanitarian projects.

He became particularly friendly with the various German and Austrian ambassadors, which gave rise to many charges of political chicanery. He was on such intimate terms with Harry von Arnim, the German ambassador at Paris whose promising career was wrecked by Bismarck's petty jealousy and intrigue, that when, early in 1874, Arnim's transfer to the Constantinople ambassadorship was announced, it was reported that Arnim had sought this post because his friend Baron de Hirsch at that time contemplated moving from Paris to Constantinople. When he turned the post down a month or so later, it was attributed to Baron de Hirsch's change of plans. When von Arnim was removed from the Paris post, Maurice quickly established connections with his distinguished successor at Paris, Prince Chlodwig von Hohenlohe, who subsequently became German Chancellor. His interesting *Memoirs* contains numerous references to personal meetings with Baron de Hirsch, ostensibly for the purpose of eliciting the Baron's opinions and information on eastern affairs. He tells of one incident when he attended a shooting party at Baron de Hirsch's Versaille hunting preserves, he driving with the Polish Ambassador, Count Potocki, and Baron de Hirsch with the Duke de Pemthierre and the Duke of Coburg. Then he adds the pointed comment: "A true sign of the times was the sight of the grandson of Louis Philippe shooting with Hirsch, the German Jew, at Versailles!"

Baron de Hirsch's friendship with Count von Wimpffen, the Austrian Ambassador at Paris who committed suicide on December 24, 1882, led to wholesale vilification and disgraceful libeling of the Baron on the part of the anti-Semitic press. Austrian interest in the Turkish railways had frequently brought the two men together, and they became close friends. When the Ambassador, fearing that he was becoming insane, took his own life, the daily papers announced at the time that he had left a letter behind, addressed to Baron de Hirsch. The next morning, Strecker's anti-Semitic organ, the Berlin *Deutsches Tageblatt,* published a fabricated text of this alleged letter. In it, Count von Wimpffen was represented as saying he was taking his life because he could not stand the disgrace any longer of having been debauched officially by Baron de Hirsch. The letter was widely reprinted and caused an enormous sensation. Fortunately, the true text of the letter had been secured by Hungarian Premier Tisza, and he was able to publicly answer the slander by producing the actual letter. In this letter Count von Wimpffen asked Baron and Baroness de Hirsch to take care of his unfortunate wife and children, begging that their departure from Paris be arranged as soon as possible. The letter advised where his securities were deposited, entrusting his estate to Baron de Hirsch for disposal.

Notwithstanding this exposure of the forgery, the fabricated version of the letter continued to be published in anti-Semitic works. It is to be found, for instance, five years later in the 11th edition of Stelli's *Der Kampf gegen das Judenthum* and it is referred to as if genuine in Drumont's *La France Jaire*. Drumont never stopped attacking de Hirsch in his paper *Libre Parole,* which had a circulation of over half a million readers daily.

It should be remarked, too, that the de Hirsches' relationship with the Jewish community of Paris, too, was somewhat strained. Unlike the Rothschilds, Clara and Maurice observed few, if any, religious practices. They were not known ever to have attended a synagogue in all the years they lived in Paris.

While the Rothschilds delighted in introducing the elite of England and the Continent to kosher cooking, Baron de Hirsch did not observe the dietary laws and at dinners and receptions in his home the finest cuisine of whichever country he happened to be in at the time was served. When he entertained rabbis or religious members of his own family, however, Clara was careful to use special dishes and to serve only kosher meat. Meat and milk were never served together when his guests were of orthodox persuasion.

De Hirsch's attitude toward religion can be summed up in a remark he once made: "Religion is born of fear and of weakness. It was spread through fanaticism and through this ignorance of people who were lead to believe that if they suffered through this life, they would be rewarded by another life after death. Priests could point to nothing good in this life and so they built the theory of an after life."

He was born a member of the Hebrew race, living in a Gentile world that looked down upon him merely because of the accident of his birth. He wanted a place in the sun. He was instinctively an aristocrat, but even though he felt that his Jewish birth handicapped him, he would not try to get rid of the Jewish stigma by baptism, as did so many of his friends in the banking fraternity.

An interesting experience that portrays the consideration Clara and Maurice always showed their orthodox co-religionists was told by G. Selikowitch in the January 13, 1920, issue of the *Jewish Daily News,* under the title, "The Seder with Baron de Hirsch." His story follows:

Translation from the Jewish Daily News, January 13, 1920.

MY REMINISCENCES.
by G. Selikowitch.

Chapter 13.
The Seder with Baron de Hirsch.

I now arrive at an important—if not the most important—incident in my Jewish life in Paris, and will describe it as faithfully as my mental hold on the past will enable me. It is my purpose to present to view, in two chapters, if possible, a row of eminent Jews, my acquaintance with whom came to pass under unexpected circumstances.

It was a week before the Passover holidays—I cannot recall whether it was in 1881 or 1882—when I received a telegram from Michael Erlanger to call at his office at 4 P.M. When I came to my noble benefactor I was handed an open envelope containing a short letter, for my perusal, I stared at him in surprise, noticing that the letter was not addressed to me, but to himself, and that it was signed by Baron de Hirsch—Baron Maurice de Hirsch!

As far as I can remember, this small letter, written in French, read about as follows:

My dear Mr. Erlanger:

I know that these few lines will startle you and you may ask in bewilderment whether I have not been converted over night into a tzadik (Baron de Hirsch spelled this word "zadik"). I would like you to find for me in the Rabbinical Seminary, of which you are Director, an intelligent young man of pleasing countenance, a student of the Seminary, who shall officiate at the Seder ceremonies in my house during the two Passover evenings. In addition to his being my guest during the entire holiday week if he so desires, I will compensate him generously, knowing that a student of the Rabbinical School can make good use of several hundred francs. Let my sudden piousness not surprise you: I have a few frum guests at my table for this Passover (I remember well that the word "frum" was used by Baron de Hirsch in German and not the French word "pieux") ; a few Wertheimers from Frankfort, my maternal relatives; Dr. Hirsch of Hamburg; my father, Joseph Hirsch from Wurtzberg; Mme. Jennie Hirsch from Berlin, and another half a dozen Hirschs. Please do not leave me in a predicament.

Your friend,
Baron Maurice de Hirsch.

After I read the letter, Mr. Erlanger stated that he had selected me to conduct the Seder. "I made this selection for two reasons. First, you will be able to converse with the guests on topics of the Torah—the other Seminarists are ignoramuses—and second, I want you to earn some money."

Though in no need of funds, I at once accepted the invitation, in order to avail myself of the golden opportunity to conduct the Seder at the home of Baron de Hirsch, and make the acquaintance of the interesting guests.

There was one point that I could not understand. Why do they need me to officiate when at their table will be seated such a pious and great scholar as Rabbi Samson Rafael Hirsch? I afterwards discovered my mistake. The Rabbi Hirsch from Hamburg mentioned by Baron de Hirsch was not Rabbi Samson Rafael, but Rabbi Marcus Hirsch.

A few days before Passover I started to prepare myself for the Seder. I spent about 200 Francs for a new suit and other triflings. I started on my visit to the Baron's palace in Passey a suburb of Paris about 4 o'clock in the afternoon on the eve of Passover. Owing to the fact that access to the palace of the Baron de Hirsch was much more difficult than to the President of the French Republic, I was supplied with all details of how to reach the inner chambers of the Baron's palace.

When I rang the door bell in a tall, brick fortress-like wall, a man in livery, with gold braid on his collar and sleeves, made his appearance. After scrutinizing my credentials he ushered me in, and signalled to two guards who were standing in a spacious garden, about thirty feet away.

Those two guards—also in special uniforms—took me to the door of the castle and announced my coming, upon which a lackey appeared, took off my overcoat, asked me to make myself comfortable and showed me into a large waiting room. I handed him my visiting card and two minutes later a handsome young man, of a princely appearance, came in and extended his hand with the words: "Follow me, Mr. Selikowitch, my father is waiting for you in the Japanese salon."

This was the young Lucien Hirsch, the only son of Baron Hirsch, who was then about my age and who died three years later, leaving Baron de Hirsch without an heir.

Without an heir? The Baron has objected to this

expression on the day of the funeral, in the following words: "It is not correct to say that I have been left without an heir. I am left without a son but I did not lose my heir, who is my people." (J'ai perdu mon fils, mais non pas mon hóritier qui est mon peuple.)

When Lucien conducted me to the Japanese salon the Baron met me and showed me to a seat. He asked me where I was born, what are my studies, shince when was I in Paris, and whether I ever was in Turkey. I answered all his questions categorically, when he abruptly stopped the conversation in French and started it in German.

"I have the pleasure of introducing to you my father, Joseph von Hirsch, banker of Wurtzberg. I am glad to introduce to you Rabbi Marcus Hirsch, Chief Rabbi of Hamburg, but born in Hungary."

"In your native land, M. Baron," I put in, in order to show that I was no greenhorn. But I missed my point, for the Baron at once corrected me by saying that he was not born in Hungary, but in Muenchen, Germany, in the year 1831 (He died in Hungary in 1896).

Rabbi Marcus Hirsch, a relative of the Baron, was a firm Orthodox. His Orthodoxy was so extreme, that the congregation at Prague, where he came as a Rabbi in the 80's, refused to keep him further in his office and because of the quarrels that took place on account of him he was compelled to return to Hamburg, a broken and disheartened man. When the Baron learned of the Rabbi's troubles, he invited him and his family to spend the Passover holidays with him and rest in his home for a few months.

Everything in the Baron's house was especially arranged for the Passover holiday. Not only were there new dishes, but also the salon, which had been used as a ball room and where the Sederim were now conducted, was thoroughly cleaned in accordance with the desire of the Wertheimers, relatives of the Baron's mother, who was herself a Wertheimer, as well as at the request of the Bischopfheims of the family of the Bar-

oness Clara de Hirsch, a daughter of Senator Rafael
Bischopfheim. This request was also made by several
of the Hirsches from Frankfort, who astonished me
with their Orthodoxy of the old type.

The Japanese salon was full of life and merriment,
most of the guests being accompanied by their wives and
daughters, who were elegantly attired in honor of the
holiday.

The palace in Passey being a summer residence was
usually closed during the winter months. His permanent
residence was in the well known palace of Fabres St.
Honore, which he purchased from the old Spanish
Queen, King Alphonse's grandmother, for 25,000,000
Francs. The Baron invested an additional sum of 12,-
000,000 Francs to make it more beautiful. In accordance with the reports of the Paris papers, the new
"escalier d'honneur" alone has cost 5,000,000 Francs.
These stairs of honor in such palaces are the artistic
staircase, which are placed in the center of a big salon
to bring the guests to the balcony of the first floor.

The Baron apparently did not want to have the
Sederim in this palace because it would have required
much work to make it suitable for Passover, in accordance with the desires of his orthodox guests. He therefore decided to use the summer palace in Passey, which
was always closed during the winter, and very often
during the entire year.

The Baron also owned summer palaces in Hungary,
which were surrounded by his own forests, where he
and his invited guests went on hunting trips. Among
those guests was counted the Prince of Wales, who
later became King Edward VII, the father of the present King George V.

The Prince of Wales was then a partner of Baron de
Hirsch trading under the name of Hirsch and Wales.
They had interests in railroads and forests. It seems
that the Baron de Hirsch managed the business, and
the Prince, poor man, shared in the rich profits. As it
is universally known Baron de Hirsch left in his will

£5,000,000 to the Prince of Wales. It is no wonder, therefore, that the English Crown Prince was a steady visitor of the Baron.

When the hour for sitting down to the seder arrived the doors of a spacious salon were thrown open where a large round table was set for a hundred guests, laden with good things—Matzos, wine and with a tower of fresh flowers in the center.

"One more guest is missing—your good friend, the English Crown Prince" jokingly remarked Joseph von Hirsch, the Baron's father.

"I could have had him here very easily tonight" answered the Baron smilingly, "but Queen Victoria, who is ill in Riviera, South France ordered her son by telegraph to come to her".

Chapter 14.

How the Baron Squared Himself with his Enemies.

There are people, men as well as women, to whom no photograph, no matter how well executed, can do justice. Their attractiveness is either immoderately exaggerated or shown less real.

The pictures of Baron de Hirsch represent him as a very handsome man. But I do not believe that any artist has ever succeeded in portraying vividly that majestic grace and aristocratic fineness which adorned the Baron when, with a steady smile on his lips, he conversed with someone. Hundreds of women on meeting him would turn around to look at "le bel homme distingue". Kindliness radiated from his eyes and there was a sort of dynamo—electric force—in his look.

The Baroness—Clara de Hirsch—was not a pretty woman, from the point of our conception of woman's beauty, but on her face there was reflected so much virtue and nobility, so much goodness and womanly charm, as if she had emerged from Jewish antiquity,— a Princess of the House of Israel, at the time when the Judean Kings reigned over the Holy Land.

They still are before my eyes—both the Baron and the Baroness—as they sat down at the head of the Seder-table. Rabbi Marcus Hirsch was seated at the side of the Baron, and the Baron's father was placed next to the Baroness. The other guests took their seats in the order previously arranged, while I was placed next to the Baron's son, Lucien, at the other end of the table facing the Baron. Next to me was seated Madame Jennie Hirsch, of Berlin, a Professor, who was also editor of a weekly Ladies Journal. Though she spoke a perfect French, her voice was somewhat shrill, which was out of harmony with the aristocratic decorum around the table.

"What a wonderful combination of color, luxury and noble figures this gathering represents;" remarked the dame from Berlin. Her phrase, however, remained unfinished, for at that moment Rabbi Hirsch signalled, by clapping his hands, that the Seder services were to begin.

I felt as if a heavy weight fell off my chest, thinking that the task which I was called upon to perform—conducting the Seder—was taken over by the Rabbi. But my joy was of short duration, for when the passage "V'he Sheomdo L'avethonu" was reached the Rabbi ordered me to continue the reading of the Hagada, which I did until supper was served.

The menu consisted of almost all the regulation Passover dishes, including even matzo-balls, and, of course, the bitter herb, haroseth, a piece of roast meat, and everything that decorates the Jewish table at the Seder.

The walls were covered with rare and expensive oil paintings of Queen Victoria, the Prince of Wales, Jules Grevy (President of the French Republic), Sir Moses Montefiore, Kaiser Franz Joseph, Sultan Abdul-Hamid, Rabbi Samson Rafael Hirsch of Hamburg, and a whole line of pictures of members of the family. In center of the room stood an easel carved out of ivory, on which rested a huge oil painting of the Baron's son, Lucien, as a child of five years, riding on a tiny white pony. I was told by Lucien himself that the pony was a gift from the Turkish Sultan when he (Lucien) was a child.

The conversation between the courses covered various subjects. The absorbing topic, however, was the departure of Israel from Egypt, as viewed from the point of modern discoveries in Egypt. The Baron asked what I though of the statement of Maspero, who, in his book "Histoire des Peuples de l'Orient", which was then quite popular, denied the story of Israel's departure from Egypt.

I explained that Maspero does not deny it. He only says that the Egyptian word "Aberu" which was translated as "Ebrim" (Hebrew) means altogether a different tribe, but the reason why Israel's departure was not recorded in Egypt was that the old Egyptians were too proud to leave to future generations records of their defeats, and perpetuated only the glories of their conquests.

The conversation was stopped by Rabbi Marcus Hirsch, who said that the Bible does not need the support of the Egyptians or the Masperos.

After the Seder ceremony, the ending of which was marked with the same enthusiasm as the beginning, the men repaired to the smoking-room, while the ladies went back to the music-parlor, where artists of music— vocal and instrumental—rendered compositions then in favor. Among the numbers rendered was Mendelssohn's "Songs without Words"; an aria from Meyerbeer's opera "Dinorah", which is known among the French under the name of "Le Pardon de Ploermel", an aria which requires the highest skill of a soprano voice.

At the request of my hosts I remained at their house during the first Seder night. On the following morning I went to the Synagogue on Rue de la Victore. Where the other guests spent the first day of Passover I do not know. I did ask them about this when I came to Passy in the evening for the second Seder, with a larger measure of impatience than on the first night. The reason for this impatience was the following:

On the first day of Passover there appeared in the daily paper *Figaro* an article of a sensational character, describing how some six months earlier the Royalist Turf Club had blackballed the Baron, who had applied for admission as a member. Three of the club members voted against his election and he was defeated. Even the fact that the Prince of Wales, who was an honorary member of that club, had resigned as a protest against the insult to his "best friend," was not divulged until the blackballing was made public. To the Parisian public the entire incident was a mystery.

Naturally, the Baron sought a way to avenge himself on his enemies, and he found one. He quietly purchased the structure where the club was housed and converted it into a stable for his horses. The *"Figaro"* reported that the Baron had paid six and a half million francs. The story of the exclusion, the resignation of the Prince of Wales, and the conversion of the anti-Semitic palace into a horse stable caused a sensation in social circles all over Europe.

I read the news with the greatest interest, and read it again in the evening papers, where it was reported with more details. Naturally, I awaited impatiently the hour of the second Seder, when I expected to hear something about the scandal. But my expectations were not realized. Not a word was said on the subject by the Baron himself. I did catch a few words uttered by the guests. "Such a desecration of God's name could have been averted," remarked Rabbi Hirsch.

"We may expect other wicked actions from the Jew-baiters," remarked one of the Franfort visitors.

I surmised what these remarks referred to, but neither the Baron nor the Baroness uttered one word regarding the sensational occurrence which had aroused Paris. One of the newspapers "Le Gaulois" even dared to state that two of the blackballs against the Baron came from two Jewish Barons, the Rothschilds, who belonged to that club.

Some people believed that the statement was true, because the Rothschilds had always kept at a distance from the Baron, whom they considered a parvenu. Others even asserted that there was a strong enmity between Hirsch and the Rothschild family. How much truth there was in these rumors I could not ascertain. The entire incident, indeed, was of little interest to me. But the fact that the two Rothschilds—Edmond and Alfonse—had not withdrawn their membership from the club as a protest, as the Prince of Wales had done— this painful act alone indicated the contempt with which the Rothschilds looked upon the Hirsch family.

It is interesting to note that immediately following this incident, Baron de Hirsch was elected a foreign member of the Royal Turf Club of England. The Prince of Wales was so incensed at this snubbing of de Hirsch by the French club that he almost created an international incident over de Hirsch while visiting Austria a short time later as a guest of the Emperor and Empress of Austria at the Royal Palace. He wanted to see de Hirsch but Jews were not admitted to the Austrian Court. The Prince insisted in his request to see the Baron and his hosts were much put out when he said that if de Hirsch was not to be allowed to come to the Palace, he would call on Baron de Hirsch. At de Hirsch's request, the Prince abandoned the whole thing, thus averting further embarrassment for the Austrian court.

Sir Sidney Lee, in his biography of King Edward VII, says on page 574 that Edward was "not disconcerted by the criticism passed in straight laced circles on the display of his broad-minded sympathies for one 'who in his view was harried by unworthy prejudice.'"

Kurt Grunwald, discussing Baron de Hirsch's relations with the royal families of Europe in *Turkenhirsch,* says;

Crown Prince Rudolf met "the French financier,"

Baron Hirsch at a shooting party in September 1886, and introduced him thereafter to his friend, the journalist Moritz Szeps, whom Hirsch helped financially to start a new (liberal) Viennese daily.

In December 1886 Hirsch had obtained an introduction to the Prince of Wales from Rudolf, allegedly in consideration of a loan of 100,000 gulden. After Rudolf's tragic death in 1889 it was said in Vienna that his debt was waived in return for nobility conferred upon Hirsch's natural sons whom his widow had adopted.

Little else is known about this relationship, to which there are only occasional references, owing apparently to its short duration. Moreover Rudolf, in face of the straight-laced court, had to be circumspect in being seen publicly in the company which he preferred.

Not so Edward. "The only shock ever administered by the Prince in Hungary to a society which was admittedly almost shockproof was caused by his attempt to introduce Baron Hirsch into its midst."

During the following London season Hirsch became part of the Prince's entourage, a frequent guest at Sandringham and the country houses of the Prince's friends. He himself had rented Bath House in Piccadilly, a shoot near Newmarket, and a country house near Sandringham where he entertained lavishly. Later that year Edward kept his promise to be Hirsch's guest at his hunt at St. Johann on the Austro-Hungarian border, arriving at Vienna on October 5 with a party including Lady Randolph Churchill, Lady Lilian Wemyss, Lord Dudley, Horace Furquart, Lord and Lady Curzon and the Arthur Sassoons. A day later the Prince gave a luncheon at the Grant Hotel for Hirsch and the King of Greece, and after lunch the party left by special train for St. Johann, while the Austrian archdukes gasped. The Prince found his few Austrian and Hungarian fellow guests congenial, although not aristocratic, and the unpretentious house most comfortable. He spent twelve days there (October 6-18, 1891).

Some years later, in October 1894, the Czarevitch,

later Nicholas II, was somewhat bewildered by the company found at Sandringham. It included, apart from turf enthusiasts, also Baron Hirsch who on this occasion "was less interested in horses or even in railway contracts, than he was in philanthropic plans to succour the oppressed Russian Jews."

11

LUCIEN

In 1888 a terrible bereavement closed the doors of the de Hirsch mansion when their son Lucien, only thirty-one, died after a few days' illness. From that time on the Baron and the Baroness made only short stays in Paris, spending more and more of their time in England, although the headquarters for the Baron's major undertakings remained in Paris. From 1887 on, they gave Bath House, 82 Picadilly, as their home address.

Clara never got over the loss. From then until the day she died she wore black, except when attending important social functions. Lucien was her only child, except for the daughter who had died in infancy, and she lavished on him all the love and affection of a mother for an only son. As a child, he had traveled with Maurice and Clara to remote parts of Eastern Europe and he was her constant companion in Constantinople, where Maurice was so busy with the complicated problems of railroad construction.

The loss of their son is said to have led the two into a life devoted to philanthropic activities. Gradually Maurice withdrew almost entirely from business enterprises and threw his energy and ingenuity into programs of great magnitude designed to improve the position of Jews everywhere, culminating in the gigantic task of trying to move millions of Jews from Russia to the Argentine and other lands. He is supposed to have said to a well-wisher at Lucien's funeral, "I have lost my son but not my heir, humanity is my heir," and he made this come true, giving away almost every cent he owned before he died.

Lucien had long been a well-known figure in the social circles of London, where he enjoyed considerable popularity with the Prince of Wales and his set. He appeared to have no interest in his father's railroad ventures, nor is there any record of his ever having been involved in business activities of any kind. He seems to have led a life centered around social activities, typical of the "idle rich" of that period. He was, though, a well-known numismatologist, considered to be an authority, and in possession of a very rich collection of antique and rare silver, gold, and other coins, which Clara kept intact after his death. In her will, she turned this valuaable collection over to the City of Brussels.

Lucien owned a large stable of race horses which his father sold on his death, turning the proceeds over to English hospitals. It was in handling the sale of his son's stable that Maurice became interested in horse racing. He acquired a large stable of champions himself, which was to make him known as one of the outstanding horsemen in England and the Continent for a number of years.

In 1889 he purchased the horse Vasistas for 6,000 pounds. In 1891 this horse won the Chester Cup. On June 29, 1890, he paid 5,500 Guineas for La Fleche, which was a record price for a yearling. She ran unbeaten as a two-year-old in 1891. She won the 1,000 Guineas, the Oaks, the St. Leger, and the Cambridgeshire in 1892. In 1893 she won the Liverpool cup and in 1894 the Ascot gold cup. Total stake winnings of La Fleche amounted to 34,585 pounds, all of which went to English hospitals. She was sold to Sir Tatton Sykes on June 30, 1896, for 12,000 guineas, a record price for a brood mare. In 1894, Hirsch paid 15,000 pounds for Match Box, which he sold to the Austrian government for the same sum. The stud of the Hirsch stables was sold at Newmarket on June 30, 1896, for 44,870 guineas.

An article in the leading sports publication, *Bailey's Magazine of Sports and Pastimes,* April, 1894 issue, says: "The memory of his son, who had been deeply attached to England, where he had made many friends, drew the Baron's sympathies toward that country. He very soon became very familiar with its language, its manners and its customs. His sojourns in London and the different sporting men's meets in England has become his favorite pastime."

Not much is known of Lucien's romances or love affairs, although he did leave a daughter, who was adopted by Clara and Maurice and raised by them. Mystery surrounds the background of this daughter, because Lucien was not known to have been married. The mother's name was Premelie but there is no record whatsoever of who she was or what her relationship was to Lucien. The Baron's will contains the following reference to the adopted daughter and makes it clear that the mother was not to be allowed in any way to interfere with her upbringing:

Before all others I bequeath one million francs to my adopted daughter, Luciena Premelie Hirsch, free of succession duty and to be secured as far as possible, as laid down in Section 18, that is to say, in so far as the law will permit.

I appoint as guardian of my adopted daughter, my brother-in-law M. Georges Montefiore Levi, Senator in Brussels. Should he on any ground whatsoever be unable or unwilling to accept guardianship, his place shall be taken by Raphael Ritter Von Bauer, Austrian Consul General in Brussels and failing him or after him, M. Jules Dietz, advocate in Paris. It shall be the duty of the guardian to look after the welfare of my adopted daughter.

The mother of my adopted daughter shall under no circumstances be at liberty to take her to live with herself or to exert any influence on her education, maintenance or the administration of her property. I further order that no relative of the mother whether by blood or by marriage shall be at liberty to exercise guardianship or undertake the education of my adopted daughter either singly or in conjunction with others.

I order that the education and raising of my adopted daughter shall be entrusted in the first instance to my sister-in-law Madame Georges Montefiore Levi and in the event of her being prevented for any cause whatsoever in the second instance to my brother-in-law, M. Georges Montefiore Levi. Failing him the education and rearing of my adopted daughter shall be undertaken by my wife and finally in the fourth instance my brother Baron James de Hirsch is begged to assume the education of my adopted daughter.

The governors or governor for the time being of my adopted daughter shall receive as recompense for the discharge of her or his duties, one half of the income of the amount bequeathed to my adopted daughter for her maintenance.

Luciena was raised with all the acoutrements of a Baron's daughter, carrying the title of Baroness, although Maurice had been unable to get the Belgian government to grant her a title on her own as he had with his own two natural sons. She married Edouard Balser, a banker in

Brussels and, so far as is known, spent her life there.

After Lucien's death Maurice and Clara adopted, on June 16, 1887, two brothers, Arnold and Raymond de Forest, both illegitimate sons of Maurice de Hirsch. One of them was an incurable invalid, on whom Clara is reported to have lavished all the pent-up love which the death of her son unleashed. Little is known of the circumstances of their birth or who their mother was. Kurt Grunwald seems to have gathered together whatever meager information is available about them. In *Turkenhirsch* he says:

Hirsch was anxious to obtain nobility for his offspring. We are told that his son Lucien (died October 20, 1888) was the first Jew to obtain a Belgian barony. Hirsch also tried hard (and apparently successfully) to obtain nobility for his natural sons, Arnold and Raymond de Forest, but was less successful in the case of Lucien's natural daughter Lucienne, who later married the banker E. Balser.

As the obituaries in the Viennese press noted, Hirsch lately had always been seen accompanied by two young boys, whose mother had been English, or American. Their name was given as Forreste-Bischoffsheim. The younger of the two, Raymond (1880-1912) died young, the older (b. 1879) now known as Count of Bendern, lives in Vaduz, Liechtenstein. The *Semi Gotha* of 1912 claims that on his mother's side Arnold, holder of a twenty year old barony which in 1900 was confirmed for Great Britain by Royal Decree, hailed from old French aristocracy, de Forrestier. And we learn from the 1956 *Who's Who* of his education at Eton and Oxford, his army and war service, and his membership in Parliament. In 1932 he became a naturalized citizen of the Principality of Liechtenstein, which made him a hereditary count and Diplomatic Counselor. A London society weekly, after referring to the sporting

achievements of this good-looking and wealthy Liberal
M. P. tells us that he was rejected by the Reform Club.
This was allegedly because of the role he played in the
agitation for land reform, which the wealthy and respectable Whig landowners abhorred. And Lloyd
George and Winston Churchill, who had sponsored his
membership, resigned from the club.

There seems also to have been some litigation or
dispute between the two brothers on the one side and
the Paris municipality on the other, concerning the
palace of Beauregard, which Hirsch allegedly had left
to Paris.

Other sources allege that it was Hirsch's widow who
had adopted the two boys, some thought after Hirsch's
death, but more likely before, as the mention of the
name Forreste-Bischoffsheim would seem to indicate.
They were also among her heirs. Here we have only a
small and insufficient clue to the character of a woman
who would justify a biography of her own, a woman
over-shadowed all her life by a husband to whom she
was not only companion and, often enough, secretary,
but probably also a sober counsellor.

A curious story concerning Lucien came to light only in
1920, when Margot Asquith's autobiography appeared in
the *London Sunday Times*. The Jewish-language newspaper, *The Day,* in its issue of August 25, 1920, ran the
following story:

Margot, the wife of the former English Prime Minister Asquith, is now writing her autobiography in the
London Sunday Times, and she tells of her meeting
with Baron de Hirsch when she was still Margot Tennant.

One evening, dining with the Bischoffsheims, (Jews)
I was introduced for the first time to Baron de Hirsch,
an Austrian who resided in Paris. The next time we met

in Paris. I lunched with him and his wife and he gave
me his opera box. A day later he invited me to dine
with him alone at the Café Anglais, and as my father
and mother were then not in town, I accepted his invitation. During the conversation he recalled our first
meeting and asked me whether I surmised the reason
for his invitation to dine with him. I answered "I did
not."

Baron de Hirsch: "Because I want you to marry my
son Lucien. He is not like me. He is
very respectable and hates money.
He likes books and collects manu-
scripts and other things and is
highly educated."

Margot: "Poor man! I don't suppose he would even
care much for me!"

Baron de Hirsch: "Oh, but you would widen his interests. He is shy, and I want him to
make a good marriage; and above
all, he must marry an English
woman."

Margot: "Has he ever been in love?"

Baron de Hirsch: "No. He has never been in love, but
many women are after him and I
do not want him to be married to a
woman for his money."

Margot: "What other English girl is there that you
would like your son to marry?"

Baron de Hirsch: "Lady Katie Lambton, Durham's
sister."

Margot: "I do not know her at all. Is she like me?"

Baron de Hirsch: "No, but you and she are the only
two girls I have met that I could
wish my son to marry."

Lady Asquith then continues:

"I must state here in fairness to the memory of Lucien that he never cared about me. He died a short time after this, and someone remarked to the Baron: 'What a fool Margot Tennant was not to have married your son—she would be a rich widow now.'

To this the Baron answered: "The one who would have married Margot Tennant would not have died".

The newspaper then attempts to judge Baron de Hirsch's attitude toward Judaism when it says:

Baron de Hirsch and his only son Lucien moved in the most prominent Jewish families in Europe. Among those Jewish families there were not only pretty, but very beautiful Jewish girls, educated and intelligent; but Baron de Hirsch did not want his son to marry a Jewish girl. He wanted an Englishwoman and a Christian to be the wife of his only son. Fate, however, decided differently and Lucien died leaving the rich Baron with his wealth. A large part of his wealth was left for Jewish purposes. Was that for the perpetuation of the Jewish nation?

Kurt Welsbach, a German journalist, relates in his book *Reminiscences* that he once had a long conversation with Baron de Hirsch concerning Jews and Judaism. The Baron suffered greatly on account of the persecution of the Jews. He was convinced that the Jews were made to suffer without cause and he had a bad opinion of the present civilization. "How can the Jewish question be solved?" he was asked by Kurt Welsbach.

"I see the best solution in baptism," he answered, "but as long as the Jews will be persecuted they will remain Jews. In the meantime, let them have a home somewhere, they must have a home, and they must be helped to build the home."

Margot's description and Welsbach's account throw light on the Baron's views. He was anxious to have his son marry a girl of a prominent English Christian fam-

ily and thus be lost among Christians. His wish would
have certainly been realized if his son had lived. He also
wished the Jews to cease to be Jews and thus stop all
antagonism against themselves. But as this was impossible he helped them as Jews. This was Baron de Hirsch
and his interesting views.

12

RUSSIA

Lucien's death almost coincided with the successful completion of the railroad enterprise and Clara and Maurice de Hirsch, after accumulating a vast fortune and becoming one of the world's richest couples, decided to fill the void left in their lives through the loss of their son by devoting their riches and their remaining years to charitable enterprises. Maurice needed some new engrossing project—a new challenge, and Clara tactfully guided his interests into helping the persecuted and oppressed Jews of eastern Europe who were so much in need of sophisticated leadership and guidance. She was determined that, if his name were to go down to posterity at all, he should be remembered as the benefactor of a suffering and downtrodden Jewish people. As a result, Maurice almost entirely withdrew from business to devote all of his time as well as the greater part of his immense fortune to charitable enterprises.

Characteristically, he entered into this new phase of life with all the gusto and enthusiasm he had shown in the business world. Using the same tactics he had employed so successfully in organizing the railroad company, he immediately sought out the most experienced social service workers in all of Europe, whether they were Jews or not, and built up a large organization established on business-like lines. He converted the first floor of his palatial Paris home into offices in which to house this staff of experts.

Maurice de Hirsch had no patience with the old-fash-ioned methods of doling out money to the "schnorrers." He was not interested in the local, communal type of charity. His natural flair for large undertakings urged him to do something big, a gigantic project to aid the whole Jewish race!

His years of hard-headed experience in the banking world had made him skeptical that social justice would ever succeed through appeals to humanity and good will alone. He was not one of those idle dreamers who be-lieved that human nature could be changed by exhortations from the pulpit or the writings of great thinkers. Only the good will of a strong government backed by laws guaran-teeing equality to all would assure Jews of permanent ac-ceptance in the Christian world.

In his *History of the Persecution of the Jews in Russia,* written in 1892, M. G. Landsberg reprints the following article by Baron de Hirsch, in which he outlines his phi-losophy of philanthropy:

> Let us give these for once the first place, which in real life they never have. These great masses of poor Jews are the eternal prototype of martyrdom, of suffer-ing, of persecution. Without law or protection they have been wandering on their thorny path like Pariahs of human society for centuries, bent under the double weight of their heavy burden and of universal contempt. People cast at them the reproach that they are not pro-ductive forces of society, but devote themselves only to trade, which brings quick profits. Granted that it is so; could it be otherwise when they have for centuries been

denied every occupation of a good citizen—especially
the tilling of the soil; shut out of honorable employment
and so forced, if they did not wish to starve, always to
seek some way to earn bread for themselves and their
families? If in this way this power and this fertility of
resources have been evolved in them at the cost of other
qualities, I believe that no one has the right to reproach
them for it.

While building his Oriental Railway, he had seen at
first hand the distressing condition of the Jews of Turkey,
Galicia, and the Balkan states, and the persecutions of the
Jews of Russia had long been a matter of great concern to
Jews everywhere. The outbreak of violence against the
Jews of Russia when Alexander III ascended the throne in
1881, which ushered in a return to medieval autocracy,
brought the plight of the Jews of the Pale of Settlement
to the attention of the Western countries in a manner so
tragic and so heart-rending that the civilized world was
shocked into action.

The first pogrom broke out at Elizabethgrad in May,
1881, setting a pattern of pillage, plunder, and murder
that spread rapidly to many of the smaller communities
throughout the Pale of Settlement—in Nyezain, Kuz-
mintzy, Plitovich, Klimov, Okhrimotzy and Lubny. In
Balta over 1,000 houses were demolished and damages
ran over a million rubles. In Warsaw two million dollars
worth of property was destroyed. Evidence was produced
at the time that established beyond doubt that these pogroms were carried out with the connivance of the government and the local police authorities. Twenty thousand
Jews, refugees fleeing the wrath of the Russian pogroms,
crossed the border into Hungary, reaching the town of
Brody, a poverty-stricken Galician town on the Austro-

Hungarian frontier. Huddling together in terror, the victims of misery and despair, broken families sought to find each other. But the Austrian authorities, fearing the outbreak of epidemics, threatened to deport the Jews back to Russia unless something was done quickly to relieve them of the almost insurmountable problems presented by the homeless refugees.

Strangely enough, not the Jewish organizations but the London newspapers were the first to take notice of the plight of these hapless refugees. It was the British authorities, too, who took the lead in organizing measures for their relief. Featured articles in the *London Times* of January 11 and 13, 1882, drew the attention of the whole world to the ruthless persecutions of Jews that were taking place in Russia. A mass meeting was called at historic Mansion House, the Lord Mayor's residence, on February 1, 1882, and a fund of 108,000 pounds was raised for immediate relief measures to take care of the refugees.

The Mansion House meeting was a memorable one. The list of names sponsoring the meeting was a veritable roll call of the world's great leaders—Charles Darwin, Matthew Arnold, James Bryce, Robert Browning, the Earl of Shaftesbury, Sir John Lubbock, John Tyndall, and Cardinal Manning. The Cardinal, on behalf of the Catholic Church, said,

Further, I may say that, while we do not intend to touch upon any question in the internal legislation of Russia, still there are laws larger than any Russian legislation, laws which are equally binding in London, in St. Petersburg, and in Moscow—the laws of humanity, of nature, and of God—which are the foundation of all other laws; and if in any legislation these are violated, all nations of Christian Europe, the whole commonwealth of civilized and Christian men, would instantly acquire a right to speak out loud. And now my Lord, I must touch upon one point which I acknowledge has been very painful to me. We have all watched for the last twelve months what is called the anti-semitic movement in Germany. I look upon it with a twofold feeling: In the first place, I look upon it with abhorrence as tending to disintegrate the foundations of social life, and, secondly, with great fear lest it may tend to light up an animosity which has already taken fire in Russia and may spread elsewhere.

In this prophetic pronouncement the Cardinal almost foretold the holocaust that was to come just half a century later in the country that originated political anti-Semitism. And he made it clear that anti-Semitism was vastly different from the old-fashioned Jew hatred that brought on the pogroms. Jew hatred was religious. All a Jew had to do was to be baptized and he was let alone. Anti-Semitism was nationalistic and political. The violence of Jew-hatred, bred of ignorance, dies of its own inertia and disappears when the fury of its attack is spent. But when anti-Semitism becomes the rallying-cry of the hoodlum and the platform of a political party, and the platform of that party becomes national policy, then come the hatred movements that spread throughout land after land, from people to people across international boundaries and wide oceans.

German universities began conducting courses in anti-Semitism. German scientists were writing books to prove the superiority of race—their race. Soon French nationalists were spreading the doctrine that Jews were alien to France and did not belong, bringing on the disgraceful spectacle of a Dreyfus case. And even in America some of these ideas caught on with the "Know-Nothing Party" and other splinter groups. The elections of 1878 in Germany, however, were to mark the official birth of the anti-Semitic movement, because the Anti-Semitic Party pledged in its platform that, if it were elected, it would disenfranchise the Jews of Germany.

With the spread of the pogroms in Russia, the problem of what to do with the hordes of refugees pouring out of Russia became almost insurmountable. Most of the European cities closed their doors to them, and there was no place to send the hapless refugees except to the few countries of Western Europe that did allow some of them to enter. England, as a result, bore the brunt of the burden of receiving most of the Russian Jewish refugees. Many of the Jews who eventually were sent to South Africa, Australia, Canada, and North and South America, passed through England, spending as much as a year or two there. When there were no more buildings to house the refugees, camps were established, where they were taken care of until homes could be found for them elsewhere. Many of the ancestors of Jews who now live in Australia, South Africa, South America, Canada, and the United States were cared for in England by the English Jewish community and by the British authorities.

The Mansion House Committee appointed a delegation made up of Samuel Montagu, afterward Lord Swaythling, Dr. Asher Asher, Scotland's first Jewish doctor, and Lawrence Oliphant, the noted Christian orientalist and author, to go to the town of Brody on the Russian-Hungarian border to supervise relief operations. Here they found several other groups already working with Leo Herzberg-Frankel, the prominent Hungarian Jewish writer, chief clerk of the Chamber of Commerce and Industry, a member of the City Council and Inspector of the

Schools of Brody. As Brody's leading Jewish citizen, he acted as a liaison contact between the many foreign delegations that had descended on Brody and the Austro-Hungarian authorities. Under his direction, a committee was set up to select the hardiest of young Jews for migration to America, thus starting the influx of Russian Jews that was to result in over 600,000 Jews coming to the United States and Canada during the next ten years. Those rejected for migration to America because they were too old or too weak for the long steerage trip were settled in Jewish communities in other parts of Europe.

Moritz Friedlander, secretary of the Hungarian Israelitische Allianz zu Wien, in cooperation with the representatives of the English Board of Deputies and the Anglo-Jewish Association, published a pamphlet in which he described the wretchedness and misery he saw in Brody, which reached Baron de Hirsch. He immediately became interested, and contributed one million francs to this relief work. At his request, the Alliance Israélite Universelle sent Chevalier Veneziani and Charles Netter to the scene to act in behalf of that organization.

In May of 1882, the infamous May Laws were passed, which sealed the fate of the Jews of Russia and made them virtual prisoners within the Pale of Settlement. They could not leave Russia, nor could they acquire land either by purchase or by lease. The May Laws, designed "to diminish the number of Jews in the Empire by converting them," induced conversions by endowing baptized Jews with all the rights accorded to Christians of the same rank, and exempting them from having to pay taxes for three years. Murderers and criminals who adopted Christianity were accorded special leniency. But the penalties that were imposed on Jews who resisted conversion were

severe. Jewish communities were to provide conscripts to
the army at the rate of one for every 1,000 rubles the
community was in arrears in its tax payments. For every
conscript not furnished at the proper time, two new conscripts were demanded. In many cases cripples and in-
valids were conscripted and placed in auxiliary service of
some sort. There are even records of boys of eight years
of age actually being taken into the army to serve terms
of as much as twenty-five years, doing all the menial jobs
in the army that were customarily filled by Jews. While
the May Laws were labeled "temporary" when they were
instituted, they remained in effect until well into the twentieth century.

Subsequent protest meetings were held in London each
time a new series of pogroms broke out in Russia. A meeting of the Guildhall on December 10, 1890, resolved "that
a suitable memorial be presented to the Emperor of all the
Russias respectfully praying His Majesty to repeal all
the exceptional and restrictive laws and disabilities which
afflicted his Jewish subjects and begging His Majesty to
confer upon them equal rights with those enjoyed by the
rest of His Majesty's subjects." This Memorandum was
not even read by the Czar and was returned unopened to
the Lord Mayor of London. In 1890, too, Gladstone
wrote in the *London Jewish Chronicle* that he had "read
with pain and horror the various statements respecting the
sufferings of the Jews in Russia and that the thing to do,
if the facts could be established, was to rouse the con-
science of Russia and Europe in regard to them."

Baron de Hirsch began to see that the plight of the
Jews in Russia offered the gigantic philanthropic project
he was seeking—an opportunity to rescue a whole people.
His first thought was to remove Russia's Jews from the

crowded Pale of Settlement to agricultural colonies within
Russia itself, which he was willing to finance anywhere in
the Czar's domains. He called a meeting in his Paris home
of certain prominent Jews of St. Petersburg and a committee was formed, under the leadership of Russia's
Baron Horace Gunzberg, to take this suggestion up with
the Russian authorities. The committee, however, met
with many rebuffs from government authorities, who
made it clear that the plan had no attraction for the
Czarist hierarchy. Baron de Hirsch then tried another
approach. He had always believed that Jews were subjected to indignities and special disabilities because the
only education they received was concentrated entirely in
the study of the Talmud, which did little to prepare them
for the difficult task of earning a living and resulted in
Jews becoming peddlers or petty traders. He told the
committee that "Jews should not huddle in ghettos but
should mix with the various peoples in various lands, remaining Jews in religion, but in all other respects assimi-
lating with the people among whom they cast their lot."
He then made his spectacular offer to the Czar to donate
the sum of fifty million francs to be used exclusively for
nonsectarian educational purposes within the Pale of Settlement, the only stipulations being that Jewish children
should be permitted to attend the schools on an equal basis
with the Christian children and that Baron de Hirsch control the distribution of the money. This the Russians were
unwilling to accept. They would make no guarantees to the
Jews. They would accept the money only if it were given
into their hands to control, with no strings attached. Any
decision to educate Jewish children would have to be left
to them. No commitments would be made. The money
would be expended as the Czar and his ministers saw fit.

In an article published by the Alliance Israélite Universelle on November 14, 1919, this whole matter is briefly summed up:

In 1887-1888, Baron de Hirsch intended to devote a sum of 50 million francs to the education of Jews in Russia. Knowing the ways of the Russian administration, he was not anxious to deliver the cash to the Government. He wanted the capital to stay in France or in England, and only the revenues of this capital would be sent to Russia for the maintenance of the future schools and the Foundation thus made would be officially acknowledged by the Government. The persons whom Baron de Hirsch had first entrusted to probe the Russian Government had led him to believe that the latter would accept this plan, but when the question was submitted to the offices of the ministries, some alleged legal difficulties arose, and finally the Government let Baron de Hirsch know that he would have to choose: he would either have to give up his project or entrust the capital to the Russian Government who would be responsible for its management and for its allotment to the proposed goals. The Baron did not hesitate; as he had no confidence in the Russian authorities, he withdrew his offer.

During the negotiations that lasted for several months, Baron de Hirsch had sent to St. Petersburg Mr. Leonee Lehmann, a lawyer of the Supreme Court of Appeals and a member of the Central Committee of the Alliance, together with the French general d'Abjas to try to induce the Russian government's favorable interest in his plan. It appears from the letters written by Mr. Lehmann and General d'Abjas to Baron de Hirsch that the ministers were favorable to the project and made all kinds of reassuring promises. But in the end none of them had the courage to give his word in fear of being disowned by the Emperor who was entirely submissive to the suggestions of the anti-semitic party, and chiefly to the general procurator of the St. Synode, Pobyedonostzev. Baron de Hirsch then decided to write a letter to the latter, in which he stresses that his goal was neither of a political nor of a religious nature, that he was only planning to give a primary education to the Jewish children and that under these conditions he asked Mr. Pobyedonostzev to support his project since he had so much influence over the ministers.

He added that, in order to prove that his project was only of a charitable nature, he was offering to him personally the sum of a million francs for the Greek Orthodox parochial schools placed under the direction of Mr. Pobyedonostzev. The latter hastened to accept the offer and Baron de Hirsch, in the hope that he would patronize his plans, handed him the million francs. Mr. Pobydonostzev not only did not do anything to promote the projects, he even worked to thwart the plan. When all the negotiations had failed, he abstained from giving the million francs back.

It is an interesting sidelight that, at the same time de Hirsch was making his offer of fifty million francs for the education of the Jews of Russia, a special financial mission from St. Petersburg was negotiating with the Rothschilds in London for a large loan. A new outburst of anti-Jewish violence in Russia broke off the negotiations when the news reached London and the Rothschild people walked out of the meeting without so much as a word.

This unreasonable attitude on the part of the Russian Government convinced Baron de Hirsch that the only hope for the salvation of the Jews of Russia was to remove them from the country entirely—and he would do it! He would become a modern Moses leading his coreligionists out of this dreary land to new, fresh lands where there were no ancient prejudices and where Jews could become farmers and artisans and skilled workmen.

In characteristic fashion he immediately began working toward that end, converting his philanthropic headquarters on the first floor of his mansion on the Champs Elysées in Paris into a gigantic migration organization and devoting all its resources to putting into immediate operation his plan for the removal of three and a half million Jews from Russia!

Clara immediately took personal charge of all the other Baron de Hirsch benevolent foundations throughout the world, devoting herself to this work from early morning until late at night. She received several hundred letters asking her assistance almost every day from individuals and societies in all parts of the eastern and western hemispheres. Endless demands were made upon her from young girls seeking dowries, from students anxious to pursue their studies, from emigrants wishing to return home, as well as larger requests from philanthropic societies of one kind and another that were insufficiently supported by the communities in which they were located.

To every appeal, no matter how large or small, she seemed to lend a willing and sympathetic ear, referring each application to the Baron's agent or correspondent in the particular part of the world from which the appeal came. She gave thousands as readily as hundreds when convinced of the worthiness of the cause.

Discussing the events that led to the momentous decision Maurice and Clara de Hirsch were about to make, the *History of the Baron de Hirsch Fund* says:

> After a year of negotiations, it became clear that those in control of the Russian government were not anxious to break down the barriers separating the Jews from the rest of the Russian people. Reluctantly, the Baron withdrew his offer.

It was this experience which led him to conclude that

emigration was the only solution if the Russian Jews were not to be abandoned to their fate. Establishment of order and method in their expatriation was the problem from now on.

The government of the Czar (he wrote) means to get rid of the five million Jews who inhabit Russian territory. Let it allow the many who, like himself, are interested in the fate of these victims of persecution and who certainly will be prepared to make the greatest sacrifices on their behalf, to save them. . . . Let a period of twenty years—let us say—be fixed; let it be agreed that every year a certain number of Jews will leave the country; but let them be left in peace until the hour of their departure arrives. If the Czar will order a measure of this character to be adopted, those who are interested in the fate of the Russian Jews will do what is necessary to provide funds for conveying to their new country the number of emigrants ordered to leave yearly. By this means it will be possible to carry out, without any great hardship and with a minimum of suffering for those concerned, the principle of expulsion decided on by the Russian government.

But transplantation of these Jewish masses was not all that Baron de Hirsch envisaged. Emigration, he hoped, would be the prelude to a physical and moral regeneration of the whole of Russian Jewry. With characteristic simplicity, the Baron laid down his final goal:

"What I desire to accomplish, what, after many failures has come to be the object of my life, and that for which I am ready to stake my wealth and my intellectual powers, is to give to a portion of my companions in faith the possibility of finding a new existence, primarily as farmers and also as handicraftsmen, in those lands where the laws and religious tolerance permit them to carry on the struggle for existence as noble and responsible subjects of a humane government."

On the matter of farming he was thoroughly convinced: "My own personal experience has led me to recognize that the Jews have very good ability in agriculture. . . . I have seen this personally in the Jewish agricultural colonies of Turkey. My efforts shall show that the Jews have not lost the agricultural qualities that their forefathers possessed. I shall try to make for them a new home in different lands where, as free farmers on their own soil, they can make themselves useful to the country. If this should not come to pass among the present generation, the next will surely fulfill this expectation."

The History of the Nineteenth Century Year By Year by Edwin Emerson, Jr., 1891, says, "In April, Baron de Hirsch notified his readiness to contribute the sum of three million pounds toward a fund for establishing in Syria and other places, colonies for the Jews expelled from Russia. In August he dispatched orders to his Argentine agents to purchase land in that country to the value of two million pounds but the first Hirsch colony, as it turned out, was established at Woodbine, New Jersey, in September."

13

PALESTINE

No sooner were Baron de Hirsch's plans made known than he was deluged with solicitations from charitable organizations everywhere, and with colonization plans for sending Jews to remote countries all over the world. Offers of tracts of land poured in from Egypt, Australia, Canada, and many other countries. The agent-general of the Province of Manitoba, headquartered in the Canadian High Commissioner's office in London, tried to interest Baron de Hirsch in a colony in Manitoba, offering farms to the settlers as free land grants. Oscar S. Straus, United States Ambassador to Turkey, and Jacob A. Schiff presented a plan that had been brought to their attention for settling Jews in colonies in Mesopotamia. Baron de Hirsch rejected this plan because his experiences with the Turkish government under Sultan Abdul Hamid had convinced him that it was impossible to deal satisfactorily with the Turkish authorities. But the greatest amount of pressure to which he was subjected was from groups interested in having him use his money to settle the Russian Jews in Palestine under plans similar to the colonies that had been established there by Sir Moses Montefiore, Baron Edmond de Rothschild, and by private groups of émigrés from Russia.

Religious Jews had never given up the dream of a return to Zion and many did go back. There are records of Jewish agricultural settlements in Palestine as far back as the year 1170. Sixty families are known to have been living in a colony in Gaza in 1481. Sporadic attempts at establishing agricultural colonies were made all through the centuries, principally by descendants of European Jews who had returned to the Holy Land to die there and be buried in Eretz Israel. But by the end of the nineteenth century there were no more than 43,000 Jews in the Holy Land out of a total population of over half a million, and of these less than 4,000 were engaged in agricultural pursuits, with fewer than 100,000 acres under cultivation.

The first of the modern agricultural colonies was not established until 1854, when Sir Moses Montefiore selected 35 families in Safed and established them on a farm colony. About 1860, two Orthodox Rabbis, Hirsch Kalischer and Elija Gutmacher, developed a plan for settling Russian and Rumanian Jews on farms in Palestine, for which they sought the support of the Alliance. Charles Netter was sent to the Holy Land to investigate. He approved of the plan but recommended that an agricultural school first be established to teach the settlers how to develop the land. The Turkish government donated 617 acres of land near Jaffa for this purpose and in 1870 the school was established at Mikweh Israel. Charles Netter died there on October 2, 1882, while on a tour of inspection, and was buried on the school grounds.

The year 1882 saw the start of a number of agricultural colonies in Palestine, mostly on a voluntary basis by small independent groups who had escaped from the pogroms in Russia. The first colony of Russian Jews was established at Rishon le Zion by six immigrants. It was one of the more successful of the early colonies and, with the help of Baron Edmond de Rothschild, the settlement grew to 266 families toward the end of the century. In 1882, too, a party of 90 Russian students migrated to Palestine to become laborers, hoping to accumulate enough money to found a colony. In 1884 they joined the Chovevei Zion colony of Chederah. At about the same time a group of Rumanian Jews founded the colony of Zikron Yaakob in Samaria, which was to become the largest and most successful of all the nineteenth-century colonies, with about two thousand persons living there at the turn of the century. Another group of Rumanian immigrants founded the colony of Rosh Pinah on 1,581 acres situated about four miles north of Safed. By 1898, some 300 colonists lived there.

The idea of creating a Jewish state in Palestine as a national homeland was not really new either. Rabbi Judah ben Solomon Hai Alkalai, a Rabbi in Semlin, Croatia, may be regarded as one of the first of the modern and practical Zionists. His book *Goral la-Adonai* (*A Lot for the Lord*), published at Vienna in 1857, is a treatise on the restoration of Palestine to the Jews through the formation of a "joint stock company such as a steamship or railroad trust, whose endeavor it would be to induce the Sultan to cede Palestine to the Jews as a tributary country, on a similar plan to that on which the Danubian principalities were governed."

On July 12, 1878, a suggestion was actually made in the Hungarian Parliament that Turkey should be forced to give up Palestine and that all Hungarian Jews should be deported there. The Turkish Government, however, declared that foreign Jews could not remain in Palestine longer than three months. In 1888 Great Britain, France, and the United States sent a protest to the Sultan asking that this rule be rescinded. The Sublime Porte then announced that this rule was meant to apply only to large numbers of Jews coming as a group at one time because Turkey was afraid that the move to establish colonies in Palestine would spread and the country would be overrun with ill-equipped Jewish colonists who would become public charges.

In 1879 Laurence Oliphant, English author, orientalist, and a former member of the British Parliament, conceived the idea of sending somewhere between 25,000 to 50,000 Jewish families to Palestine as a start toward reestablishing a Jewish nation there. He went so far as to found a Jewish settlement in Giliad at the upper end of the Dead Sea as a commercial speculation, pointing out that in addition to it being farmland there was some possibility of mineral deposits being present there. It was in connection with this project that he wrote his book *Land of Giliad* in 1880. Although he had the support of Disraeli and the semi-official approval of the British government, he was unable to secure the Sultan's consent to his large-scale project of Jewish immigration and colonization in Turkish territory. He spent the latter years of his life in Palestine, living in a community of Jewish immigrants until his death in 1888. It is interesting that this was the same Laurence Oliphant who had been appointed administrator of the fund raised by the London Mansion House Committee in 1882 for the relief of Russian Jews escaping into the town of Brody in Galicia. He was to become well known, too, as Baron de Hirsch's emissary to Russia to supervise the selection of emigrants to be moved to the colonies in the New World.

An attempt was made by the Chovevei Zion of London

and the Paris branch to bring Baron Edmond de Rothschild and Baron de Hirsch together on a project to
sponsor emigration to Syria and Palestine. On July 29,
1891, a meeting was held in Paris for the purpose of discussing this question, attended by several members of the
Central Committee of the Alliance Israélite and Rabbi
Mohilever of Bialystok and Dr. Hildesheimer of Berlin.
Baron de Hirsch was at Carlsbad at the time and the
suggestions made at the meeting were forwarded to him
there. The delegation suggested sending a commission of
expert engineers and social workers to investigate the possibility of organizing a mass movement of Russian Jews
to Palestine and other countries in Asia Minor.

Baron de Hirsch replied with the following memorandum, setting forth the reasons why Palestine seemed to
him to be inadvisable as a land for emigration, and why
he felt that the Argentine was so much more preferable:

> Concerning the project of Russian Emigration and
> the creation of a (Agra) Farmers' Trust Bank in As-
> iatic Turkey, I have taken note of the minutes of the
> meeting held at Paris, July 29, 1891, and composed on
> the one part of several members of the Central Com-
> mittee of the Alliance Israélite Universelle, with Mons.
> Zadoc Kahn, Grand Rabbin of France, as their spokes-
> man, and on the other part by delegates of Russian
> Societies in favor of Palestinean Colonization. These
> latter proposed to and, in fact, did obtain from the
> Alliance its approbation and its moral support in favor
> of a project having as its object:
>
> (a) The creation of Russo-Jewish colonies in Asiatic
> Turkey, particularly in Syria and Palestine.
>
> (b) The establishment of a Farmers' Trust Bank in
> order to facilitate such colonization by all available
> means.
>
> I have been called upon at Paris by several of the

delegates of the Russian Societies who orally put before
me their idea and their project; they have, besides, so as
to gain my assent and support, addressed to me a letter
accompanied by a memorandum, setting forth the plan
of the enterprises projected. On the occasion of their
call, I explained to the delegates the reasons why it is
not possible for me to share their point of view, or to
approve without reservation, the project of colonization
in Asiatic Turkey. They do not ignore that, if they wish
to follow my advice, they ought partly to modify the
standpoint hitherto taken by them exclusively, namely,
that of religious memories and historical traditions.
However grand and honorable these traditions may be,
they do not constitute a sufficiently solid basis where-
with to secure the immigrants in their new fatherland
against new vicissitudes and new misforenues. The delegated gentlemen know that I think it to be the duty of
all who have in view the real welfare of our co-religionists only to entertain the project of colonization in
Asiatic Turkey with the express proviso of a provisional
and very careful investigation of which I shall speak
later. After having expressed to them my opinion I
added that I am quite disposed, in order to prove to
them my great desire to be helpful to them, to assist
them in the negotiations to be undertaken at Constantinople, adding to their delegates of my own choice,
who are to enter on the spot in an investigation of the
localities more seriously to be considered for an eventual choice, as well as to obtain of the Turkish government the best possible terms.

One cannot, indeed, start colonizing haphazardly,
and the movement should be preceded by a preliminary
serious and careful investigation. First of all, then, a
commission should be appointed, composed of experts,
three or five for example; their mission would be, in
the first place, to choose those localities and lands most
suitable for colonization purposes, next to put themselves in touch with the authorities in order to acquire
the selected lands on the best possible terms. Surely, if

the principle of colonization in Asiatic Turkey be granted, that should be the way to go about it; only thus will those charged with the selection of the lands and wishing to assume the responsibility of this work, have the opportunity to inform themselves exactly by personal investigation of the means whereby they subsequently can conduct the negotiations with a full knowledge of the subject. This provisional investigation, urgently needed as it is insofar as colonization, pure and simple, is concerned, is not less so as regards the establishment of a Farmers' Bank.

According to the project submitted to me by the Russian delegates, this Bank should serve:

1. To advance interest bearing loans on good security in form of mortgages, to wit:

(a) To new colonists whose own means are insufficient to provide for cultivating their lands, planting and sowing, and such other farm work as is necessary up to the time of harvesting or reaping; (b) To the already installed colonists to aid them in improving and enlarging their lands.

2. To provide a shelter and living for the destitute that will seek employment as farm laborers in the colonies or on the private farms.

3. To enable the purchase of lands in Asiatic Turkey on the part of Jewish colonists coming from Russia.

4. To direct the hitherto so ill-regulated and planless emigration movement towards the latter country in a safe and systematic manner.

This program is excellent in theory but, before deciding upon the creation of such an institution and fixing a priori its different departmental functions, it will be very necessary to know whether the organic conditions of that colonization work necessitates so extensive a program.

It should first be known what will be the area and consequently the importance of the lands to be acquired; before all, it should be ascertained whether it is not possible by means of an understanding with the govern-

ment, to obtain lands for cultivation through concessions without payment of a purchase price.

If this latter alternative should eventuate, a Farmers'
Trust Bank would certainly lose much of its interest. In
these circumstances, and until these preliminary questions have been settled satisfactorily, it appears prema-
ture to discuss the subject of a Farmers' Trust Bank,
and especially, to follow the Russian delegates into the
details of its functional organization. The above suffices
to demonstrate the necessity of a serious preliminary
investigation of the project of colonization in Asiatic
Turkey. It may be well for me briefly to point out, in
the following, the chief reasons that have convinced me
that to be sure of success, colonization ought to be tried,
in the first place, in the new world, and, especially, in
the Argentine Republic. And, first, from the agricultural viewpoint and that of economic life, the superiority of this latter country may be thus shown. No one
is unaware that agriculture in Turkey does not prosper.
The causes are known.

In the Argentine Republic, on the contrary, the soil
is of a proverbial fertility; the climate is excellent;
thanks to the financial crisis, at present prevalent in that
country, one could buy there considerable lands at re-
munerative prices. The Argentine Republic is the true
land of the future; there thousands of millions have
hitherto been spent for railway constructions, river en-
largements, harbor works; all that has been done at
large cost and all this exists; the new colonists will
profit thereby under exceptionally advantageous conditions.

Aside from the agricultural and economic status, the
political social life aspect of the colonies in Argentina, I
maintain, offers the Jews a point of concentration which
they will hardly find elsewhere. The area of this country is nine times that of France, while its population
does not reach the figure of four millions. Consequently
there is room and a future for an unlimited number of
Jews.

From the moment that Jews emigrate, it should be done with the view, not of gaining only a few years of tranquility and respite, but with the firm purpose of securing for their posterity rest and stability in the future. Are they sure those that propose to direct the Russian emigrants towards Asiatic Turkey, that these very ones will see any useful result from their labors, and their efforts crowned with success? Are they not afraid to expose them once more to collisions, soon or late, with their present persecutors, the Russians? Have they considered that they thus tend to disperse the emigration movement, instead of concentrating?

The central idea, then, the principle whence I believe the work of emigration ought to start, is as much as possible concentration. But, as I have said at the start, if the deputation of the Russian Societies persist in their project, I am quite disposed to place at their disposal both my influence and my active co-operation with the Imperial Ottoman government. I merely feel bound to demonstrate to them the necessity of having their project preceded by a preliminary careful investigation and the superiority of colonization in the Argentine Republic above all other hitherto proposed systems. This preliminary investigation is for me a question of so high importance that it outweighs all others; it is, moreover, an absolute condition of my prospective intervention, I must be sure of it.

Since this note has been drawn up, I was visited by M. J. Navon, who, as you know, has had relations with M. Erlanger of the Alliance on the subject of immigration into Asiatic Turkey. I have had a long talk with him and I am well convinced, although he is ostensibly very enthusiastic about the immigration into Asiatic Turkey, that at bottom he would not hesitate to give the preference to the Argentine Republic, had he not beforehand embarked upon the other project. The conversation I had with M. Navon is summed up as follows:

I have made him understand the danger entailed in

conducting haphazardly the immigration movement into Asiatic Turkey, as well as to treat at random with the government, without having before investigated, in the most careful manner and on the spot, the localities eventually most suitable for colonization. M. Navon believes and, it appears to me rightly so, that, provided Palestine be waived, the Turkish government will accept a limited number of Jewish immigrants and furnish them gratuitously, or nearly so, the necessary lands. I for my part would prefer to have these lands acquired for private ownership.

To resume, M. Navon understands the absolute necessity for the sending of a commission of three to five members who shall be charged with thoroughly investigating the question of the lands to be selected and asked of the Turkish government.

These delegates should act as much in the name of the Alliance as in my own name. M. Navon preferred that it be in my name especially. I admit I feel some hesitation to present the matter as coming largely from me, for the reasons above set forth; nevertheless, I shall do my share, if such become indispensable, not wishing to spare, as I have said, neither my influence nor my active co-operation. These delegates will have to place themselves in touch with the persons competent to select the proper lands for colonization. They will have to visit these lands, inspect them with care, examine also which is the best organization to be given to the immigration, in a word, draw up a veritable plan of campaign, as I have done for the immigration to the Argentine Republic through the labors of Dr. Lowenthal. Their plan once fixed, they will, lastly, have to negotiate with the Turkish government, in order to fix the terms of purchase, those of duration, taxation, etc.

This most highly important investigation ought to be made in an extremely conscientious manner. The delegates and the members of the Central Committee of the Alliance who have signed the minutes of the meeting of July 29, 1891, will not have to make their choice, in constituting this commission, of truly capable men, well posted on the matters that they will have to examine, and proof against the intrigues by which they will not fail to be surrounded. As to the delegates to be chosen by me, I reserve it to myself to appoint them; after I shall have been informed of the delegates chosen by the Alliance and by the Russian Societies I shall act thereon.

I shall furnish these delegates the necessary instructions and references

(signed) *Maurice de Hirsch.*

Carlsbad, August, 1891.

Baron de Hirsch had always been skeptical about settling Jews in Palestine because he feared that the country would one day come under Russian domination. Oscar Straus once pointed this out in explaining why de Hirsch looked only to the Western Hemisphere. "The late Baron de Hirsch," he said, "was profoundly impressed by the belief that Palestine was destined to fall into the hands of Russia. And it was this, and this alone, as he himself assured me, that led him to fix upon Argentina, rather than the Holy Land, as the scene of his great experiment in Jewish agriculture."

Nevertheless, he did send Veneziani and a group of engineers on a tour of Palestine in 1887 to investigate its potential for colonizing purposes. The report Veneziani brought back was discouraging. It pointed out that the agricultural communities that had been established in the Holy Land could hardly be considered shining examples of successful colonization and that, if it were not for the charitable donations of a handful of Jewish millionaires, they would actually have been dismal failures. The report also made pointed reference to the danger of epidemics and recurring plagues if thousands of Jews were to be brought into Palestine in a few years' time. Describing the health conditions it found, the report said, "From various causes the death-rate at Jerusalem is, to European notions, abnormally high . . . hardly anybody escapes fever once or twice a year; ophthalmia is caused by the glare of the sun against the white stone walls, and the chilly mornings and evenings are accountable for a good deal of rheumatism. It is particularly painful to see the puny and wizened babies, and boys and girls, sharp and clever but looking prematurely old. The offspring of too early marriages is always sickly, but the chief causes of the ill-health are the poorness of the water supply and absence—or rather, presence—of drainage."

This report confirmed Baron de Hirsch's thinking that it would take more money than he and all the wealthy Jews of the world together could muster to make a habitable land out of Palestine. There was the hazard, too, of having to deal with the Turkish government and the further danger that Palestine might some day fall into hands that were antagonistic to the Jews. He decided to look elsewhere and he looked west. He saw thousands of miles of unsettled land in the New World, hungry for settlers who would penetrate into the wilderness and create prosperous farm communities on soil now overrun with jungles and virgin forest. His attention was called to several groups of Russian Jews who had settled in Argentina in 1889 and, after incredible hardships, had succeeded in establishing successful agricultural colonies there. He sent an expedition to the Argentine, under the direction of Professor Guilliaume Lowenthal of the University of Lausanne, an authority on hygiene, for the purpose of investigating the country. The expedition returned in March,

1891, with a report that Argentina presented climatic, political, and social conditions most favorable to the development of the contemplated project of Jewish colonization. Baron de Hirsch decided that his first colonists should be sent to the Argentine Republic.

Baron Edmond de Rothschild, explaining why he continued to sponsor Palestinian colonies even though he was aware of the many disadvantages that the Veneziani report had disclosed, told Isaac Naiditch, as reported in his profile of Baron de Rothschild published in 1945, that

> Later came the projects of Baron Moritz Hirsch to settle Jews in countries more highly developed than Palestine, where it would be easier to find a livelihood. Baron Hirsch and I started out with two opposed philosophies. Hirsch was a great philanthropist. But his idea was to enable Jews to engage in productive work in different countries in the world and by no means to concentrate them in one. According to him they could assimilate only if they formed a small minority rather than a large community. But my idea was not merely to provide them with work and a livelihood but also to create such conditions as would make it possible for them to maintain Judaism and Jewish life and to further their growth. That is only possible if Jews live in compact masses and are not scattered in various far places. That is possible in our Holy Land where our Torah was given us and where our Prophets and the great spiritual teachers of the later days of our history lived.

14

J.C.A. COLONIZING

It was apparent that any plan of colonization was dependent on Russian cooperation in allowing Jews to leave the country and in making arrangements for the selection of emigrants. With this end in view Baron de Hirsch sent Arnold White, a Member of the British Parliament, to St. Petersburg as his representative to negotiate with the Russian Government, and commissioned him to travel through the Pale of Settlement to find out whether Jews living in ghettos there could be made fit for agricultural colonization in a pioneer country such as Argentina. White arrived in St. Petersburg in May and was received by Pobyedonostzev and several Ministers. These high dignitaries, incensed by the protests of the civilized world against Russian atrocities that they considered to be interference in their internal affairs, gave full vent to their hatred in their conversations with White and his party. Pobyedonostzev at one point said, "The Jew is a parasite. Remove him from the living organism in which and on which he exists and put this parasite on a rock—and he will die."

White visited Moscow, Kiev, Berdychev, Odessa, Kherson, and the Jewish agricultural colonies in South Russia.

Wherever he went he saw men who were "sober and industrious, efficient artisans whose physical weakness was merely the result of insufficient nourishment." He was more than convinced of the fitness of the Jews for colonization. "In short," he said, in his report, "the perverted type of Jew which had been painted to him in St. Petersburg was evolved from the inner consciousness of certain Orthodox statesmen, and has no existence in fact. If moral courage, hope, patience, temperance are fine qualities, then the Jews are a fine people. Such a people, under wise direction, is destined to make a success of any well-organized plan of colonization, whether in Argentina, Siberia, or South Africa."

White returned to St. Petersburg to negotiate for permission to organize emigration committees in Russia and to secure the necessary passports for the Jews to leave the country. He unfolded before the Russian authorities the far-reaching plans of Baron de Hirsch, who intended "to transplant 25,000 Jews to Argentina in the course of 1892 and henceforward to increase progressively the ratio of emigrants, so that in the course of twenty-five years, 3,250,000 Jews would be taken out of Russia." After months of discussion and deliberation, the Czarist government finally agreed to the plan, sanctioning the establishment of a Central Committee of the Jewish Colonization Association in St. Petersburg, with local committees in the great centers of Jewish population in the provinces. The Central Committee included many prominent Russian Jews, among them Baron G. Gunzburg, Baron David Gunzburg, M. I. S. Poliakoff, M. Sack, and the Messrs. Passower and Raffalovich, members of the St. Petersburg bar. David Feinberg of Konigsberg, well known and respected by Jewish communities throughout Russia, was appointed General Secretary to the Committee, charged with the responsibility of selecting the colonists who were to go to Argentina. The Russian authorities further promised to issue the emigrants free permits to leave the country, and to relieve them from military duty on condition that they never return to Russia. The Committee undertook to take care of all the details necessary to assure the safe departure of the colonists from the country.

Thus, at one man's insistence, the barriers that had for centuries held the Jews in the Pale of Settlement were broken down. No longer was it a crime for Jews to try to leave Russia! No longer was it necessary for them to steal across international borders! From now on Jews could leave the land of the Czars without risking the loss of their personal effects, and without physical danger! Had Baron de Hirsch accomplished little else for the betterment of his fellow Jews, this one act alone should have earned him their eternal gratitude.

Dr. Max J. Kohler, a director of the American Baron de Hirsch Fund, during Memorial Services held on April 25th, 1901, at the Baron de Hirsch Trade School in New York, said:

It required the large experience, the far-sighted acumen of a great financier and a man of world-wide renown and influence to open a new path of liberty and light, of self-emancipation and self-help to millions groaning under the yoke of oppression from without and within, and lay out the plan of salvation for a whole race on a scale such as Baron de Hirsch conceived of and carried into effect. It almost seems as if all the grand successes and privileges, the enviable friendship and companionship of princes he enjoyed, and even the sports and pastimes of the high life he indulged in, were but the means of fitting him for his great task, for an undertaking which no one else ever dreamt of, devising means and measures of education and elevating the Eastern Jews and rolling the shame and humiliation of centuries from their inner and outer life. While Baron de Hirsch had no sympathy or regard whatsoever for the Talmudic Jew and his learning, he was but carrying out one of the fundamental maxims of the Talmud when he insisted that the children of the poor should learn a trade, because training to self-support and self-respect is the only correct mode of offering aid and instruction to the helpless and downtrodden.

News of the planned exodus from Russia quickly spread over the civilized world, bringing joy and high expectations to some areas and consternation and concern to others. There was certain to be somewhat less than enthusiastic response from government authorities and Christian groups in the countries to which Baron de Hirsch intended to send his impoverished Russian Jews, and almost instantly protests were registered in many countries throughout the world that suspected that they were to be selected as targets for the emigration. One would scarcely expect, however, that the Jewish communities in these countries would protest. But, as with the integration movement that has swept the United States within the last several years, where most of the people in favor of integration expect it to take place in someone else's neighborhood, there was worldwide support among Jewish organizations for Baron de Hirsch's scheme only as long as the refugees were being shipped to some other country. Typical of this reaction is the protest of the Australian Jewish community as reported in the *London Jewish Chronicle*:

Baron de Hirsch's selection of the Anglo-Jewish As-

sociation to represent the Jewish community in England
in the distribution of his shares, may perhaps be traced
to an incident which occurred in connection with an
unfounded rumour of his intention to send a large number of Jewish emigrants to Australia. When the report
reached Melbourne it created immense excitement; the
press was up in arms, meetings were held in denuncia-
tion of the project, and the Melbourne Branch of the
Anglo-Jewish Association even went so far as to send a
resolution of protest to the parent body in London. To
this protest the Council sent a dignified and proper
reply, pointing out that it was the duty of Jews throughout the world to assist in sharing the burden cast upon
them by the persecution of Jews in Russia, totally re-
gardless of the feeling that might be entertained by
fellow-countrymen of other creeds. The protest of the
Melbourne Branch was communicated to Baron de
Hirsch by the Agent-General for Victoria in London,
and the Baron, unwilling to believe that views such as
were expressed in the resolution could be held by a
Jewish body, caused enquiries to be made at the London
office of the Association as to the authenticity of the
protest, and if true, the nature of the reply sent by
the Council. A copy of that reply was forwarded to
the Baron, who expressed his hearty appreciation of the
tone which the Council had assumed.

American Jewry, too, was concerned. The *New York
Herald* sent their Paris correspondent to question Baron
de Hirsch about a rumor that Pennsylvania had been
selected as the site of one of the colonies. The following
interview was reported in the April 29, 1891, issue of that
paper:

New York Herald, Editorial. April 29, 1891.

BARON DE HIRSCH'S PHILANTHROPY.
Our Paris correspondent has had a very interesting

talk with Baron de Hirsch, and sends the results to the *Herald's* readers by Commercial Cable.

A report having been published in certain papers that Baron de Hirsch, the great benefactor of the Jewish race, had arranged for the establishment of a Jewish colony in Pennsylvania, where the Jews who are being expelled from Russia might establish themselves, I called upon the Baron at his magnificent residence yesterday in the Rue de L'Elysée, for which he gave, it is said, five million francs.

Baron de Hirsch is a very active man. He begins receiving at eight o'clock in the morning, and for two hours his time is fully occupied with callers. He is a man of medium size, with a large moustache, which is turned upward, good features and dark brown eyes, full of kindliness and good nature. He speaks in a low tone, but with forcible expression. Such is a brief description of the man who has become so well known during the past few years.

In answer to my inquiry as to the Pennsylvania colony, he said, "No. It is not to be Pennsylvania. That is a mistake. I have just sent a commission to the Argentine Republic, and have decided to establish my first colony there, but later on, as the movement develops I shall send colonists to Brazil, LaPlata, and other South American countries."

"Why have you chosen the Argentine Republic?"

"Because the commission reported that there is excellent agricultural land there. I want none but the very best farming soil and we can get any quantity of it in the Argentine Republic. Already we have four hundred families established there, and they are doing very well."

"How are they occupied?"

"On the land. The colonization is entirely agricultural. No money is given for trade.

THE ANNUAL EXODUS.

"How many will you send?"

"The first year we will send one thousand, the next

year two thousand, and the third year three thousand, and so on up to ten thousand. They will receive assistance at first, but, of course, every attempt will be made that the colonies will become self-supporting as soon as possible.

"You had intended forming a colony in the United States, had you not?"

"Perhaps, but we thought they had enough Jews there already."

"You have read some articles concerning the Jews in the *Herald* of Russia, stating that they lived upon the Slavs?"

"All that is pure fanaticism, it is the work of the synod. They would act in the same manner toward Protestants, if they dared. The head of the Orthodox Church went to the Czar, saying, "You have five million Jews and eighty-five million orthodox subjects, one or the other must go." Thus it was that the Jews were cruelly driven away from all the trades and isolated, in districts where they could not live. There are thousands and thousands of them simply starving, and in abject misery. Such a condition of affairs could not exist in any other country except Russia."

"It is not true, then, that the Jews will not engage in agriculture?"

"They will engage in agriculture when admitted. In Russia they have not been given a chance."

"Will the Russian Government help the Jews to emigrate?"

"They want to get them over from the frontier that is all. They won't help them to pay their passage."

"Then your passage will form a very heavy item in your colonization scheme."

He added reflectively, "I suppose I shall spend all my money in this movement. But, after all, what is the use of money unless you do some good with it." And with these simple words the conversation ended and the man who is prepared to give fortunes away in aid of his poor fellow creatures hurried away to attend to the multitude of affairs awaiting his attention.

15

THE EXODUS

In May, 1892, the constitution of the Jewish Colonization Association was ratified by the Czar. Alarming
rumors of imminent persecutions, on the one hand, and
exaggerated news about the plans of Baron de Hirsch on
the other, resulted in huge masses of refugees flocking to
Berlin, Hamburg, Antwerp, and London, imploring to be
transferred to the United States or to the Argentinian
colonies. Everywhere Relief Committees were organized
rapidly, but there was no way of transporting the emigrants to their new homes, particularly to Argentina,
where the large territories purchased by de Hirsch were
not yet ready for the reception of colonists.

Baron de Hirsch issued a special appeal in pamphlet
form, printed in Yiddish and Russian, asking them to bide
their time, and warning that undue haste might bring down
the wrath of the Russian Government on their heads. The
pamphlet, which was sent to all Jewish communities in
Russian lands read:

> To my coreligionists in Russia—You know that I am
> endeavouring to better your lot. It is, therefore, my duty
> to speak plainly to you and to tell you that which it is
> necessary you should know.

236

I am aware of the reasons which oblige many of you to emigrate, and I will gladly do all in my power to assist you in your hour of distress. But you must make this possible for me. Your emigration must not resemble a headlong, reckless flight, by which the endeavour to escape from one danger ends in destruction.

You know that properly organised committees are shortly to be established in Russia, with the consent and under the supervision of the Imperial Russian Government. The duty of these committees will be to organise the emigration in a business-like way. All persons desirous of emigrating will have to apply to the local committees, who alone will be authorized to give you the necessary facilities.

Only those persons who have been selected by the committees can have the advantage of the assistance of myself and of those who are working with me. Any one who leaves the country without the concurrence of the committees will do so at his own risk, and must not count on any aid from me.

It is obvious that in the beginning the number of emigrants cannot be large; for not only must places of refuge be found for those who first depart, but necessary preparations be made for those who follow. Later on the emigration will be able to assume larger proportions.

Remember that I can do nothing for you without the benevolent and gracious support of the Imperial Russian Government.

In conclusion, I appeal to you. You are the inheritors of your fathers, who for centuries have suffered so much. Bear this inheritance yet awhile with equal resignation.

Have also further patience, and thus render it possible for those to help you who are anxious to do so.

I send you these words of warning and of encouragement in my own name and in the name of thousands of your coreligionists. Take them to heart and understand them.

May the good God help you and me, and also the many who work with us for your benefit with so much devotion.

(signed) *M. de Hirsch*

Baron de Hirsch was concerned, too, about overcrowding the countries to which his Russian protégés might emigrate and, of his own accord, and without waiting for restrictive immigration laws to be invoked, he took measures to regulate the exodus. He continually impressed his agents and the emigrants with the importance of directing their energies to handicrafts and agriculture so that they would become sturdy citizens in the countries in which they settled. He realized that colonizing, like planting a forest, required time and patience. He felt that as the colonies became firmly rooted in different parts of the world, they would draw greater and greater numbers from Russia, so that in one or two generations Russia would materially suffer from the loss of the energy and activity of her Jews, and would either fully stop the exodus by according full civil rights, to those who remained, or would fall, as did Spain, the logical victim of her own intolerance.

The following excerpt from the *New York World* presents a memorable picture of Baron de Hirsch as he was interviewed in 1891:

New York World Aug. 2, 1891

IS IT LIFE OR DEATH.
HOW MANY JEWS WILL EVER LEAVE RUSSIA ALIVE. BARON DE HIRSCH, THE JEWISH PHILAN- THROPIST SPEAKS IN AN INTERVIEW WITH A *WORLD* CORRESPONDENT. HE GIVES A GRAPHIC OUTLINE OF THE PRESENT CONDITION OF HIS

PEOPLE IN RUSSIA. HIS PLANS FOR PRESENT AID AND SPEEDY REMOVAL.—"IF ONLY I HAD THE TIME," HE LAMENTS BUT THE NEED IS IMMINENT, AND HIS COLONIZATION PLANS CANNOT BE CARRIED OUT IN A DAY—OTHER INTERVIEWS—DISTRESSING SCENES—RUSSIAN INHUMANITY.

The policy of persecution which the Russian Government has adopted against the Jewish subjects is engaging the attention of the civilized world. Whatever the motives which have prompted it, there can be no doubt of the relentless barbarity of the Russian Government. Proofs of this are being accumulated every day, and it is plainly seen that the persecution is nothing short of persecution death.

The Czar denies to his subjects the right to emigrate. That is granted only as a favor. And yet hundreds of thousands of Jewish people are being driven into the towns in the Pale of Settlement with no prospect before them save starvation. But even if the autocrat of all the Russias could be induced to facilitate the expatriation of a people whose extermination he has decreed, and if the corrupt officials of Russia could be compelled to waive their privilege of despoiling them from depression, whither shall they go? England is growing alarmed over the number that have come to her already, and the United States looks askance to an invasion of Russian Jews, and yet the migration has been thus far but a fraction of what it must be if the towns of the old Polish provinces are to be kept from becoming vast charnel houses, and famine and pestilence are to be prevented from counting more victims than a great war.

In this hour of their supreme need, a man of their own race has arisen for the deliverance of the Jews of Russia, if the Czar will only allow them to be saved. He has millions ready to devote to the task which he has undertaken, and he has a plan large enough to effect the desired end if due time only be given to its execution. With a view to ascertaining what this scheme was, a *World* correspondent called upon Baron de Hirsch. The owner of millions and a friend of the Prince of Wales is not easy of access, but the interview was secured, and the Baron has expressed his views.

THE BARON.

An arrangement was made with Dr. Sonnefeld, the director of the Baron's Bureau de Bienfaisance, 31 rue de Bellechasse, Paris, who promised to secure this interview with the Baron in London, and fortified with a berth with M. Furth, Baron de Hirsch's secretary, the correspondent was to meet him at the Hotel Albemarle, Picadilly. When the correspondent called the Baron was engaged with a visitor. A few moments and he was admitted to his sitting room. It is on the second floor of the hotel, with two windows looking out on Albemarle St. Baron de Hirsch was sitting at his small table, which was now littered with his morning's mail. He rose, and without offering his hand, bowed slightly, and motioned me to a chair close at hand. He is a compactly built man of fifty-three or four, standing about five feet ten and who would be up to the beam of 170 lbs. He is square shouldered, and with a very slight protuberance in his abdominal section. The face of Baron de Hirsch is not a notably strong one. His clean shaven face is ruddy, and his head pretty bald on top, only a few silvery hairs clipping out from his reddish scalp. The rest of his hair is thick, strong and black, and plentifully sown with white. His forehead is large and very slightly retreated, while projecting over his smooth well marked eyebrows. His eyes, large, round and brilliant, are of a clear greenish shade, with the white of the eye balls, showing a slight tendency to be blood-shot. His nose is a well shaped aquiline feature, broad at the base of the nostrils. A heavy crinkling moustache also plentifully interspersed with gray, adorned the upper lip of his moderately wide mouth.

His teeth are large, regular, and of a yellowish tinge.
His hands are neither large, or small, the fingers being
a little square at the extremities, and the smooth skin
of his hands was marked with a few pale freckles. His
feet are small and well shaped.

Such was the first personal appearance of Baron de
Hirsch, as he stood and extended the hospitality of a
chair. He wore a suit of plain, slate colored cloth, the
coat being a "cut away," open in front. A small margin
of white pique showed at the neck of his waist-coat, and
he wore snowy "spats" with his brilliant patent leather
shoes. His neck scarf was a steel colored silk "ascot,"
with a small pin, representing a running grey-hound, in
tiny diamonds. He wore no watch chains and his hands
were without rings. His dress was exceedingly quiet and
simple, and nothing more than a clerk on a $1,000 sal-
ary would wear in America. One feature of the Baron's
hands was the shapely nails which were manicured so
that they glistened like crystal.

"Baron, I would like to get some idea of your scheme
for relieving the Russian exiles," I said, as I seated myself across from him.

"Oh it is not such an enormous one," he replied
easily, speaking in English, and with little accent and
perfect fluency. His voice was rich and full, pitched in
a rather deep tone, and his utterance was slightly thick.
"The only difficulty is that I have not time enough. If
I could devote five or ten years to it I could accomplish
it in full. But there is need of instant action. They are
coming out too fast; Russia is treating these people
with the greatest severity. She wants to get rid of them,
but it is like shutting the door on people in a room, and
then ordering them out. I said to them: what do you
want. If you wish to kill them it would be quicker and
less brutal to do so at once by electricity." My object is
to help these poor people out."

"Have the Russians met your overtures in a friendly
way"?

"Yes, they are willing to allow these measures of

relief to be extended to them. My idea is to get 100,000 of them to Argentina, settled there on farms, or engaged in pursuits of artisans. They are poor. It is work or die with them. I have given a good deal of study to this question and there is no doubt that they will be able to use their capacity as agriculturalists or builders. There is a settlement of them already there in Argentine. Many of them who did not know how to put one stone upon the other have in a short time become such successful builders that they have been engaged by others to put up buildings."

THE ARGENTINE REPUBLIC

"Why did you select the Argentine Republic, as your colonizing scheme, Baron?"

"Because the climate there is very temperate, and there are very large stretches of land, which can be secured for farming purposes. They can put up any sort of a dwelling at first, which will be sufficient protection at the start. The trouble is that the land there is in the hands of different owners, so that to secure it these individual proprietors have to be dealt with. There are no lands there to be taken by colonists through the claim of first occupancy. And the titles are not as clear as they might be where some of these native land owners hold hundreds of acres.

"My idea is to put the matter upon a business basis," the Baron went on, "by organizing a company, which shall advance what is necessary to the immigrants to secure the land, and set it out with seed and vegetable. With good crops they could repay in a year the help that would be thus advanced to them. This makes them independent and saves them from being mendicants.

"If they get well rooted there and comfortably settled, they will write such letters back to their relatives and friends that others will follow in the lead of those pioneers. They would exercise a force like a magnet in drawing the rest of their people there. It would be an impossibility in transplanting five millions anywhere."

"I see that Egypt has been suggested by a writer in the Jewish Chronicle as a good place for these Russian exiles. Did you consider that as a possible field?"

"The climate is too warm" said the Baron at once. "And then the best land for agricultural purposes there has already been pre-empted."

"Is your knowledge of these people in Russia derived in the main from the report which Mr. Arnold White made to you of their character, condition, and ability?" I inquired.

"I knew already of their capacity, and I knew how they were treated there," answered Baron de Hirsch. "But, Mr. Arnold White's report has confirmed me in my views and belief. I selected him to go there because he is a man of philanthropic sentiments himself. And then," added the Baron with a slight smile, "Mr. White is anti-Semitic in his feelings and prejudices, so I could count on getting a report from him which would not be colored by too much interest in their favor."

"What do you think of the aggressive spirit on the part of the Russian Government?"

"It is a spirit of fanaticism. It is largely due to Pobyedonostzev, and is based on religious intolerance. He was the tutor of the Czar, and has a great influence upon him. He is in the Russian Church, and he represents to the Czar, that the Jews are undermining the people. Why I have known of those who have served as soldiers for twenty years or more, and who have been decorated for their fidelity, to be hunted out of their homes and driven off."

"Baron, I would like, if it does not seem an indelicate question, to know what sum you are prepared to devote to this purpose of assisting these exiles."

AN ENORMOUS SUM.

"I should be willing to spend between $16,000,000 or $17,000,000 for this purpose," replied this millionaire philanthropist, as quietly as if he were speaking of $100,000. "It is my desire to spend my wealth in doing something to make the lot of the miserable easy. If one could take his money with him where he went he might not care to dispose of it in this way," he said, with dry humor, "but it seems much better to me to look to its beneficial distribution myself than to leave it to be disposed of by bequests. I have no family," he added, with a touch of regret in his voice. "I had a son, but he died," he added with perfect simplicity. "I have two adopted sons, but they need no help. So there are only my wife and myself."

"Is it true that the Russian Government relieves these people if they are baptized, of all disabilities?"

"No, they do not want them to be baptized," said Baron de Hirsch. "But the best religion a man can have is to lead an honest life, and I want to help them do that. There are a number of wealthy men who would be glad to assist in my plans and scheme, which looks to the alleviation of this misery. There will be no difficulty in finding the men to assist them. The meeting at the Guildhall in December, where the Duke of Westminster and the Earl of Meath headed the meeting called by the Lord Mayor at an earlier stage of the persecutions, was resented by Russia as foreign interference with her administration of her own domestic affairs. At that time it was thoroughly thought by many here that the Czar would not be fully cognizant of the measures which were being carried out against the Jews. But it is known now that he fully endorses the treatment of them."

"The main trouble is having so many of these Russian exiles to deal with at once. It is difficult to look after the large host at the same time, though I am doing everything possible to enable them to escape from the hardships of their fate. I want to help them to such conditions and environment that they will lead an honest, independent existence. Though the Argentine is not wholly free of the prejudice against them, the conditions there seem to me favorable. They are so poor, these exiles that, if they are put into a position where labor will produce profits to themselves and their families, there would be no doubt they will embrace the opportunity presented to them and profit by it. Mr. White has told of the excellent conditions of the agricultural Jews in Russia in the province of Cherson before they were abolished in the reign of Czar Nicholas. They present a marked contrast with the people who have lived in cities and towns."

"When these poor fellows get into cities they are used as they use them down in Whitechapel. A "sweater" gets hold of them and gives them a shilling a week for their work, and then gets eight or nine shillings a week for it himself. Mr. White is familiar with this phase of life here, and has given testimony of what these unfortunate men have to endure. How can they support families on a pittance of that kind? If they have agricultural pursuits they can establish a home for themselves and secure some of the comforts of life, as well as the bare necessities."

"Jews have an abundance of fortitude," he continued. "That is the reason they can bear so much and will not break down. When with this inexhaustible energy, they find themselves put where it is merely a question of honest labor to provide for themselves decently as opposed to starvation and misery, they will surely respond."

"And now," said Baron de Hirsch, rising and casting a glance at the letters on the table, "I must attend to some matters which call to my consideration, and you will have to excuse me. I have already given you more time than I expected," he said, as he accompanied me to the door. "Are you an American?"

In my answering that I had that distinction, he said: "I am interested in America. I am going over there to see it."

He extended his hand, and bade me goodbye with greater cordiality than he had manifested at the beginning of the interview.

16

ENGLAND

Perhaps it was because their son Lucien had been so deeply attached to England that they began to think of making their home there. Or perhaps it was because Maurice felt that his close friendship with the Prince of Wales, so well demonstrated to the world in the incident of the Club de la Rue Royale when the Prince resigned because of the blackballing of Baron de Hirsch, would assure them a prominent place in London society. In any event, they soon began to spend more and more time there, even though the headquarters for their major philanthropic undertakings was still located in Paris.

The Prince of Wales had often said that he was attracted to Baron de Hirsch by his enthusiasm for the turf and for his wide knowledge of financial affairs throughout Europe. It was common gossip, however, that the friendship ripened when the Baron carried the Prince along with him on some of his more successful speculations, and there were even rumors that they planned to form a partnership, an investment company to be known as Hirsch and Wales. Queen Victoria is supposed to have squelched this idea when she interceded with her son to stop this venture. Although the Prince was a frequent guest of the

Baron's, especially at his estate in Hungary where he said the hunt was the best on the Continent, Baron de Hirsch was often snubbed by some of the socialites who traveled in the same circles as the Prince of Wales and his coterie, but who simply did not like him or his social-climbing tactics. It is curious, too, that the Prince was equally friendly with the Rothschilds, who never mixed socially with Baron de Hirsch. In fact, they did not mix at all. It was well known that each studiously avoided any business dealings in which the other was involved, their hostility even extending to their philanthropies, for they were known not to have been interested in each other's pet charitable projects. It is interesting, too, that Maurice and Clara were never able to attain the position in the social world that the Rothschilds held almost without trying. Sir Philip Magnus, in his biography of King Edward VII, says of Baron de Hirsch, "He was richer than the Rothschilds, but unlike them, never assimilated socially. He was excluded from the Jockey Club, cold shouldered or, at best, was treated with mortifying condescension by most archdukes and great magnates and never received at Court." Clara and Maurice de Hirsch, if they were to be accepted in London's most exclusive social circles, would have to offer some attraction other than themselves and their money. The Prince of Wales became that attraction.

To launch their introduction to London society, Maurice and Clara acquired the famous Bath House, built in 1821 at 82 Picadilly on the site of the old original Bath House. It was one of the finest mansions in Picadilly, an area of fine mansions. The English Rothschilds all lived there—Leopold at Five Hamilton Place, Alfred at One Seamore Place. It was here that Disraeli, who had become

Lord Beaconsfield when he was retired as Prime Minister, lived with Alfred de Rothschild. Lord Ferdinand Rothschild resided at 143 Picadilly, his sister at 142, and Lord Mayer Rothschild at 107. Lionel de Rothschild lived at 148 Picadilly, next door to Apsley House, which had been the Duke of Wellington's residence.

Bath House had once been the home of Lady Harriet Montagu, daughter of the sixth Earl of Sandwich, who had made it a literary center through her friendship with many notable writers of the day. Maurice and Clara tried to revive the tradition of Bath House as a literary center but they were not successful, probably because neither of them could claim a real interest in literature. Bath House was to regain its reputation as a social center, however, because of the stupendous parties and entertainments they gave there, with the Prince of Wales, the Duke of Devonshire, Lord Curzon, Earl Grey, and many other highly-placed notables as principal attractions. For their first dinner party they were able to send out invitations "to meet their Royal Highnesses, the Prince and Princess of Wales."

More likely than not, the real reason for making the move to England was economic. Every banking center in Europe was constantly being disturbed by threats of war. The Napoleonic upheavals, the revolutions of 1848, the Russo-Turkish War, the Franco-Prussian War, and the many other localized conflicts had taught the money powers of Europe that the most logical place for the safe-keeping of capital was London's Lombard Street. The British Empire was stable, its government sound. It had the world's largest mercantile marine and the most powerful navy. No country in the history of the world had ever occupied a position in international trade and commerce such as England now held. International capital was transferred into English funds, deposited in English banks or invested in British Empire undertakings, and the British pound sterling had become the standard of currency around the world.

Paul H. Emden, in *Money Powers in Europe in the 19th and 20th Century*, says,

> An account in London was a necessity for the big merchants overseas and for the banks of the whole globe, and was the pride of the wealthy private citizen on the Continent. It was a matter of common knowledge that the German Government kept a very considerable amount with the London Joint-Stock Bank and that the Hapsburgs maintained important deposits here. This country had the most stable of all governments, while the thrones of all other countries were exposed to constant changes . . . and so Lombard Street which received money from one part of the world and lent it to the other, became, and perhaps in no other way could have become, a world conception.

Baron de Hirsch had brought Ernest Cassel into his company as his chief assistant and right-hand man in 1884, and it was at his insistence that he transferred his major holdings to English banks. It was at his insistence, too, that the Anglo-Jewish Association was chosen to be the principal holder of stock in the Jewish Colonization Association when Baron de Hirsch incorporated that organization in 1891. Cassel, who was to become the famous Sir Ernest Cassel of World War I fame, was the son of Jacob Kassel, who conducted a small bank in Cologne. Since 1874 he had been with Bischoffsheim and Goldschmidt, where he was principally involved in handling railway financing in which the bank was interested. One of

his outstanding successes in this capacity was the reconstruction of the Erie Railway Company, operating in New
York and Ohio, which was financed by Bischoffsheim and
Goldschmidt and which had failed in 1875. When he
joined Baron de Hirsch, he not only lent his brilliant
talents to the Oriental Railway Company but he entered
into a number of other activities in partnership with de
Hirsch. One of the first of these was in a syndicate with
Kuhn, Loeb and Company of New York, in which he
worked closely with Jacob H. Schiff in reorganizing the
Louisville and Nashville Railway Company. The part-
nership also took a leading interest in the Mexican Central
Railway and in 1893 negotiated a large loan for the
Mexican Government. Ironically, however, it was in
Egypt that Cassel earned his reputation as an empire
builder, for he is generally credited with being the finan-
cial genius behind the reconstruction of modern Egypt.
Emden says of him,

> Ernest Cassel fits into no category and cannot be
> classified under any rubric; he was not a banker nor
> the head of a great business house nor did he preside
> over any board, and yet for very many years he was
> the strongest European financier. He combined the art
> of a finished diplomatic negotiator with the gifts of a
> never failing visionary; he lacked all sense for any kind
> of speculation and, perfectly straightforward in his
> methods, was innocent of the slightest trickery. It was
> his business to make money, and he made it on an
> immense scale—the main part of it in Egypt, but only
> through enriching the whole country itself, not by ex-
> tracting money from it—and the financial genius of this
> immigrant was never directed to any other aim than
> the service of the Empire. The enormous fortune which
> Cassel made in a relatively short time gave him an

extraordinary power over men and institutions, and to his credit it must be said that this power was not once misused by him.

Ernest Cassel kept up the friendship with the Prince of Wales that Baron de Hirsch had started and an intimacy developed between the two that lasted until the King died on May 10, 1910. Two weeks before ascending the throne, Edward assisted at the wedding of Cassel's daughter Maud to Wilfrid Ashley, and later, as King, he was godfather to their daughter, Edwina. Immediately after the Baron's death in 1896, the Prince turned over to Ernest Cassel the difficult problem of bringing order into his monetary affairs, which de Hirsch had been handling. So well did Ernest Cassel handle this assignment that, when the Prince ascended the throne on the death of Queen Victoria, the Commission that was appointed to inquire into the financial position of the new sovereign heard a report by Sir Deighton Probyn, official manager of the King's finances, that "Edward VII had ascended the throne unencumbered by a single penny of debt, which may safely be placed to the credit of Cassel as the advisor behind the throne."

As Sir Ernest Cassel he worked tirelessly in an effort to stave off World War I by promoting a lasting peace between England and Germany, and he established the Anglo-German Foundation for that purpose. In Germany his efforts were supported by Albert Ballin, founder of the German Mercantile Marine, a conforming Jew who also worked fruitlessly for the establishment of good relations between his native country and England.

Ernest Cassel, the son of Jacob Kassel, an orthodox Jew of Cologne, became a Catholic as a result of a promise made to his dying wife, to whom he had been married just three years—from 1878 to 1881. She was Catholic and she wished her husband to accept the Catholic faith, which he did after much study of Catholic dogma. He never became a practising Catholic, however, and few people knew that he had converted from Judaism to Catholicism. The story is told that when he was being sworn in to the Privy Council as Sir Ernest Cassel, the clerk of the Council did not know whether he was still a Jew or if he had become a Christian, and he was not sure which Bible he should have on hand with which to administer the oath. Many people were surprised years later when, on his death in 1921, funeral services were held in the Jesuit church of the Immaculate Conception in London.

It did not take Maurice and Clara long to become thoroughly familiar with English manners and customs. Their sojourns in London were more and more frequent and of longer duration, and attending the different sporting meets in England became the Baron's favorite pastime. His racing stable ranked among the first in the United Kingdom, and the use to which he put his winnings at the races contributed more than a little to his popularity in turf circles, for he let it be known that "Baron de Hirsch's horses raced for charity." He made it a rule that all his winnings should go to the London hospitals. When, in 1892, his horse La Fleche won the three major racing events of the year, the Oaks, the St. Leger, and the 1,000 Guineas, he turned over the entire $200,000 he had won to be divided among the Middlesex hospital, the Great Ormond Street Hospital for Children, and the Kilburn Refuge of Mercy.

Baron de Hirsch took no active part in English politics

and little is known of his party affiliations, but an interesting incident throws some light on his attitude toward the socialist movement that was sweeping over Europe. It was told by a correspondent of the London *Daily Chronicle,* who wrote in the issue of April 24, 1896, after the Baron's death,

> On one occasion I accompanied Baron de Hirsch to one of those vast meetings in Hyde Park, where 80,000 or 100,000 people demanded the abolition of the House of Lords, or some other political boon. After marvelling at the absence of troops or police, we drew up to listen to one of the Socialist orators who was addressing the crowd in a really able manner. After listening for some time, Hirsch turned to me and said, "I agree with every word that man has said. I will talk to him." And so he did, and an excellent thing it was to see the Not-have and the Have arguing over the wrongs of the people.

The same article goes on to say:

> From the time that Baron de Hirsch became partially a resident in London, the heads of Jewish philanthropic institutions have made repeated attempts to obtain from him contributions towards their respective funds. With one or two exceptions, all these attempts proved failures. The Baron invariably replied to these persistent applications, made sometimes through friends whom he would have wished to oblige, that he was not as the *London Chronicle* reported, "disposed to relieve the Jewish community in England of any of its obligations for the maintenance of its poor and its benevolent institutions. Mr. S. Simons, Chairman of the Loan Committee of the Board of Guardians, twice obtained donations of 500 pounds from the Baron, the last occasion being less than a fortnight back, and it speaks

well for Mr. Simons' diplomacy, as Mr. B. L. Cohen informed the Board meeting last week, that he had succeeded where others of his colleagues, some of them personally known to the Baron, had failed. The Anglo-Jewish Association was another exception, the Baron having given annual donations since he became a Vice-President, and a third was the Jewish Convalescent Home, of which his niece, Mrs. H. L. Bischoffsheim, is President.

In connection with the Anglo-Jewish Association, we may recall the fact that to this body belongs the credit of having been the only institution in England which had the advantage of Baron de Hirsch's presence at a public gathering. It was at the annual meeting of the Association, held on the 9th of July, 1893, that the late Sir Julian Goldsmid entered the Council Room of the United Synagogue, accompanied by a gentleman who was a stranger to all but one or two individuals in the room. Great was the interest aroused, when Sir Julian announced that the visitor was no other than the great Baron de Hirsch. During the proceedings, the Baron was asked by the President to address the meeting, which he did in English, and in the following terms:

"I have to thank the Chief Rabbi for the kind way in which he has referred to me in connection with the unfortunate persecutions in Russia. I do the best, all I can, to alleviate the sufferings of my oppressed brethren. The beginning of any task is always difficult, and beset with many dangers, but I hope for a successful issue to the scheme of colonisation in Argentina. It has been said of the Jews that they do not make good and useful citizens, and that they are nothing but traders. I want to prove that assertion untrue. Argentina has been selected as a land in which to form Jewish colonies consisting of persecuted refugees, and I have asked my agents only to select those who are likely to make good colonists. In this way we will endeavor to help the scheme on to success. Of course I know it is impossible to remove the whole of the Jewish population from

Russia. I was too well aware of the insurmountable difficulties of such an undertaking. What I hope to see is a great number of the refugees prosperous and happy as agriculturists, and then by pointing to them as a proof that Jews can be good and useful citizens, we hope to prevail upon Russia to discontinue its disastrous system of persecution.

"In the lands where Jews have been permitted to acquire landed property, where they have found opportunity to devote themselves to agriculture, they have proved themselves excellent farmers. For example, in Hungary they form a very large part of the tillers of the soil; and this fact is acknowledged to such an extent that the high Catholic clergy in Hungary almost exclusively have used as tenants Jews on mortmain properties, and almost all large land holders give preference to the Jews on account of their industry, their rectitude and their dexterity. These are facts that cannot be hidden and that have force; so that the anti-Semitic movement, which for a long time flourished in Hungary, must expire. It will expire because every one sees that so important a factor in the productive activity of the country, especially in agriculture—cannot be spared. My own personal experience, too, has led me to recognize that the Jews have very good ability in agriculture. I have seen this personally in the Jewish agricultural colonies of Turkey; and the reports from the expedition that I have sent to the Argentine Republic plainly show the same fact. These convictions led me to my activity to better the unhappy lot of the poor, downtrodden Jews; and my efforts shall show that the Jews have not lost the agricultural qualities that their forefathers possessed. I shall try to make them a new home in different lands where as free farmers, on their own soil, they can make themselves useful to the country."

It has been said that the best history of nineteenth-century England is to be found in the cartoons of *Punch,* and a citation from this comic paper may give a more vivid impression of what people felt about Baron de Hirsch and his exodus plan than a sheaf of solid newspaper articles. In *Punch* of September 28, 1891, a cartoon appeared in which the Baron, with his elegant clothes and heavy moustache, is leading a horde of grimy, battered Russian refugees toward the Promised Land. Accompanying the picture were the following verses:

The Modern Moses . . . Money-lenders of the village
　　　　　　　　　　Now will turn to honest tillage
　　　　　　　　　　Wring their sustenance with toil
　　　　　　　　　　From New Jersey's stubborn soil.

　　　　　　　　　　Hardly even Hirsch's money
　　　　　　　　　　Will extract the milk and honey
　　　　　　　　　　From mosquito-haunted sand
　　　　　　　　　　Of New Jersey's Promised Land.

The *London Jewish Chronicle,* in the obituary issue of April 24, 1896, gives a complete report of the objectives of the Jewish Colonization Association, and the make-up of its first board:

> The nominal capital of the Company is £2,000,000 (the stamp duty paid being £2,000), divided into 20,000 shares of £100 each. The Baron took 19,900 shares, and on the formation of the Company one share was taken by each of the following gentlemen: Lord Rothschild, the late Sir Julian Goldsmid, Mr. Ernest Joseph Cassel of Messrs. Bischoffsheim and Goldschmidt (then Baron de Hirsch's London representative), Mr. F. D. Mocatta, M. S. H. Goldschmidt, President of the Alliance Israélite Universelle, M. Salomon Reinach, of Paris (described in the Memorandum as "Attaché des Musées"), and Mr. Benjamin L. Cohen, M. P. We published at the time the full text

of the Memorandum of Association; it will suffice if we reproduce here the main objects for which the Company was established:

To assist and promote the emigration of Jews from any part of Europe or Asia, and principally from countries in which they may for the time being be subjected to any special taxes or political or other disabilities, to any other parts of the world, and to form and establish colonies in various parts of North and South America and other countries for agricultural, commercial, and other purposes.

To purchase and acquire, by donation or otherwise, from any Governments, States, municipal or local authorities, corporations, firms, or persons, any territories, lands, or other property, or interests in or rights over territories, lands, or other property, in any parts of the world, and all concessions, powers, and privileges which may be necessary or convenient for developing the resources of the same and rendering the same available for purposes of colonization.

To accept gifts, donations, and bequests of money and other property, on the terms of the same being applied for all or some one or more of the purposes of the company, or on such other terms as may be consistent with the objects of the company.

Baron de Hirsch throughout took the utmost personal interest in every matter, even of the minutest character, affecting the development of his great work. Whether in Austria, London, or Paris (where the administrative work is carried on), he allowed nothing to escape his personal attention or his personal control. On one occasion he came into direct contact with a small group of emigrant agriculturists from Bessarabia, who passed through London on their way to South America. It was on the 1st of March, 1893, that the Baron received the party at his residence, Bath House, Piccadilly. With him were the Chief Rabbi, Mr. F. D. Mocatta, Mr. H. G. Lousada, the London representative of the Colonisation Association, Mr. Arnold White, whom the Baron had in 1891 sent on a mission

to Russia to pave the way for the colonisation movement, Dr. Sonnenfeld, the Baron's Secretary in Paris,
and Herr David Feinberg and Herr Rapoport, who
had accompanied the emigrants from Russia. The interview lasted upwards of two hours, during the greater
part of which Baron de Hirsch went most closely with
his protégés into details connected with their future.
He earnestly impressed on them the duty of continuing
steadfast Jews, faithful to their grand religion, and
promised that every facility would be afforded them for
carrying out all its observances. In this connection we
may reproduce the telegram which Baron de Hirsch
himself caused to be sent to us, to contradict statements
alleged to have been made by him to an interviewer.

Baron de Hirsch has given too many proofs of his
devotion to Judaism and to the Jews to be suspected of
hostility to the cause he has defended with so much
spirit and supported with such munificence. Profoundly
afflicted at seeing so many Jews reduced to extreme
misery, by religious or racial hatred, he desired simply
and plainly to tell the anti-Semites that in persecuting
the Jews they were going directly against the object
they seek, viz., an assimilation more or less complete:
that it is not by violent proceedings they can attain this
end, but, on the contrary, persecution stimulates religious sentiments. The Baron declared: remove every
barrier, admit your Jewish compatriots to every right
and advantage of social life, and there will be more
chances for effecting the fusion which you appear desirous of witnessing. This is what happens in France and
England, and indeed, wherever Jews enjoy the same
rights as their fellow-citizens.

In recognition of his confidence in the Anglo-Jewish
Association, the Council elected Baron de Hirsch a Vice-
President, this being the only office he held in any Jewish
institution except the Alliance Israélite Universelle, on
which he had a seat at the Central Committee.

17

ARGENTINA

The report brought back by the Lowenthal Commission had painted a glowing picture of Argentina, pointing out that "the country has a population estimated at only 2,500,000 people in an area as great as all of Central and Western Europe combined, abounding in remarkably fertile plains, or pampas, with rich alluvial soil four or five feet thick formed by decay of luxurious vegetation. The province of Buenos Aires is the most populous of the 14 provinces, with over half a million population, largely European, attracted there by the fertility of the soil and the prosperity and free institutions of the Republic. In 1891," the report went on, "there were 212,000 people of foreign birth occupying 2,000,000 acres of land in the province of Buenos Aires alone, owning 35 million sheep and multitudes of horned cattle acquired in a few years by men who, on arrival, did not own a dollar. . . . Twelve lines of steamers run to Europe, the passage occupying 29 days. The Republic has about 4,150 miles of railway and 13,619 miles of telegraph, besides Atlantic cable communication with London. The government is a Federal Republic, modelled on the Constitution of the United States, except that the ministry is responsible to

Congress, an adverse vote in the Senate and House leading to the formation of a new Cabinet. The laws are the
same for all, native and foreign; immigrants are free to
naturalize themselves as Argentines or maintain their
foreign nationality."

By August, 1891, the Jewish Colonization Association
had acquired 3,000 square leagues of land, roughly 17
million acres, for which it paid $1,300,000. Three thou-
sand colonists arrived in 1891. Eight hundred were sent
to Moiseville, a colony that had been established by a
group of Russian Jews in 1890 and was now being reorganized by the Jewish Colonization Association; about
a thousand went to Mauricio (named after Baron de
Hirsch), while the colony of Clara in the Province of
Entre Rios, named after the Baroness, absorbed 1,500 of
the settlers.

Dr. Lowenthal was named the first Director; almost
immediately he ran into trouble with the colonists. He
was replaced shortly by Dr. Adolfo Roth, who also experienced difficulty in working with the early immigrants.
Misunderstandings and distrust characterized his relationship with the colonists and he was soon recalled. Most
of the troubles experienced by both administrations were
caused by the religious practices of the settlers, whose
background of orthodox Judaism ran headlong into conflict with the assimilationist ideas the administrators tried
to introduce right away. The colonists, for religious
reasons as much as for any other, wanted to live in villages, so that they could enjoy the same sort of communal
life built around the synagogue as they had had for centuries in the ghettos of Europe, and they did not like the
pattern generally followed throughout the Americas of
living in farm homes miles apart from each other. The

administrators, on the other hand, objected to the colonists living in villages similar to the Russian style, because too much time would be lost going from home to farm and back.

The third and most successful administrator was Colonel Albert Edward Goldsmid, an Indian Jew, born in Puna, Bombay, India, about 1845. He was a professional army man, to whom leave of absence was granted by the British War Office so that he could accept the appointment as Administrator of the Argentine Colonies. Colonel Goldsmid arrived in Argentina in April, 1892, and at once set to work organizing a system of self-government in the colonies, eliminating the causes of friction and the irritations that had characterized the previous administrations. When he retired from this position in 1894 to become commander of the Welsh regimental district of Cardiff, troubles developed again and Baron de Hirsch decided to establish a Board of Management in Buenos Aires, consisting of three experts, two of whom came from the Alliance Israélite Universelle. Samuel Hirsch had formerly been Director of the Alliance Agricultural School at Jaffa, while David Cazes, noted Moroccan educator and writer, had been Headmaster of the Alliance's famous school at Tunis. Even these outstanding administrators, with years of experience in Jewish colonizing efforts, were unable to cope with the religious problems; contradictory stories continued to find their way back to Europe of the dissatisfaction of the farmers with the administration and of the administration with the farmers. Rumors were widespread of hundreds of defections from the colonies. Unable to adapt themselves to an agrarian way of life, the immigrants had deserted the farm colonies and gone to the cities.

Baron de Hirsch, in an article entitled "The New Moses," which appeared in the *London Daily Graphic* on July 7, 1894, is quoted by the author, Lucien Wolf, as saying:

"The initial difficulties have been overcome, though some were greater than had been anticipated. My hands were forced by the suddenness of the Russian persecutions.

"You must remember that with all the success I have had, I am only at the beginning of my enterprise. The land I have will not accommodate more than from 10,000 to 15,000 people. And what is that? A trifle. I must have a larger tract of land. A special committee will shortly be dispatched by me to study a scheme of colonization on a large scale, and to purchase three or four million acres at least. Meanwhile, I shall continue to send out four to five thousand people a year, and in two years' time I hope to be able to invite the leading representatives of the European and American press to visit my colonies and see for themselves whether the Jews aren't fit for something better than mere trade."

"Is there any hope of brighter days for the Jews in Russia?" Lucien Wolf asked. "None whatever—at least for a very long time. The persecution of dissenters is inherent in the present state of things in Russia. But when my scheme is a success it will bring shame to the cheek of every Russian. The time will come when I shall have from three to four hundred thousand Jews flourishing on their homesteads in the Argentine, peaceful and respected citizens, a valuable source of national wealth and stability. Then we shall be able to point to them and contrast them with their brethren who have been demoralised by persecution. What will the Jew-haters have to say then? I have made up my mind not to stop in this work. If my energies or my fortune could accomplish it, believe me, the whole Jewish population of Russia would be taken out of the country."

The mounting criticism of the whole Jewish Colonization Association program and the many contradictory and
conflicting reports he was getting from Argentina were of
great concern to Baron de Hirsch and he decided to get a
firsthand analysis from people he trusted and in whose
opinions he could place complete reliance. He delegated
David Feinberg, Director of the Central Emigration
Association, who had originally made the selections in
Russia of the colonists who were sent to Argentina, and
Dr. Sonnenfeld, Secretary of the Paris office of the Jewish
Colonization Association, to go to Argentina, and make a
complete survey of conditions there, and to determine
when and where more colonies could be established. The
findings of these two indicated that immigration should be
stopped until the colonists already settled in Argentina
were completely absorbed, with the colonies functioning
properly. Feinberg issued the following statement to the
press:

> My general impression is most favourable to our
> colonists. It was with joy that when I passed from one
> colony to another I was able to convince myself of the
> marvellous aptitude of our co-religionists for the hard
> work of the fields. It was I who selected the colonists
> in Russia. They were for the most part, small mer-
> chants, shopkeepers, subordinate employees, and in
> general people who had never been engaged in agri-
> cultural pursuits. But evidently the fault, if fault there
> was, was not theirs. And the proof is that when they
> have been given the means of cultivating the soil, they
> have shown a zeal and ardour which, in less than two
> years have made them suitable agriculturists.
> In the course of my journeys through the colonies,
> I came across several families whom I had personally
> known in Russia. I recognized them no longer. It was
> not the lean and pitiful-looking Jew, with hollow cheeks

and bent shoulders, as though a heavy load pressed on him, with a visage full of an indefinable expression of sadness and constant care, in a word it was no longer the man seeking his daily bread without ever gaining it, whom I saw before me. These people now cultivate their land, and every evening they make an inspection of their fields, on horseback, as though they were born agriculturists. The free and healthy air of the country, physical labour and etc., have completely transformed them. It is comforting to observe how rapidly this assimilation has been effected. I did not believe that the Jewish peddler could be so quickly transformed into an agriculturist. To-day the doubt is no longer possible. And it is here that Baron de Hirsch's work is so grandiose.

I will not hide the fact that there are some exceptions in the Jewish colonies; there are people who will not take to work. But this element exists only in the proportion of 10% to 15%. We have made it a rule to eliminate this element from our colonies, and in this respect we are absolutely pitiless, for it injures the development of our operations and everyone will agree that the general interest must be considered first.

The colonists are divided into two categories—those who have been established for two or three years, living in the larger colonies, numbering about three hundred families, and about eight hundred families of newcomers. The first category leaves nothing to be desired. They are accomplished agriculturists in every acceptance of the word. The colonies have at their heads two Russian Jews; one M. Lapine is an experienced agriculturist who is most devoted to his co-religionists and is therefore much liked by them. The other, M. Kahn of Odessa, is regarded in his colony as a father; the colonists hold him in high esteem. It is the establishment of the newly-arrived colonists which still presents all manners of difficulties, but these will disappear in time and in proportion as the work progresses. For the moment, it is not our intention to recruit new colonists in Russia. We desire that the 1100 or 1200 families already in the Argentine should be definitely installed, and that the colonists of the second category should attain the same degree of perfection in agricultural labour as the first. This will occupy us at least two years. We shall then recommence our work and perhaps even in much greater dimensions."

Actually, after four years, a meagre 1,222 families were settled in the several Colonies with only 18,210 hectares of land under cultivation out of the 189,023 hectares (472,562 acres) owned by the Jewish Colonization Association.

Simon Dubnow, in his *History of the Jews in Russia and Poland,* says,

Ere long Baron Hirsch's dream of transplanting millions of people with millions of money proved an utter failure. When, after long preparations, the selected Jewish colonists were at last dispatched to Argentina, it was found that the original figure of 25,000 emigrants calculated for the first year had shrunk to about 2500. Altogether, during the first three years, from 1892 to 1894, the Argentinian emigration absorbed some six thousand people. Half of these remained in the capital of the republic, in Buenos Ayres, while the other half managed to settle in the colonies, after enduring all the hardships connected with an agricultural colonization in a new land and under new climatic conditions. A few years later it was commonly realized that the mountain had given birth to a mouse. Instead of the million Jews, as originally planned, the Jewish Colonization Association succeeded in transplanting during the first decade only 10,000 Jews, who were distributed over six Argentinian colonies.

A more optimistic outlook was expressed in a book on

Argentina by a Christian writer, which appeared around 1899. The author, Dr. Martins, who for many years had edited two Argentinian newspapers, seems to feel that the experiment in colonization was successful, and he expresses surprise that the Jewish Colonization Association had been able to do what, at the time of its organization, no one considered possible. It had made people whose former way of life had fitted them only for petty trade and peddling into successful farmers.

Dr. Martins agrees that the first years were discouraging.

Although the colonists were given free transportation from Europe and found ready-built houses on fenced-in farms with the corrals filled with cows and oxen, and they were supplied with farm implements, plows and harvesters, and even some hard cash, some of them abandoned house and farm, sold the implements and live stock and preferred to earn their living as peddlers or cattle dealers, or moved into Buenos Aires.

Despite this, most of the colonists struggled through the first year or two and just these few years have sufficed to bring about a complete change of attitude. The colonists have realized that a brilliant future is in store for them, and that on their farms they will do far better in a very short time, than they ever dreamed. . . . They no longer need pecuniary aid. They have been able to save money out of the produce of their farms, and they have cattle, some as many as a hundred head. Every colonist is both produce and stock farmer, raising cattle for the market.

Many young colonists who had been living with parents or relatives applied for land concessions and settled down independently. A number of colonists even sent for their relatives from Russia to come at their own expense. The colonists have until now (1897) not even been asked to pay off their indebtedness to the Associa-

tion and Baron de Hirsch released them from 25% of
their obligations before his death.

And of the young people, he says:

Riding their horses with the grace and ease of the
gauchos, clad in the cape and sombrero of the gaucho,
dirks and revolvers in their belts, they present a gallant
picture; to all appearances wild Indians rather than
respectable Jewish boys and girls.

To infer that Baron de Hirsch's enterprise proved
to be a failure would be a great mistake. Even suppos-
ing the merely hypothetical case that all the colonists
were to leave the colonies belonging to the Jewish Colonization Association without paying their debts, the
Association would come out with a handsome profit.
The increased price of land, as well as the fact that the
land was bought at the time when gold stood at 350,
whereas at the end of 1898 the exchange was 270, and
considering that the originally virgin soil is now under
cultivation, would bring a large profit.

Perhaps the best description of the Argentinian colonies
is contained in a book, *Jews In Many Lands,* published in
1905 by Elkan Nathan Adler, who traveled all through
the colonies shortly after the turn of the century. His
analysis of the conditions he found there is probably the
only constructive, independent opinion of why the project
failed. The chapter in his book that deals with the Argentinian colonies follows.

A Visit To Moisesville

THE PAMPA
What most impresses the European traveller about
the Province of Santa Fé in general and Moisesville

Colony in particular, is the treeless flatness of the place. It forms part of the endless pampa. The soil is very rich, and produces six to eight crops of lucerne or alfalfa grass every year. There is no lack of water, though it is said that since the ground has been culticated, one has to dig two or three times as deep for it as one used to, but it is always found within nine metres of the surface. When I was there, there was, unfortunately, too much water. Tropical rain-storms had destroyed two months' crops of alfalfa and most of the wheat, and only the maize was still promising. The colonists were much depressed.

The heat was terrific; there was no shade, and it was obvious that even the cattle, some of which were fine English beasts, suffered from want of shade. Each colonist is allowed a few Eucalyptus trees gratis, and as many Paraiso trees as he wants. Paraiso trees have the advantage of being distasteful to the locust. But our colonists are either too poor or too lazy to plant trees except when an immediate profit is in sight, and so the fine Durham cows and even the native horses languish and deteriorate. Only one of the colonists at Moisesville keeps sheep, although I saw some good flocks in the part of Palacios not yet acquired by the Jewish Colonization Association, where also were some fine avenues of trees planted perhaps twenty years ago. And there are some trees round the administration building and the synagogue.

PROSPECTS

One cannot help feeling somewhat discouraged at the prospects of Moisesville or the aptitudes of the Jewish agriculturist there. Perhaps he has more chances at Mauricio, which is in the Province of Buenos Ayres itself, and only eight hours from the capital. Land there is constantly appreciating in value, and is now worth three times what Baron de Hirsch gave for it. But at Moisesville and, indeed, throughout the Province of Santa Fé, a succession of bad years has kept the value of land stationary, and even the great English cattle-breeding estancia of St. Cristobal (two or three stations to the north of Moisesville) is said to be doing badly. The scattered colonies in Entre Rios, on the other side of the River Plate, are said to be not more satisfactory. I met a Government Inspector of Agriculture on the railway, and he told me that hitherto the direction of our Colony had been bad, and altogether he was not very optimistic as to its future. This was the more disappointing after the congratulatory tone of the letter of Senor Iturraspe, the Intendente of Santa Fé, who visited the Colony in January, 1902. It is published in the Jewish Colonization Association Report of June 22, 1902, but, of course, allowance should be made for the inevitable exaggeration of a polite Castilian visitor.

The Jew seems to be too speculative to make a good agriculturist even in the Argentine. He is too fond of putting all his eggs into one basket. Lucerne grass paid very well, indeed, in 1901, and so he has devoted himself this year almost exclusively to lucerne. The rain spoils the crop, and he is down in the dumps, and, especially if a Roumanian, quite prepared to throw up the game and go to Rosario or Buenos Ayres and start a business in the town, or open a shop, or travel the country as a colporteur. If he went in for dairy-farming as well as for agriculture proper, if he cultivated different kinds of crops at the same time, he would, under favorable conditions, make a little less, but the least favorable would do him no irretrievable damage, and he would have no need to be discouraged by a single failure; he would divide his risks.

And agriculture *is* risky in the Argentine. Nature is in some respects very kind. The soil is of almost incredible richness. There is rich loam or vegetable earth many centimeters deep all over Moisesville, but the tropics are too near to justify one in placing any reliance on the climate. One year there is drought, locusts ravage the pampas in another year, and next year heavy rains, out of season, spoil the harvest. And yet it is wonderful to

see fifty-acre fields, neat and trim, with clouds of yellow
butterflies hovering around, where, fifteen years ago,
fierce pumas prowled and wild Indians successfully beat
back the timid advances of civilization. For the improvement, candor must praise the railway as much as
the Jewish Colonization Association, but even the Jewish Colonization Association may do something with
the second generation of its *protégés*. The children of
our colonists have nothing of the ghetto bend about
them. Fearless and high-spirited, the boys and girls ride
the horses bare-backed, and they at least are really
attached to the land.

RUSSIANS AND ROUMANIANS COMPARED

There is a great difference, they say, between the
Russians and the Roumanians. The Russian gets on
better than the Roumanian—at first. His standard of
comfort is lower, he is less extravagant, more easily
satisfied with small mercies, and less discouraged by
the rebuffs either of nature or of man. But the Roumanian is more intelligent, and gets on better with the
natives. His language is not very different from the
Spanish, and a year suffices to make his Castilian fluent
and even classical—no mean advantage, when it is remembered that all the year round Spanish persons have
to be employed on the farm, and during harvest time
every colonist has to engage at least three or four to
aid him in preparing his produce for market. Hired
labor, however, is expensive, and, if anything, the
Roumanian's family is smaller than the Russian's, and
so he has less gratuitous help. He finds it very difficult
to make both ends meet, especially in a bad year, and so
he gravitates to the towns.

A different case, leading to the same result, came
under my notice when I left Palacios. At the next station a young man boarded the train whose friends had
driven him about ten miles from Moisesville to see him
off. It turned out that he was a widower with a furniture
shop in Buenos Ayres, who had spent the last three days

in the Colony making the acquaintance of a young lady
(an attractive young Jewess of sweet seventeen) to
whom he had just become engaged to be married. The
farewell was affectionate in the extreme, and he was to
come back again in a couple of months to fetch his bride.
He was a Caucasian from the neighborhood of Rostow,
and his father had been an original colonist of Entre
Rios, where they kept a Kosher butcher shop. A Span-
iard in his cups had knifed a Jew called Abraham Bond-
arow, or some such name, and had threatened to treat
my friend in the same way. He thought discretion the
better part of valor, and got his people to leave the
Colony to the tender mercies of the unpunished murderer. They migrated to Buenos Ayres, and still grum-
ble that the Jewish Colonization Association allowed
them only three hundred dollars for unexhausted improvements, the value of which they estimate at ten
times that sum. But they have done very well.

JEWS IN ARGENTINE

Whatever one's opinion may be about the value or
success of the Colonies themselves, there can be no
doubt that it is almost exclusively owing to them that
there is a Jewish population of thirty thousand in the
Argentine, of which a third are to be found in the capital. They have two synagogues there, both in the
Calle Liberdad. In the rest of the mainland of South
America there are hardly any Jews. In Panama there
are a few, who have a burial ground of their own, the
Hebrew inscriptions on which gave me a turn as I
tramped one appallingly hot day from the Bocas to
that city. In Peru there are perhaps a dozen, including
the Jamaica-born daughter of an Englishman married
to a dentist from the Danish Island of St. Thomas. In
Chili there are hardly more, and in Brazil, although
there used to be an agent of the *Alliance Israélite* at
Rio, till he died a few months before my visit, there is
neither synagogue nor Minyan to be found throughout
the Continent, except perhaps on Kippur. But the

Argentine constitutes a notable exception, and judging from the analogies which Buenos Ayres, with its rapidly increasing population of eight hundred thousand, presents to New York, it would not be surprising to find the Jewish millionaire as frequent there a generation hence as he is now in the United States. But as to his agricultural future I am far less sanguine. For the rest, the central office of the Jewish Colonization Association in Buenos Ayres is located in a handsome mansion in the Calle Callao, where reside the two joint directors, about whom, to their credit be it said, rumor has never suggested that they have ever had a difference of opinion. The one is Mr. Cazès, formerly Director of the *Alliance Israélite* Schools at Tunis, and author of a bibliography and history of Tunis Jews. The other is Mr. Hirsch, sometime Principal of the Agricultural School at Jaffa, Mikveh Israel.

The Hope of Israel is hardly to be found in South America. My visit did not elate me, and after making every allowance for the personal equation, and for the unfortunate damage to the crops which I witnessed, not to mention the personal torment inflicted by the mosquitoes and flies, which positively swarmed over the damp soil, my prevailing sentiment was one of disappointment tempered by the interest excited by the strange birds—owls and cardinals, bustards and scissors birds—one saw, and by the snakes which were not seen but rumored. Perhaps Mauricio would have been more encouraging.

18

NORTH AMERICA

U p to the year 1890 the influx of Jews from Eastern Europe into the United States had been just a mere trickle, with somewhere between 15,000 to 20,000 Jews a year reaching American shores. The year 1891, however, saw the beginning of immigration that brought over half-a-million Jews from Eastern Europe to North America by the end of the century. Simon Dubnow in *History of the Jews in Russia and Poland* says:

> The main current of Jewish emigration flowed as heretofore in the direction of North America, toward the United States and Canada. In the course of the year 1891, with its numerous panics, the United States alone absorbed more than 100,000 emigrants, over 42,000 of whom succeeded in arriving the same year, while 76,000 were held back in various European centers and managed to come over the year after.

Statistics furnished by A. S. Solomons, General Agent of the Baron de Hirsch Fund Committee, revealed that

> Jewish arrivals in the port of New York from 1885 to July 1, 1893, aggregate 285,894, of whom up to January 1, 1893, 205,416 were exiled Russians. These

273

people naturally gravitate toward the central body of their compatriots already residing chiefly in the Tenth Ward. This ward is the most densely populated area in the world, averaging 25,000 people to the acre. When one hears that one double tenement house contains 297 tenants, one can conceive somewhat of the crowding. In a house in Essex Street, which I visited some time ago, the building, front and rear, was occupied by fifty-two families, composed of from three to ten members, besides an almost equal number of lodgers.

While Baron de Hirsch's interest lay principally in his Argentinian colonies, he recognized that the thousands who were fleeing Russia on their own were also in need of help. With most of them flocking to the United States and Canada, Russian Jewish immigration into both countries began to assume such massive proportions that it soon became evident that temporary arrangements would no longer suffice and that something would have to be done on a much larger scale, and of a more enduring nature. If the Jewish immigrants, so recently released from the confining life of the Russian ghettos, were to become self-supporting citizens in the countries of their adoption, a fresh approach to life in this new land that offered freedom and opportunity was needed. Again, secular education and occupational training was the answer, with the emphasis on farming.

Through Oscar Straus, Baron de Hirsch was induced to place his confidence in Michael Heilprin, head of the Hebrew Emigrant Aid Society, and together they worked out plans for establishing an organization to be known as the Baron de Hirsch Fund, which he endowed with $2,400,000, to be used "to educate the immigrants from Russia, Rumania and other Eastern European countries;

to teach them trades and to pay them while learning; to supply the tools they would need to work at the trades they learned; to afford instruction in agricultural work to those interested in farming; and to give all of them some schooling in the English language."

The Baron de Hirsch Fund was incorporated under the laws of the State of New York, February 9, 1891, with an outstanding group of Officers and Trustees: Myer S. Isaacs, President; Jacob H. Schiff, Vice President; Jesse Seligman, Treasurer; Dr. Julius Goldman, Honorary Secretary; and as Trustees, Henry Rice, James H. Hoffman, Oscar S. Straus, all of New York, and Mayer Sulzberger and W. B. Hackenburg of Philadelphia.

The Baron's donation of $2,400,000 was an enormous sum of money for that period, especially when one considers that it took less than $1,000,000 a year to support almost all of New York's Jewish institutions. Madison C. Peters, in his *Justice to the Jew,* published in 1899, says, "Our Jewish fellow-citizens successfully conduct charities covering every conceivable case of need and suffering. In New York City alone, for their twelve leading institutions, the Jews contribute upward of seven hundred thousand dollars a year."

The same book describes the events leading to the formation of the Baron de Hirsch Fund and the scope of its activities:

Between 1889 and 1891 a plan was under consideration, between Baron de Hirsch and those who were to become the trustees of his fund, with reference to the proposition of the former, to devote ten thousand dollars per month for the amelioration of the Russian and Eastern European immigrants. In 1891 a deed of trust was executed by which the sum of two million, four hundred thousand dollars was placed as capital in the hands of the trustees of the Baron de Hirsch Fund, the interest of which was to be used for the education and training of emigrants from Russia and Eastern Europe. Among the provisions was authority to disburse two hundred and forty thousand dollars of the capital for acquiring and improving land, allotting farm holdings, and erecting buildings for manual and agricultural training and general education. The income of the fund, $100,000 per annum, is used in sustaining an agricultural colony founded in 1893 at Woodbine, New Jersey, and the schools established there; a trade school and English classes established in New York City, an employment, transportation, and relief bureau in connection with the United Hebrew Charities of New York City, and public baths (Hon. A. S. Solomons is the efficient general manager). In addition, local committees in Philadelphia, Baltimore, Boston and St. Louis received sums for similar work in connection with employment, transportation, relief, and education. To some of the several hundred Russian Jewish farmers who bought abandoned farms in the New England States, the fund made loans on bond and mortgage upon a strict business basis. It assisted colonies which were in need in Dakota, Colorado, Michigan, and other States. It has made loans also to students to enable them to complete their college course.

The booklet published by the Baron de Hirsch Fund on the occasion of its seventy-fifth anniversary says,

Even more important than the Woodbine experiment were the many services offered by the Jewish Agricultural Society to prospective Jewish farmers. This Society, founded in 1900 by the trustees of the Baron de Hirsch Fund, had among its objectives, the "encouragement . . . of agriculture among Jews in America. . . ."

In establishing the Jewish Agricultural Society the Fund carried out the dearest wishes of the Baron because among other expressions of interest in agriculture he said "the object of my life . . . is to give a portion of my companions in faith the possibility of finding a new existence, primarily as farmers."

The idea of settling immigrant Jews on farm colonies was not new in America. The first known Jewish agricultural colony, "Sholom," was established as far back as 1837 at Wawarsing, New York, founded by thirteen Jewish families who left New York City to become farmers. This colony lasted only five years. In October, 1881, a group of Russian Jews, twenty-five families who had fled the Elizabethgrad pogroms and thirty-five families from Kiev, were settled in a colony on Sicily Island near Bayou Louis, Louisiana, by a New York committee of prominent Jews working with the Alliance Israélite Universelle. Mississippi River floods in the spring of 1882 washed away the settlement at a loss of about $20,000.

In July, 1882, Herman Rosenthal, who had been president of the Louisiana colony, started another settlement in Cremieux, South Dakota, settled by twenty families, all financing themselves. Shortage of water and lack of railroad transportation caused this colony to fail and in 1885 it was deserted. Soon after this twenty-five unmarried young men founded another South Dakota colony, Bethlehem-Yehudah. This was a communal plan settlement that also failed after several years.

On May 9, 1882, twelve Russian families were sent to Cotopaxi, Colorado, by the Hebrew Immigrant Aid Society to start farming on government land there. At about the same time, forty Russian Jews established a colony some 265 miles south of Portland, Oregon, near the town of Glendale on the California border, which they called New Odessa. This colony was abandoned in 1888. Toward the end of 1882 a colony was established near Bismarck, North Dakota, when twenty families were each given 160 acres in a community known as Painted Woods, sponsored jointly by the Jewish Community of St. Paul and Baron de Hirsch.

In August, 1891, sixteen families of Russian Jews were placed in a settlement called Palestine in Huron County, Michigan. In 1891, too, an agricultural colony sponsored by the Jewish community of Washington was started in nearby Virginia when nineteen Russian Jews and their families established a settlement called Washington. Other colonies were started at various times in Virginia, but none of them lasted. In Connecticut, farming communities sprang up at various times at New London, Norwich, Chesterfield, Colchester, and Montville. A colony was started in California in 1882 in Calaveras County.

In 1894, Joseph Krauskopf, an American Rabbi who had gone to Russia to make a study of the Jewish Agricultural School at Odessa, was so impressed by it that he established a National Farm School at Doylestown, Pennsylvania. It had some success for a few years, but eventually was abandoned.

Canada, too, was experimenting with Jewish farming communities. The Citizens Committee of Montreal and the Jewish Colonization Association were the principal founders of agricultural communities, working with Sir Alexander Galt, Canadian High Commissioner in London, who acted as trustee for the Mansion House Fund. Together they established a colony, New Jerusalem, at Moosowin, 220 miles west of Winnipeg, when thirty families settled there. Each family received a grant of

160 acres of land, cattle, implements, and food to last till
the third harvest, but by the time the three years were up,
the colony had been abandoned. The colony of Hirsch was
founded by Baron de Hirsch's Jewish Colonization Association in 1891 in South Assiniboia, about 12 miles from
the United States border, on land given by the government
under the Dominion Lands Act. Forty-nine families were
settled there in typical farmhouses, with cattle, horses,
implements, seed, and food for three years. Twenty-four
additional farms had to be laid out to take care of friends
and relatives who found their way to Hirsch a year or so
later. At the end of three years, after advancing more
than $50,000, which was to be repaid in twelve annual
installments, the trustees announced that the colonists
would henceforth have to be self-supporting. Most of the
settlers sold their equipment during the next few years
and moved to Winnipeg and to cities in Minnesota.

Canadian Jewry was disappointed when it learned that
the Baron de Hirsch Fund was enjoined by its charter
from sending any money outside the borders of the United
States. Harris Vineberg, President of Montreal's Young
Men's Hebrew Benevolent Society, directed a letter to
Baron de Hirsch on May 20, 1890, calling his attention
to the fact that Canada had been overlooked and that
many of the Jews who were finding their way into Canada
had to be cared for by the Society. He pointed out that
unless they were given help, they would have to limit the
number of refugees they could receive in Montreal. In
reply, he received the following letter from Baron de
Hirsch:

To the President
Young Men's Hebrew Benevolent Society
Montreal, Canada

I received your communication of May 20th sent to Vienna and in reply I regret to say that the mission of the Board of Trustees that managed my American Foundation does not allow of extending their activity beyond the United States.

However as I appreciate the usefulness of your action and the objects you pursue, I am ready to contribute the sum of $20,000 which I enclose in a cheque. I shall be glad to hear from time to time about the progress of your work and may perhaps in a future time further assist you but cannot with this respect take any engagement.

Yours truly,
(signed) M. De Hirsch

The Fund also established the Baron de Hirsch Trade School in 1895, for the thousands of immigrants who chose to remain in New York City. This school, the first of its kind under nonpublic auspices, offered training in various trades. To qualify for admission, applicants had to pass aptitude tests and demonstrate the physical fitness required for a particular trade. Among the trades taught were printing, painting, carpentry, house painting, sign painting, and machine and electrical work. The building on East 64th Street, between 2nd and 3rd Avenue, built at a cost of $150,000 donated by the Baroness in 1897, has been turned over to New York City and is now attached to the neighboring high school.

The properties in New Jersey have been disposed of, too. In 1941, the Baron de Hirsch Fund, after selling off land to individual settlers, turned over its remaining acreage to the Borough of Woodbine. The Agricultural School was donated to the State of New Jersey and is now a state-operated mental hospital.

The Baron de Hirsch Fund still carries on and in 1966

celebrated its seventy-fifth anniversary. A display in the B'nai B'rith building in Washington, D.C., portrayed the many services the Fund had supplied to impoverished immigrants fleeing Hitler's Germany and reaching America's shores in destitute condition. The interesting booklet explaining the Exhibit says:

Just before and after the second World War, the Society entered on its period of highest activity because of the great desire of many of the refugees and displaced persons to become farmers. Prior to the war, a large proportion of German refugees to this country was made up of business and professional men who could not re-establish themselves in their original occupations and turned to farming—usually poultry farming—with the aid of the Society. Between 1946 and 1953, when there was a large influx of displaced persons from Europe, an estimated seven percent went to the farm, many with the aid of the Jewish Agricultural Society. In 1951 the Society helped settle 236 families on farms, 159 of them displaced persons or refugees. In that same year the Society granted 285 loans, 155 to displaced persons and refugees. New Jersey was the principal state of settlement, but many newcomers also went to New York, Connecticut and California.

With the decline in immigration in the last decade and the decrease in the number of small farmers, the Society's operations in this direction have lessened. It is now turning to other activities, principally to a scholarship program for Jewish farm youth who need financial aid while attending college or university. In 1965-66 it awarded 134 scholarships, with money provided by the Baron de Hirsch Fund. It continues to work with the reduced number of Jewish people who are operating farms.

The Fund also makes substantial grants to agencies which assist Jewish immigrants admitted to the United

States. Among these agencies are United HIAS, New York Association for New Americans, and ORT's Bramson School.

Perhaps a million American Jews owe a debt of gratitude to Baron de Hirsch, whose generosity enabled their parents or grandparents to settle successfully in America.

19

HERZL

One morning early in May, 1895, a letter came to Baron de Hirsch asking for a meeting "merely to have a Jewish-political conversation. I wish to discuss the Jewish problem with you. It is not a question of an interview, still less a direct or indirect money matter. I want to discuss with you a Jewish political plan, the effects of which will perhaps extend to days when you and I are no longer here." The letter did not go into detail, but merely asked the Baron to set a time when they might get together. It was signed Theodor Herzl.

It was only to be expected that the man to whom Theodor Herzl would turn with his visions of a Jewish State, after being completely ignored by the Rothschilds, was Baron de Hirsch, who, as Herzl says in his *Diaries,* "concerns himself about the Jews in such an astonishing and millionaire manner." He realized that the Rothschilds were no more than charitable philanthropists while Baron de Hirsch was not interested in just feeding the poor. He wanted to eliminate the causes of poverty and he was the only one who had shown that he understood that what the Jews needed most was a new start somewhere where the habits of the ghetto could be quickly forgotten and historic prejudices would not be present to hold them back. And he had boldly undertaken, single-handedly, to deliver the Jews of the Russian Pale from their misery and transport them to new lands where freedom and a decent standard of living awaited them.

Herzl had felt sure that he would get the support of the Rothschilds but, except for Baron Edmond de Rothschild, not one of the family even bothered to answer his request for an interview. Baron Edmond, head of the French Rothschild family, had become intensely interested in Palestine when Rabbi Samuel Mohilewer of Byelostok, founder of the Chovevei Zion and one of the early Russian Zionists, prevailed upon him to finance a colony of 101 Russian Jews who had settled not far from Jaffa. Over the years he went on to establish many colonies in Palestine and to help financially others that had been started on their own. Of the seven Jewish agricultural communities in Palestine in the middle 1880s, he at one time or another saved them all from bankruptcy. But even Baron Edmond declined to meet with Herzl, declaring that "my activities in Palestine are a matter of philanthropy and not of nationalist politics." Herzl, discussing the Rothschilds in the *Diaries,* complains, "How is one to negotiate with this collection of idiots!"

Isaac Naiditch, in his profile of Baron Edmond de Rothschild, published in 1945, tells of an interview he had with him in Paris in 1919, in which he explained his refusal to help Herzl. "I must tell you the truth about that first meeting with Herzl," he said. "When he explained to me his idea of convoking a Congress and starting a public agitation among Jews and non-Jews for the creation of a Jewish state, I was frightened. I thought it was a dangerous road to take. I thought that, first of all, it was difficult

on account of the possible repercussions in the attitude of
the Turkish government towards our efforts. Besides, I
thought it was harmful to the welfare of the Jews all over
the world, since the anti-Semites would raise the cry that
the Jews ought to be made to go to their own country.

"I felt that the colors could be raised over a house only
after it had been built, and that there was no point in
hoisting the flag when there was still no edifice and when
even the land for the edifice had not yet been provided.
That was the reason for my opposition to Herzl. But
history has shown that it was Herzl who was right
and not I."

It is indeed a strange anomaly of fate that, although
none of the Rothschilds lent any encouragement to Herzl
or contributed to his cause (although they did help his
family after his death), and the London Rothschilds
actually took an active position in the Anti-Zionist League
of British Jews, the Balfour Declaration came to the Jews
in the form of a letter to a Rothschild.

Baron de Hirsch, too, paid little attention to Herzl's
letter. How could he find time to wonder what a relatively
unknown newspaper correspondent could have in mind
that could be of such importance to the Jewish world? He
did set up an appointment for Herzl, however, little realizing that this was the man who would relegate him to
obscurity, he who had been called the "Nineteenth Century
Moses" to whom thousands looked for escape from the
Russian pogroms. How could he foresee that this obscure
writer of plays, this Viennese newspaper correspondent,
was to take from him the mantle he had worn for so long
as the savior of his people, or that it was Herzl's name
instead of his that was to sound throughout the world,
awakening Jews from that lethargy which had held them

in its grip for 1,000 years, calling them back to the Holy Land, with Herzl the new Messiah who would lead them there. Little did he realize that the name of Baron de Hirsch, the first practical Zionist to lead the exodus from the land of the Czars, would not even appear in the annals of Zionism, and that another would reap where he had sown.

The first and only meeting between Theodor Herzl and Baron de Hirsch must have presented an interesting study in contrasts. Both men were visionaries. The banker, with the money and power to put into motion the fantastic schemes he envisioned, lacked that basic understanding of humanity which the novelist and playwright possessed to a remarkable degree. Baron de Hirsch recognized but two classes of Jews, the ghetto Jew—coarse, ignorant, fanatical in his religious observances—and the assimilated Jew. All that was necessary was to remove Jews in large numbers from the first group into the second group and anti-Semitism would vanish. For the Jewish intellectuals— the writers, the scientists, the politicians—he had little respect, and he would not allow himself to become associated with any Jews who were identified with strange new political or philosophical ideologies. He could not condone Jews who demanded their rights from Gentiles, and he looked with dismay on the writers who wrote that "anti-semitism is a Christian problem, and what are you Christians going to do about it?"

Seldom does destiny produce two such fundamentally different personalities, each with the same dream of saving an entire people, but differing completely in their approach to the problem—the conciliatory as opposed to the fanatical, the assimilationist against the nationalist, the advocate of evolution versus the proponent of revolution.

Herzl, the intellectual, was the man of wider vision, the dreamer whose head was governed by his heart, while de Hirsch's horizons were far more circumscribed. Herzl had the zeal of the fanatic. He imbued his drive for the Jewish State with his whole being, and to it he imparted the full force of his dynamic strength. Baron de Hirsch was the practical realist, scrutinizing everything that came his way with the cool detachment of the banker. He was not the man to sweep the Jews off their feet into a current as rapid and as full of dangers as the Zionist movement appeared to be. He was an assimilationist, a fighter against backwardness, a leader away from traditionalism into a higher, freer, more humane community of mankind, in which the Jew would be welcomed as an equal among all men.

Each had what the other needed—de Hirsch the power and the money, and Herzl the zeal of a Messiah. Many have speculated that the two might have reached an accord in time. Baron de Hirsch had been receiving discouraging reports from his Argentinian colonies, and he was close to admitting that his plan had met with failure. After years of work, and after spending many millions of dollars, he had barely scratched the surface. Jews were still living in unspeakable misery in Czarist Russia and the pogroms were increased in scope and in fury. And the sickness was spreading all over Eastern Europe! Now Rumania was being heard from and life for the Jews there was fast becoming unbearable. But to Baron de Hirsch, Herzl was an unknown quantity, an interloper, and his Jewish State idea was new and radical. How could he follow Herzl in his headlong plunge into political Zionism when it was contrary to everything he stood for? It was a step backward, a roadblock in the path of total assimilation, which was the only hope for the Jews in the modern world. To Herzl, on the other hand, the Baron's schemes "looked like enlarged charitable programs, with the schnorrers being dragged half way around the world." He, Herzl, offered the Jews an ideal. He offered them Zion. As he wrote to the Baron, "The settlements in Argentina were a failure because when you want a great settlement, you must have a flag and an ideal." To Herzl, the flag and the ideal could only be Palestine.

Herzl did not know that Baron de Hirsch had long ago investigated the possibility of resettling Jews on agricultural colonies in the Holy Land on a large scale. Nor did he know of the Veneziani Report of 1891, which stated that it was the opinion of the Commission that Palestine was not suited for settlement by European Jews, and that no further consideration should be given to establishing agricultural colonies there. He had no knowledge either of the memorandum on Palestine as a refuge for Russia's Jews that the Baron had written, both to the representatives of the Chovevei Zion and to the committee that had attempted to enlist his and Baron Edmond de Rothschild's support for the establishing of Palestinian colonies. Jacob de Haas, in his biography of Theodor Herzl, says: "In his interview with Herzl, the Baron made no allusion to the existence of his curious memorandum on Palestine. Herzl knew not of the existence of this document. Had it been mentioned by either, *The Jewish State* might never have been penned, but the Jewish homeland might have been established by the joint efforts of the journalist and the millionaire." Had this happened, Herzl, comparatively unknown to the Jewish world, would probably have been completely outshone by the magic of the Baron's name. Baron de Hirsch might have become the "father of Zionism," and Theodor Herzl might easily have remained in the almost complete obscurity from whence he came.

The famous meeting took place on the morning of June 2, 1895, in the Baron's mansion on Rue de l'Elysée. Herzl admits to being nervous, and a "little fearful in the presence of a person of such high rank and exalted position. I had purposely broken in a pair of new gloves the day before," he says in his notes of the meeting, "so that they should look slightly worn, not brand new. One must not treat rich folk with too much deference." He was impressed by the de Hirsch mansion. He noticed the details carefully and reflected, "Wealth affects me only in the guise of beauty; and here everything was genuinely beautiful. Men of my kind are not thinking of these effects of wealth when they speak of it disparagingly."

Herzl began the interview apologetically, explaining, "I never thought I would busy myself with the Jewish Question. So you, too, never imagined that you would one day be the Patron of the Jews. You were a banker . . . I have been since youth a writer and journalist. . . . But my experiences and observations and the growing pressure of anti-Semitism have forced me to the problem."

And then he went into his central theme that political action had to replace philanthropy, and that the ideal that Jews everywhere would follow was the return to the Promised Land—to a Jewish State. He did not present his case well. As he subsequently wrote in a letter to the Baron explaining why he had reached only page six of his twenty-two pages of notes during their meeting, "I am always nervous in the presence of strangers, a weakness I diligently try to conquer. I can explain myself more fully in writing."

He started his presentation haltingly. "Some of the

things I have to say you will find too simple, others too fantastic. But it is the simple and the fantastic which leads men. Throughout the two thousand years of our dispersion we have lacked unified political leadership. I consider this our greatest misfortune. It has done us more harm than all the persecutions. It is this that is responsible for our inner decay. For there was no one, not even a king inspired by selfish motives, to educate us as men. . . . If we only had a unified political leadership . . . we could initiate the solution of the Jewish question."

But first there would have to be complete repudiation of the principle of philanthropy. "You breed beggars," he told the Baron. "Among no other people is there so much philanthropy and so much mendicancy as among the Jews. It is impossible to escape the conclusion that there must be an organic connection between these two phenomena. Philanthropy debases the character of our people." With this observation Baron de Hirsch was in agreement, adding, "The rich Jews have no capacity for large giving or for great undertakings," a truth that Herzl did not realize until many years after.

He then went on to attack the Argentine colonization program. "You transport these Jews as plough-hands. They naturally feel that henceforth they have a claim on you, and this certainly does not promote the will to work. Whatever such an exported Jew costs you, he is not worth it. And how many individual samples can you transplant in any case? Fifteen thousand, twenty thousand. There are more Jews in one street in the Leopold district of Vienna."

"What you have hitherto undertaken was as magnanimous as it was mistaken, as costly as it was useless. Hitherto, you have been only a philanthropist, a Peabody. I will show you a way by which you can become greater."

What would Herzl substitute for philanthropy? "Great
ideals, daring enterprises and incentives to improve themselves, to improve the mass character among Jews
wherever they happened to be. "They must be made
strong as for war, filled with the joy of work, penetrated
by high virtues." What did he think de Hirsch could do
about this? Here Herzl faltered. He had nothing to sug-
gest except that the Baron "should offer prizes for
achievements in science and art, for distinguished moral
actions. The annual prizes will themselves be of little importance. What is of importance is the wide-spread effort
which will be made to be among the prize-winners;
through this the general moral level will be raised."

Here the Baron interrupted him impatiently: "No, no,
no. I don't want to raise the general level. All our mis-
fortunes come from the fact that the Jews aim too high.
We have too many intellectuals. My aim is to discourage
this pushiness among the Jews. They mustn't make such
great progress. All the hatred of us comes from this."
And he then went on to expound his favorite theory that
the only avenue through which Jews might achieve equality among their neighbors was secular education. He was
sure that if they could be taught to work and live like
their neighbors and weaned away from the Talmud and
the Cheder, could be educated out of the habits and practices of the ghetto, anti-Semitism would soon disappear.
Assimilation was the answer.

To Baron de Hirsch the explanation of anti-Semitism
was as simple as this. He firmly believed that the intellectual attainments of Jews created a fear of them and this
in turn spread anti-Semitism. He had no understanding of
the complex nature of Jew hatred, based on an incredible
fund of fact and fiction, of history and legend, which had

been accumulated through the centuries about the Jew in Christian literature and folk-lore. Nor did he understand that the Jew had come to be regarded as the anti-Christ, the heretic, the ritual murderer, the usurer, the power-seeker, the intriguer, the very enemy of Christianity itself. He had no insight into the sick nature of the uneducated Christian mind when it dwelt on the Jew. In the simple explanation for Jew-hatred that his mind had conceived, there was no place for wonderment at the readiness of the Christian world to believe any accusation against the Jews, no matter how fantastic or how ridiculous it might be. This readiness he attributed to the medieval mind, which still persisted in many places but which, with the advance of education and enlightenment, would disappear from the European scene along with the mysticism, the witchcraft, the barbaric cruelties, and the many other practices of the Middle Ages still in evidence in the more backward regions of the Continent.

After these remarks, Herzl considered it useless to unfold his ideas any further. "You do not know," he said, "what fantasy means, and you do not realize that it is only from a certain height that one can perceive the great outlines of men."

In the *Diaries* he gives his impression of Baron de Hirsch. "I was not disappointed, but rather stirred. All in all a pleasant, intelligent man—vain, par excellence!— but I could have worked with him. He makes the impression that with all his self-opinionatedness he is reliable."

In his notes Herzl continues:

Hirsch said that migration was the only way. "There is land enough to be purchased. . . ."

I almost shouted at him: "Certainly! Who told you

that I'm against emigration. Here it is, in these notes.
I will go to the German Kaiser; he will understand me,
for he has been educated to the reception of great
ideas. . . . I will say to the German Kaiser: Let us go
forth. We are aliens here, they do not let us dissolve
into the population, and if they let us we would not do
it. Let us go forth! I will show you the means and
methods whereby this migration can be carried out
without causing an economic upset, without leaving a
gap behind us."

Hirsch said: "Where will you get the money?
Rothschild will donate five hundred francs."

"The money?," I said, smiling scornfully. "I will
create a national loan of ten million marks."

"Fantastic," smiled the Baron. "The rich Jews will
give you nothing. The rich Jews are bad, they display
no interest in the sufferings of the poor."

"You speak like a Socialist, Baron Hirsch," I said.

"This won't be our last conversation," the Baron
suggested.

He left the door open for further discussion and asked
that Herzl submit a detailed explanation of his plan, in
writing. If he approved of the plan, or felt that its merits
would warrant further discussion, he would arrange another interview at a later date.

That date never came, for Baron de Hirsch died before
Herzl could submit his proposal. The report that Herzl
was preparing for the Baron, however, became the first
draft of *The Jewish State,* which was to create so great a
sensation on its publication, and which revolutionized all
previous Jewish thinking. It was the Magna Charta of the
Zionist movement.

In his biography of Herzl, translated from the German
by Maurice Samuel, Alex Bein says:

"Herzl's first attempt to win this great power over by

storm had failed. Had he set about it in the right way? Had it been wise of him to try and compel this man to new ways of thought? We can, without presumption, assert that he had not set about it in the right way; he had not approached him from the practical angle, he had not given due weight to Hirsch's positive achievements. He should have come to this cool, practical man with a more specific plan of action, on which they could have united. The larger theoretical aspect could have been introduced later, and by degrees. As it was, he began by bringing to focus their theoretical divergence, with the result that Hirsch felt he was dealing with an interesting dreamer, but a dreamer nevertheless."

Herzl, too, recognized this, for he said in the *Diaries,* "We two are spirits who mark the beginning of a new era—he is the financial, I am the intellectual condottiere. If this man will go with me, we can really revolutionize the life of our day." And when he learned of the Baron's death, he said; "Of the rich Jews he was the only one who wanted to do something for the poor. Perhaps I did not know how to handle him rightly. It seems to me that today we have become poorer."

Herzl realized that he had mishandled this first meeting and he immediately wrote the Baron a long letter, setting forth some of the ideas he had in his twenty-six pages of notes but which, in his nervousness, he had not discussed. He wrote:

> You are the Jew of great wealth; I am the Jew of the spirit; hence the difference in our roads and methods. . . . What you seek is to hold a great human group down to a specific level, in fact, to repress them. . . . Man has struggled much from his original condition to reach his present culture. And he shall

climb ever upwards despite everything and for all
time, ever higher, higher and higher, through changes
to be brought about among the masses by training, by
tremendous propaganda, the popularization of the idea
through newspapers, books, pamphlets, lectures, pictures, songs. All these works are to be directed purposely and farsightedly, from a single center. But then
I should have had to speak to you finally about the flag
which had to be unrolled and under which the movement was to march. And then you would have asked me
mockingly: "A flag—what is that? A stick with a rag
at the end of it." No, Monsieur le Baron, a flag is a
great deal more. It is with a flag that people are led
whithersoever one desires, even to the Promised Land.
For a flag men live and die; indeed, it is the only thing
for which they are prepared to die in masses if they
have been brought up to it.

Where would he get the money to do all this?

    I will launch a Jewish national loan. There's always
plenty of Jewish money for Chinese loans, for Negro
railroad enterprises in Africa, for the most extrava-
gantly adventurous ideas—and will we be unable to
find money for the deepest, most immediate, and most
tormenting need of the Jews themselves?
    Certainly this national fantasy must rest on practical
foundations. But whence have you the impression that
I have no practical ideas for the details? The exodus to
the Promised Land presents itself as a tremendous
enterprise in transportation, unparalled in the modern
world. What, transportation? It is a complex of all
human enterprises which we shall fit into each other like
cog-wheels. And in the very first stages of the enterprise we shall find employment for the ambitious
younger masses of our people; all the engineers, architects, technologists, chemists, doctors, and lawyers,
those who have emerged in the last thirty years from

the ghetto and who have been moved by the faith that they can win their bread and a little honor outside the framework of our Jewish business futilities. Today they must be filled with despair, they constitute the foundation of a frightful over-educated proletariat. But it is to these that all my love belongs, and I am just as set on increasing their number as you are set on diminishing it. It is in them that I perceive the latent power of the Jewish people. In brief, my kind. . . .

Do you know that you have adopted a frightfully reactionary policy—worse than that of the most absolute autocrats? Fortunately your powers are not great enough to carry it out. You mean well, parbleu, je le sais bien. That is why I want to direct your will to the right channel. Do not permit yourself to be prejudiced by the fact that I am still fairly young. At thirty-fiive men become cabinet ministers in France, and Napoleon was Emperor at that age.

He closes the letter by declaring that he is ready to continue the conversation as soon as de Hirsch desires. But he makes it clear that the movement does not depend on the consent of the Baron. "Very definitely I should like to find, through you, an existing and recognized force, the short-cut to my plans. But you would only be the beginning. There are others. And finally, and above all, there is the mass of the Jews, to which I shall know how to find my way."

Alex Bein, in his biography of Theodor Herzl, says:

On April 20, 1896 Herzl drafted a long letter to Max Nordau, the famous German writer, son of an equally famous Rabbi, and Herzl's first lieutenant, suggesting that the latter attempt to make connection with Baron de Hirsch. Perhaps the Baron could be persuaded to contribute a couple of million francs to the cause. This would "make a ringing impression on public opinion," and at the same time they would have the baksheesh needed for negotions with Turkey. How far he had outgrown his own pride in thus proposing to approach once more the man who had so coolly let him leave Paris! The next day he completed the letter and sent it off. An hour later he learned that Baron Moritz de Hirsch had died the night before on one of his estates in Hungary. He recalled the letter telegraphically. "What a strange coincidence," he noted in the *Diaries*. "For months the pamphlet has been ready. I gave it to everyone except Hirsch. The moment I decide to do it, he dies. His cooperation could have hastened our success tremendously. In any case, his death is a loss to the Jewish cause. Among the rich Jews he was the only one prepared to do something big for the poor ones. Perhaps I did not know how to handle him. Perhaps I should have written that letter to Nordau fourteen days ago. For it was always in my mind to win Hirsch over to the plan." And he says in the *Diaries*, "The Jews have lost Hirsch, but they have me, and after me they will have someone else. It must go forward. I conceive the same matter differently and I believe better, more strongly, because I do it not with money but with the idea."

20

DEATH OF BARON
DE HIRSCH

It is our mournful duty to record the death of Baron de Hirsch, the distinguished financier and large-hearted philanthropist whose colossal gifts to Jewish and general charities and notably his Scheme for emigrating Russian Jews to agricultural colonies in the New World, have placed him foremost among the philanthropists of the century. He died unexpectedly in the night of Monday, while on a visit to the country house of a friend, Herr Ehrenfeld, in the neighborhood of his estate of Ogyalla, near Neuhausel in Hungary. This immense property was only lately bought by the Baron in substitution for his famous shootings at St. Johann, which he sold last year to Prince Hohenlohe for £300,000. During the evening of Monday he complained to his host of feeling unwell and retired early to rest. The next morning a servant found him dead in bed. An autopsy which was made on Wednesday showed that he had succumbed to an attack of apoplexy. The Baron was in London at the end of January and had expressed his intention of returning to Bath House, Piccadilly, for the season.

The body reached Vienna yesterday on its way to Paris, where the interment will take place on Sunday with the simplicity usual at Jewish funerals.

With these words the London Jewish Chronicle announced to the world the death at the age of 65 of Baron Maurice de Hirsch auf Gereuth, on Tuesday, April 21, 1896.

Clara was in Paris at the time and was notified of Maurice's death by telegram. Immediately she was surrounded by friends and relatives. Wires and letters of condolence started pouring in from important people everywhere. Special services were hurriedly arranged in almost every synagogue in the world—in Russia, in the United States and Canada, in England, and in all the countries of Europe. A report from Buenos Aires describes the reaction of the Argentinian colonists there to the news of the Baron's death:

> The sad intelligence of the death of Baron de Hirsch was made known here privately before noon on the morning the mournful event took place. About an hour afterwards the afternoon papers had telegrams from Hungary, Paris and London confirming the news. The consternation felt by all classes of the Jewish community here was very great and the directors of the Jewish Colonization Association were constantly interrupted by reporters of the press anxious to give a correct account of the late Baron's life and great charitable deeds. The press spoke most highly of the philanthropist, and the *Nacion* and *Pressa* gave portraits of the late Baron.
>
> Funeral services have been held by the German and Spanish congregations, the Societies "La Espanza" and "Obereros" and in the Russian colonies in the provinces of Buenos Aires, Santa Fe and Entre Rios. Over 10,000 Jews in this Republic have paid homage to his memory.
>
> The memorial service in the synagogue of the principal (German) congregation was held on April 26

and was attended by far larger numbers than usually assemble on festivals or even on the Day of Atonement. The synagogue Ark, the reading desk, and the pulpit were entirely draped in black, and numerous handsome wreaths were hung with inscriptions of letters of gold "May he rest in peace." The curtain concealing the Ark also contained the words in large letters of gold "Baron Mauricia de Hirsch." In addition to the ordinary illuminations, several tall candles were lit. The entire scene was both impressive and imposing. Among those present were Mr. David Cayes and Mr. Samuel Hirsch, the representative here of the J.C.A., as also Dr. Sonnenfeld, secretary of the Society in Paris and Mr. David Feinberg of Konigsberg, both of whom are here on an official mission to inquire into the condition of the colonies.

The great and the near great, kings and princes and the nobility of almost every country in the Western World called or wrote to pay homage to one of the greatest figures of the nineteenth century. Rabbi Zadoc Kahn, Chief Rabbi of France, Honorary President of the Alliance, and Chevalier of the Legion of Honor, officiated at the funeral which took place on Monday, the 27th of April, from the mansion at 2 Rue de L'Elysée, attended by the family and those who had been especially invited to participate. The Chief mourners were Baron Emile de Hirsch de Gereuth, Theodore and James de Hirsch de Gereuth, all brothers, Arnold and Raymond de Forest, his adopted sons, his brothers-in-law Henri Bamberger, Jonas de Hirsch de Gereuth, Ferdinand Bischoffsheim, Leopold Goldschmid, George Montefiore Levy, and his uncle, Solomon Goldschmidt. There were no flowers or wreaths; neither were military honors rendered. Burial was in Montmartre Cemetery.

Baron de Hirsch was on intimate terms with Prince Ferdinand of Bulgaria, a circumstance which led at one time to much speculation. It is to be noted that on the day of his funeral, the Prince, who was visiting in Paris, called on the Baroness in the morning to pay his condolences.

In its obituary of April 24, 1896, the *London Jewish Chronicle* said:

> Baron de Hirsch was the master of many millions, and the architect of many vast financial and industrial enterprises. The practical instincts and wide views which had given him his colossal fortune, he brought to the service of the philanthropic schemes he so lavishly endowed with a largeness of heart and a quickness of sympathy which were truly phenomenal. It is the loss of these qualities which will be most severely felt now that he has passed away. At the same, a towering and picturesque personality will be missed from our midst— a singular combination of Jay Gould and Wilberforce, of Count d'Ossay and General Booth, of Sidonia and Monte Cristo. It is no exaggeration to say that in many respects Baron de Hirsch was one of the most remarkable characters of a century which has been rich in remarkable men. . . .
>
> Any other man, in face of the attitude taken up by the advisers of the Czar towards the Educational Scheme which he proposed to them, would have dropped the Russian problem in despair; but Baron de Hirsch was not so easily deterred. Something had to be done, and he resolved that what he could do, however little it might be, should be done with heart and soul. Thus he embarked on his great plan for transplanting the Russian Jews and enabling them to recast their lives as tillers of the soil in the New World. Of course it was impossible to organize an Exodus en masse, and it is scarcely necessary to say that he himself never dreamed of any such enterprise. But he established the beginnings of a new life for his persecuted brethren, and there can be no question that if his Scheme is managed wisely it will, in process of time, exert a very powerful influence of good, not only on the Russian Jews who emigrate under its auspices, but even on those who stay at home. It should be remembered that the Baron kept the threads of his great schemes in his own

hands, and now that he is dead, it will not be an easy task to pick them up. Unity of purpose and responsibility must be maintained at all hazards. If many masters are to be substituted for one the result will be disastrous. Nor will the great personal interest he devoted to his various enterprises be easily replaced. His schemes, however, he has bequeathed, with ample resources, to men who have a wide experience of the problems he was anxious to solve, and whose sympathy with the sufferings of their coreligionists is not a whit inferior to his own.

Baron de Hirsch was, perhaps, one of the first of the practical sociologists, for he believed that true charity was not the giving of alms, but giving in such a way as to make almsgiving unnecessary. He was one of the first to realize, however, that mere philanthropy was not enough, and that far more constructive steps would have to be taken if the lot of the Jews was to be permanently bettered. He had nothing but scorn for the "mitzvah" type of charity which was so widely practised by the prominent Jews of the period. The scheme which he finally evolved was so revolutionary, and so breath-taking in scope, that it was considered foolhardy and visionary by most of the Jewish communal leaders and by the charitable organizations that had been working on the problem.

He felt that the Jews must get away from petty trading, out of their ghetto shops where they sat amid musty surroundings waiting to pounce on the first customer that came along for fear their competitor would get him first. The emancipation movement could only reach its zenith of fulfillment when more and more Jews took to ploughing the fields and harvesting the grain. The farmer is a freeman, far superior to the petty trader and the ghetto merchant. Where the ghetto walls still stood, there Jews remained in the same degraded position they had been in for centuries, steeped in Talmudic lore but ignorant of the ways of the world. Hence, the answer was to educate the Jews for assimilation into the general population. Keep their religion if they must but at least, drop the customs of the ghetto.

"We Jews always borrow from our environment," he once said. "Anyone transported into a synagogue could, from the style of the decorations and the character of the music, at once tell whether he was in a Catholic, a Protestant, or a Mohammedan country."

Baron de Hirsch was not a man of profound intellect in the scholarly sense of the word. But if he was not profound he was certainly a clear thinker. When he made plans, whether it was in building his railroads or in following his charitable impulses, he always worked out in his own mind every detail of the course he was going to take. He did not follow hunches. He made no move without first thinking out thoroughly the advantages and disadvantages which would develop as a result of his move. He had the ability to understand what his actions would lead to and of making others see exactly what he was thinking. Muddled thinking antagonized him. He disliked the dreamer who knew what he wanted but did not know how to attain it. Nor had he any use for the "special pleaders," those professional speakers, and newspaper editors who sought to make much of each new atrocity against the Jews—the calamity howlers who had little to offer as a solution except to berate the Christians among whom Jews were forced to spend their lives.

Because of his distrust of intellectuals, many of whom sought his support for their activities, de Hirsch was skeptical of all movements that relied on an appeal to the masses for their support. He preferred to be guided by the Alliance and the few other organizations in which he had confidence. Because of this he was thought to be aloof, to be condescending, to be interested only in furthering that which would create of the Jew merely an emancipated peasant.

What did he owe to his blood, to the country of his origin, to the age in which he lived? To the Jewish spirit, undaunted through eighteen ceturies of persecution he undoubtedly owed his independence of spirit, his stubbornness, his intensity of purpose, his flair for showmanship coupled with a curious reserve, his strong sense of justice. To his mother, Caroline Wertheimer, he owed the deep religious background that was to make him everconscious of his Jewishness, which kept him loyal, albeit lukewarm, to Judaism all his life. To his father, the daring speculator, he owed his penchant for financing risky projects, his delight in plunging into highly speculative deals, and his consuming imagination. To the city of Munich, which had seen a new birth of activity and building during the early years of his life, he owed his flair for large undertakings. And to the age in which he lived, ushering in, as it did, the new freedoms, the new belief in the rights of all men, and the new capitalism that was to make economic freedom possible along with the social and political freedoms, he owed his strong belief in the power of education and economics to undo the injustices that had beset the Jews for two thousand years.

The *New York Evening Journal* of June 28, 1891, quoted an interview with Baron de Hirsch in which he said:

There is, in my opinion, no possibility for doubt that

the possession of great wealth lays a duty on the possessor. It is my innermost conviction that I must consider myself as only a temporary administrator of the great wealth I have amassed, and that it is my duty to contribute in my own way to the relief of the suffering of those who are hard oppressed by fate.

I contend against the old system of alms-giving, which only makes so many more beggars; and I consider the greatest problem in philanthropy is to make human beings who are capable of work, who would otherwise become paupers, into useful members of society. Philanthropy, in its proper sense has, no doubt, a higher purpose, and can find its best action in the creation of free libraries, green parks, beautiful churches, etc. This is Mr. Carnegie's idea, which he has demonstrated again and again.

New York's *Yiddish—Jewish Gazette*, August 22, 1919, also compares Baron de Hirsch with Carnegie, when it says,

The death of the great philanthropist Carnegie reminds us of our own philanthropist Baron de Hirsch. Baron de Hirsch could not give so many millions to charity as did Carnegie. No rich man in Europe could dispense charity of such imposing size. Baron de Hirsch, however, in certain respects excelled Carnegie: Baron de Hirsch is the only rich man in the world who gave away *all* that he possessed for charity.

INDEX

307